UNCOMMON GIRLS

UNCOMMON GIRLS

CARLA GRANT

Bink Books
Bedazzled Ink Publishing Company • Fairfield, California

978-1-945805-71-4 paperback

Cover Design
by
TROUT + TAYLOR
www.troutandtaylor.com

Bink Books
a division of
Bedazzled Ink Publishing Company
Fairfield, California
http://www.bedazzledink.com

I dedicate this book to all the single moms out there on
crappy Plenty of Fish™ dates . . .
Who can't drink to cope . . .
Who have an autistic transgender teenager, a hockey player,
and a toddler at home . . .
No? Just me?

Then, I dedicate this book to Gramma ♥

Preface

October 4, 2012, was a day that seemed to change everything.

Eliot: Did you know that gender reassignment surgery is now
covered by Alberta Health & Wellness?
Me: Oh? I don't think I knew that.
Fuck. Really? Odds that this was a randomly googled fact?
Very small . . .
Don't miss your bus.
Phoned my psychologist, on speed-dial, to put her on retainer.

That was one of the many days I would categorize as "big" in my
life. The double blue lines on the pregnancy test would be on the list,
along with the day we got a diagnosis of autism and the day I checked
into Rehab. There were many other days on the positive side of the
spectrum of "life changers" that I'd have to consider for my list. Like
being chosen valedictorian, celebrating Jackson's first hat trick, and
rescuing my first dog.

That day, in Eliot's 12th year, wasn't even really the start of our
gender journey. It's hard to pinpoint an exact beginning. Maybe it
was when he fell into hysterical sobs when he wasn't permitted to
wear the princess dress in the dress-up box, or buy the pink patent
slippers at the shoe store when he was four, likely even before that,
perhaps even in utero. It was all so intricately intertwined with our
other life journeys that the signals were hard to distinguish from the
static.

I never kept a diary growing up. Most of my journals started
with "okay, okay, I'll write it down" and then had three pages of
scribbles before the glaring blank pages of lack of self-discipline
began. On a fundamental level, I believe my writer's block stemmed
from both a belief that problems are not often solved by the same
brain that created them, and that I would be disappointed at the
end of it because no one else would read it to give me a coveted
Gold Star ★.

So why now? This memoir was written with the intention of sharing it. It's honest and thorough, with a few liberties taken to temper anything that would harm my children's opinions of important people in their lives, and honour their right to privacy. Refraining from criticism breeds mutual respect and harmony—both things that I value and uphold. I have also chosen to name specific places and people simply by their descriptive noun in their proper forms. Rehab has a real name, as do the Arts School, Dr. Gender, the Family Psychologist, the Metropolis, and others. I assure you this was not done to hide, but rather to generalize.

My man, Arthur, tells me I share too much. This book could well be the epitome of oversharing. I impart my experiences, strength, and hope, knowing that they may uplift, enlighten, reinforce, encourage, or normalize so many things that seemed to be quite scary and very, very odd at the time.

#Throwbackthursday is a blessing and a curse on social media. People post older photos to gloat about how far they have come, to lament having not progressed at all, or to briefly access a charged memory from long ago. It feels to me, as a zealous organizer, like flipping through my filing cabinet and coming across an old love note, or cleaning Jackson's room and unearthing a precious masterpiece created at daycare. Memories are state dependent— meaning they are more easily accessible when you are feeling the same way you did when the event took place. This is why roaring laughter with old friends easily leads to funny story after funny story, and why raging at a spouse easily slips into reminding them about every single thing they have done wrong. Ever. Many events in recent years have done just that for me; my experiences led to vivid blasts-from-the-past which I have often included.

You may notice I exist most comfortably in logistics and action plans. I don't think that stems as much from being 87% left-brained as it does from becoming queasy around the touchy-feely aspects of life. Strong emotional experiences induce a physical lump in my throat—likely a psychosomatic block in the pathway between my heart and my head. Emotions are hard for me to name, brutally hard for me to share, and allowing myself to experience them is often an impossible task. I am not a robot, I am deeply sensitive and often empathic. Know that it took mammoth effort to insert the sentiments attached to events in my own life into these pages.

I considered adding a disclaimer here about "not knowing what it is like to be a trans person", or that "my experiences do not even begin to depict the vast array of issues and roadblocks facing alcoholics", or that "I do not speak for all of the autism community".* That stems from my own fear of people not liking my ideas. This book is a request for others to join me in a journey of digging deeper, miles beyond the sensational appeal of "the" surgery, behind the scenes of Rehab reality shows, past the stereotype of *Rainman*, into the real life of my family. I won't press the issue further. Take what you like, and leave the rest.

#throwback #2009 #readyforrehab

---

*   British folk and American folk can't agree on ". or ." so you're getting both!

Learn

2011

When you assemble a list of your best personality traits for Plenty of Fish™, you will catch what you lure. I tried my best to avoid men posting selfies taken on iPhones while they were in public washrooms, tag lines that included #hookup, and other obvious deal-breakers.

My top three self-described personality attributes were quite simple to identify: I could earn a good living, I could run a tight house, and I could have sex. I'm not sure why it took years of failed relationships with variants of the same guy for me to figure out that I was attracting men who needed me to earn the money, to organize their lives, and who expected a fantasy-like sex life.

I was challenged by my Alcoholics Anonymous sponsor to go on *10 first dates*. She was under the impression (and rightfully so) that I had no idea what I wanted or needed. It was an exercise in letting go of the voice inside saying, "This *HAS* to be the guy . . ." Everything I let go of had claw marks all over it.

I dug deeper and stripped the top three from my tackle box. But, when you lose the best personality traits, what are you left with?

Username: cg999
Catch line: Uses a machete to cut through red tape

Profile:

You will find me at Home Depot, not Holt Renfrew. You will find me riding elephants, not riding in a Corvette. You will find me in a hostel, not at the Hilton. You will usually find me in jeans, but I can dress it up for a fabulous night on the town.

I save wisely and spend freely. I'm deeply spiritual but not religious. I work in a health care profession and enjoy my days working as much as my days off.

I love beds that feel like clouds and the very first sniff out of a fresh tin of coffee. I save the best part of the Nanaimo bar for last . . . the yellow stuff. I soak up big waves and long for warm ocean days.

I am a busy mother of 2 fabulous boys. I am searching for someone to be the cherry on top of the already complete Carla cake.

Johnny

I met Johnny at an exclusive restaurant opening I had crashed years earlier and we had dated happily for months. Johnny was a ridiculously wealthy workaholic. He took me to concerts in limos, broke spontaneously into show tune songs, bought swanky prizes at silent auctions, and tried his best to keep up with someone slightly older than his daughter. I went away on a trip to Thailand and things fizzled out after I returned. I thought I'd try again.

> iPhone Me: Hey Johnny! I think I'm about 3 years late for that birthday dinner I owe you!
> iJohnny: How did you remember it was my birthday? ☺
> *I hadn't! Lucky break.*
> iMe: Meet me. Wednesday evening?
> iJohnny: Absolutely. 7pm. Earl's.

We met, reminisced, and flirted. I ordered the extra fancy stuff on top of my steak which I often deny myself, certain he would pick up the tab. Johnny ordered something soft because of his new braces . . . his vanity hadn't waned. Much had happened in the preceding few years. My life had imploded and I had fallen deeply into the clutches of alcoholism, eventually landing in a residential treatment centre. His life had accelerated and he had launched himself into the entertainment world, in addition to growing his construction empire. He looked well, but old—I tried to block this obvious truth out of my mind.

Our second date, this time around, was an invitation to see his new home. It was a breathtaking rebuild in an opulent neighbourhood. Granite cook tops for the BBQ, hand rubbed hardwood, the plastic grass you never need to water or mow . . . every luxury imaginable. I reluctantly took my dog Monty (newly rescued) with me at Johnny's request so our pups could play together.

We kept toasty outside by a fire and the dogs frolicked. Inside, he sang and played his grand piano with intensity; my adoration soared. Monty, on the other hand, must have been frightened enough to shit on the new *white* silk shag area rug. Johnny discovered the surprise when he stepped in it, tracking it across the carpet, and because his sock was covered in the slippery mess when he hit the hardwood floor, he wiped out. I almost died of embarrassment. I spent the remainder of the evening cleaning up dog crap on my hands and knees.

Johnny cancelled our next date. He never asked me out again. Monty RUINED my chances at the "good life".

#icomewithshit #nottrophywifematerial #easytolovearichman 💩

Bert

I spotted Bert in the parking lot of the bookstore while I was finding a spot. I was alarmed immediately because, although he looked very much like his profile pictures, his stature resembled that of my ex-husband Iain. This didn't bode well.

He had two children and a working relationship with their mother. This was a good thing, right? It was also the moment I became consciously aware that I had very little desire to deal with other people's children. There are many days I struggled to even like my own. We discussed parenting plans and techniques, and I did come away with a few ideas to try. The conversation went something like this:

Bert: So, tell me about your spirituality.
Me: Ummm . . . it's hard to articulate. It's an all-encompassing energy flowing with colours and various intensities, passing through life, and beings, and decisions. The birther of the Universe. *Ask me about my powertools first!! Then you can ask about my spirit . . .*
Bert: I'm painting my house in earth tones.

#cantstandotherpeopleskids #tooedgyforearthtones

Jason

Jason had potential on paper. He was a tall, 40-ish operations manager at a large building material supplier. I was impressed; he was late for our dinner by a few minutes because he was flying back to town from a business meeting. The flip side of the jet-setting was that he forgot his wallet on the plane, so I had to buy our meal, in addition to giving him money to get his vehicle out of the parkade.

To a sane person, this would have been a warning sign, unfortunately, when dating, I'm not sane.

We enjoyed a few more lovely meals together, and a few evenings of passion, and then, "the talk".

Jason: I think we should slow down our physical relationship.
Me: You'll need to explain.
Jason: I have been in so many relationships that start out hot and heavy and never work out.
Me: Why don't you tell me about all the relationships that were NOT hot and heavy and DID work out?
Baffled.
If you don't want to have sex with me, how will I know you like me?
Did I actually just say that out loud?

I couldn't help myself and dropped a bottle of AstroGlide® in his mailbox one afternoon to remind him I was thinking of him . . . old teasing habits are hard to break.

Jason: My mother seemed distressed when she came and made my dinner this evening. She asked me when mailmen started giving out sample products.

End of relationship.

#sexdoesnotequallove #single40yearoldscantshare
#everyoneknowsajason

Gavin

His witty texts gave me butterflies. Gavin and I met for breakfast as soon as we could. He was a smart, engaging, fit, handsome, and available stock broker with a completed family. He was by far the best catch I had made. Who wouldn't want someone who had it all? I envied his simple life with big ambitions.

We had come up with a nice division of labour through our conversations:

Vice President—Fitness	Gavin: the obvious choice as he was training for a marathon. I had given up jogging eons earlier when my cigarette kept going out.
Vice President—Food	Me: a day in the kitchen cooking for someone who enjoyed eating, it really filled my cup.
Vice President—Furry Friends	Me: Gavin said, "tried but just CAN'T love them."
Vice President—Procurement	Gavin: anxiety seeped through my pores when I even entertained the thought of shopping . . .
Vice President—Finance	Dual appointment? Gavin with obvious monetary skills and myself, born an accountant at heart, with an unhealthy love of Excel spreadsheets . . .

While out for dinner on our second date, I received a text from SuperJen, the kid-sitter, who was minding the boys and post-surgery Monty after his second prolapsed eyelid repair operation.

iSuperJen: Monty is really after his eye . . .

I can't get the cut on Jackson's head to stop bleeding, but I think it looks worse than it is.

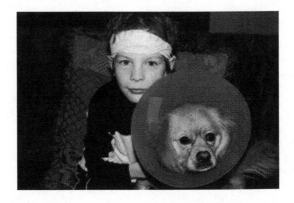

Back to reality.

#mustlovedogs #mywalkingwounded

Dean

Me: What do you do?
Dean: I'm a video executive. I produced shows on public television for years before I started doing contract work.
Me: Cool. What kind of stuff?
Dean: Uh . . . I'd rather not talk about it on a first date.
Me: *It had to be porn. What else wouldn't he want to talk about?!?* Porn.
Dean: Well, not *exactly*. It's a *"reality"* show. For Playboy television.
Me: And the difference is?
Dean: I'm producing a show filming a teenager who is trying to start a porn business in his basement with his friends . . . he is a pizza delivery guy for extra money.

I was no porn star. I decided that it would be a good idea to assess whether he had picked up any useful skills during his time in "the industry". My conclusion was . . . *not*. I woke up next to an ordinary man in a creepy Darth Vader-like sleep apnea machine mask.

#awkward #understandablydivorced #walkofshame

Daniel

I was blown away by his charisma and intriguing interests . . . Our phone calls were lengthy, and we truly connected on our first couple dates.

But there were warning signs . . .

- He jumped for joy that I was in AA because he had just celebrated three weeks clean
- Pocket dialed at 02:17 the night before he vanished for two days
- Ditched on Valentine's Day because he had been pulled over in an unregistered vehicle

#cocaineisanastyhabit #getyourshittogether
#tiedthoseredflagsintoabeautifulscarf

Arthur

Arthur was a nice mix of tattoos, motorbikes, international travels, grenades, and doggy love. He was a little lispy, and quite round. Property manager, with a couple of university degrees, married once for 13 years, no kids.

Arthur: I was SO nervous waiting here . . . I even drove here with all my windows down and asked the waitress if my cologne is too strong.
Blush.
Tell me about your day?
Me: It's crazy that we connected today because I had a sitter booked with plans that had fallen through—I know you don't know me yet, but the odds of having an available kid-free evening are unfathomable! But then that sitter's car broke down, so I tracked down another . . . and my dog bit me this morning, in a frantic effort to free a stuck paw, so I spent the day alternating between icing my hand, tending Monty, and painting a wall green . . . Eliot has a film project and needed a green screen so I demolished the den. Luckily, I got that done before I had to take

Jackson to an outdoor hockey practice and drop him at home, because the second sitter doesn't drive. Sorry that I'm a few minutes late.

If he doesn't go running after that recap of an average day, I'll be amazed. I'm still covered in "Traffic Light Green" paint flecks and have a bitten hand I need to keep elevated.

Arthur: Wow, big day.

Me: And I just started Weight Watchers™, again, so I have saved up 15 points for our sushi supper! I'm starving. Tell me about you!

Funny from the little girl speaking to a large man . . .

Maybe this could work.

#broughtmeflowers #onlinedatingsucks

May 12, 2012

I had finally organized the trip I had been dreaming of for years. California, with grandparents and kids old enough to frolic in the ocean. Big holidays were difficult to orchestrate as a single parent, not just the time and money, but logistically—who waits with the child that doesn't want to go on the ride?

When I envisioned Disneyland, I was expecting corn dogs, stale beer spills, and vomiting children—more like the Calgary Stampede. I must report that I was very wrong—it truly was the happiest place on earth. The boys, nearly 10 and 12, had saved their own spending money and were thrilled to blow it on bags of candy (Jackson) and framed animation cells (Eliot). Ride after ride, meal after meal, day after day, we all soaked up the fun and sun. Gramma rode California Screamin' three times, and Papa navigated and enjoyed his family.

We enjoyed the Getty Museum and Universal Studios, where we caught a glimpse of the Bates Motel to satisfy Eliot's Hitchcock obsession. Jackson tried out the chicken fingers and fries at every restaurant we could find.

Iain and I had both made a concerted effort to share great parenting moments with each other even from afar, ones that would have otherwise been lost as the result of our collapsed marriage. Though Iain was not "my guy", he was my co-parent; he was the father of my children.

iMe: We're on Hollywood Blvd . . .

Eliot told some crazy dressed up lady that he had enough sunscreen on that "he wasn't gonna' look like Snooki . . ."

And Jackson bought him the "Best Drama Queen Academy Award . . ."

August 2, 2012

I was into my seventh year of major home renovations. "The Gemstone", affectionately named by Eliot because of the broken bits of coloured glass embedded in the rock-dash stucco, was bigger than I could manage, and older than I knew what to do with.

The Gemstone was built in 1937 and was originally the farm house of a local pioneer. Year after year, I tackled what I could: foundation, windows, electrical, plumbing, squirrels, a cistern of water under the basement floor, mice, and cracks in the lath and plaster. My house was "that house" to people who were familiar with the neighbourhood. I loved the original hardwood floors and the triangular knee-wall spaces, used mostly for kid sleepovers. It was my money pit and my labour of love.

Arthur listed and sold his house at a loss, a hasty decision to try to lose some of his emotional baggage. This involved moving an entire house of furniture into a house that was already full of furniture. We worked feverishly to organize the completion of the basement and second bathroom so he would have a functional shower. We both dug deep to cut the strings of attachment to furniture we had accumulated over time, and trinkets that no longer fit in our combined space. My house, now our home, was infused with a new energy—2 adults, 2 kids, and 4 dogs!

August 24, 2012

I never wanted a giant rock. They were impractical, got caught on everything, and I feared losing valuable things. I vividly remember the white gold cross molded from my parents' wedding rings falling irretrievably down a shower drain. The remorse has always stuck with me.

But I gotta' tell you, stepping into a ring store makes a $20,000 ring look pretty damn attractive! I spent hours Googling rings. I schooled myself in clarity, colour, and cut. I checked out every ring at the counter at work. I tried to rationalize the decision with people in my life who could tell me "you deserve it!" and "it only happens once!" and "you will love it forever!". I now understood why people say bridal fairs are the worst possible place to take a bride.

The ring I couldn't stop looking at was a vintage 1950s white gold vine-y design with a white diamond and two blue diamonds. It had been hiding on consignment in an antique store. Arthur proposed on our 6-month anniversary at the sushi restaurant where we had had our first date; I accepted with love in my soul.

September 1, 2012
Jackson was geared up on his relatively new BMX bike. He had asked permission to go to the skate park for the first time, and I hesitantly agreed; after all, it wasn't far away. I hoped some other parent would have stepped up to the plate and accompanied their child; I was "tired" and "busy". Somebody in this community would likely be present to reduce the chances of my 10-year-old smoking with some hoodlum skateboarders.

> *Phone rings—I typically don't even answer the home phone, but instinct insists. A friend's father on Jackson's cell calling from the skate park.*
> Father: Is this Jackson's mom?
> Me: Yes . . .

My heart sinks— everyone who loves someone knows this feeling.
Father: He took a spectacular bail off his bike. I think he's okay, but
he'll need to be cleaned up.
Me: I'm on my way.

Time stood still while I drove the three blocks to the scene of the
accident. I was stopped at a green light waiting for an ambulance,
the sirens piercing my eardrums, on its way to Jackson. It cleared the
intersection en route to my baby . . . then time sped away from me
. . . I couldn't catch my breath. It occurred to me then how bad it
could be.

When I reached my Jackson, he was being attended to by many
paramedics, clearing his spine, assessing his bloody little body for
broken bones. I confirmed for them that "I am Mom," and felt a
crushing sense of guilt for not having been there to protect him.

Road rash had scraped the freckles and smile off half of his face.
Doctors in the emergency room scraped the dirt out of the wounds
with what looked like a nail brush. Laughing gas took the edge off,
and lidocaine numbed his skin. We do chuckle at the ripped shirt he
was wearing which read "I do my own stunts".

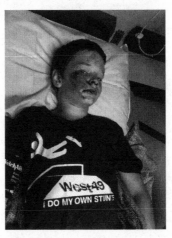

I tried to redeem my worthiness as a parent, after having missed
his first big injury, by tending to his wounds with the best possible
pharmaceutical products and specialty bandages available every few
hours, night and day. The wounds inevitably healed; his flesh and my
heart. With the healing came some recognition that kids will do what
kids do.

September 3, 2012

Almost exactly ten years earlier, Iain and I moved across the country into what was a tough house for everyday living, especially during the stormy winter. We had wood stoves for heat, lost power almost weekly, a shallow well produced minimal amounts of apple juice-coloured water, and ocean storms that forced the windows to bow.

I shivered in baths of yellowish well-water just barely deep enough to cover my ears and muffle out the sounds of crying babies and my own breathing. I can still recount the plans to end my suffering wallowing in my first undiagnosed post-partum depression. They were very dark, lonely days for me.

Eliot was terribly two and Jackson was just six weeks. I began taking the boys to a playschool in the mornings for some mama reprieve. Eliot wasn't quite three, so I stayed, watching him tromp around in a pair of thigh-high cowboy boots, which slowed him down only slightly. He was a smart, headstrong child who enjoyed identifying the make and model of every vehicle in a parking lot and carefully lining up his dinky cars. He was mostly interested in fans, the household oscillating variety, and frilly dress-up clothes. We never made it through circle time without a tantrum, and I always felt it necessary to excuse ourselves after our hour of "socialization" was up.

Months passed, and I celebrated the day I could leave Eliot and his crazy blonde curls alone at playschool with his teacher Linda. I went home and celebrated with bottles of red wine. It hadn't been but 4 weeks before the teacher pulled me aside.

Linda: Today he insisted we change all the words in "Head, shoulders, knees, and toes" to "Cranium, clavicle, patella, and metatarsals"!
We love Eliot. And don't want him to leave. Most kids settle once they have explored everything. He never does. He escalates. The waiting list is long for "assessments" and maybe if you got his name on the list now, if we still have concerns in a year you won't be behind again.

Me: Thank you.

I imagine the teachers had engaged in long discussions amongst themselves about whether I would be receptive to their suggestion or not. Who wants to tell a mother there is potentially something "wrong" with their beautiful child?

I cried and cried. We stopped at the blueberry patch on the walk home for a few extra minutes, to indulge Eliot's desires. They were tears of relief. Someone else had finally noticed how much harder I was working than all the other moms at the playground.

Friend: Linda has seen a lot of kids; she is a pretty good judge of the bell curve of "normal".

Me: I trust her, for sure. And the doctor did think falling on the backs of his hands to avoid the dirt touching his palms, his diet of cold spaghetti and soya sauce eaten with chop sticks, lining up objects, and the intensity of his determination was a bit unusual. He's referred us to a pediatrician.

Friend: He reminds me a lot of a friend's son who was just diagnosed with Asperger's Syndrome.
Me: Never heard of it.

When I read the page on the computer that popped up on my pre-Google search for "Asperger's", I was blown away. "Children with Asperger's syndrome are generally awkward in social situations and often have difficulty interacting with peers. They may develop eccentric or odd repetitive behaviors. Children with this condition often have unusual preoccupations or rituals and may develop an intense, almost obsessive, interest in a few areas." That was my Eliot. How could I have not known?

I had thought knowing all his letters and numbers at 14-months-old was a sign of brilliance, not of a diagnosable mental health disorder. He was so cute, and he talked so well! On some levels, it was hard to believe there was anything wrong. The more I learned and the more I connected with the online Asperger's community, the surer I was and the more wine I drank.

What followed were years and years of public and private assessment with psychiatrists, psychologists, occupational and physical therapists, early interventionists, and many others. It was years of specialized programming at home and at school, and one of fighting for funding for aides and for supports in a regular classroom. It was years of sly looks from other parents saying with a glance, "can't you control your child?" and "my child would never do that." It was years of joy, and exhaustion, parenting a very special little spirit—probably a book in itself now wrapped into this small paragraph.

Eliot completed kindergarten through grade 2 with a full-time aide, grade 3 with a part time aide and then began to fail in grades 4 and 5 when he was left to his own devices. It was a cruel test in "Wow, he is doing so well while supported, let's pull the funding and see how well he does." It was a story every parent of a child with special needs will understand.

He was later enrolled in an Academic Challenge program in Suburbia Junior High. The class of 12 exceptionally smart quirky kids was a good fit for him—lead by a teacher named Ellen who really "got" the odd child. He would rather have been in grade 7 in the other junior high with ALL his "friends," but this was where he needed to be.

September 11, 2012

The dogs, like the rest of us, had some sorting out of personalities and neuroticisms to do.

Arthur's three dogs—Snazzy, Benny, and Angie—moved in as soon as the fence was up to safely enclose them. Snazzy, the deaf Dalmatian, was the eldest and thus was entitled to a special spot on the sleeping couch in our room. Benny, affectionately named Lick-Licky McDicky, was the anxiety-plagued Chihuahua/Jack Russell cross obsessed with his genitals and stealing my underwear. If you could coax him out from under the couch where he hid growling at feet, he really could give the best hugs. Angie was truly man's best friend, an ever-gentle sweet lab companion who tolerated all sorts of jackassery from the other mutts. My Monty was aloof and disinterested in his new friends.

They were all rescues. They all came with fears and habits developed from experiences we will never hear about. Then, as now, I err on the side of compassion when I deal with their devious doggy behaviours.

Snazzy was drooly, loving, and gentle. I adored her soft coat of hair and oddly shaped spots, but especially the heart shaped one on her back, and the way she religiously waited outside Arthur's shower door while he cleaned up. He was the only man she trusted.

Her hind legs were failing at 14 years old, her mind was certainly demented, and she had a 2-hour bladder. I made the dreaded appointment and took a day off work. Could she have lived more days? Probably, but as each day got marginally worse than the one before, and the flicker of life faded from her confused eyes, it simply felt like the right time.

I wish we could be as humane to humans. Snazzy was surrounded with love and people she knew and trusted. We quietly witnessed her exhale her last breath.

September 22, 2012

I peed on a few sticks and the lines were a brilliant blue. I carefully hid the box and wrappers in toilet paper before disposing of them at work to keep my new secret carefully hidden. The nausea and fatigue were no lie . . . I was pregnant!

The hours until I would share the news with Arthur dragged painfully on—a mix of nervousness and elation. We went for sushi at the restaurant that had now become the "location of important events".

Me: Handed him a card and 2 wrapped packages.
Open it! It's your birthday present.
Arthur: My birthday isn't until next weekend; I'll open it then.
Me: No, no. I don't want to wait. Open it!
Arthur: It's not my birthday, I can't.
Me: Arthur, please open it. Next weekend we'll be at my Mom's for Thanksgiving, and it isn't appropriate to do it then.
Arthur: No. I'll wait.
Me: OPEN IT.
Elevated to an estrogen induced mini-rage only a pregnant woman would relate to.
Arthur: Fine.
Opens the card and examines the printed screenshots of Draw Something® I had been saving for months.

Me: *He seriously has no clue yet.*
Arthur: *Opens the card and read all the way through . . .*
He gets to where it says, "We are having a baby" before he clues in.
SERIOUSLY?!?
Me: Baby Z should be due in the beginning of June . . .
Arthur: *Jumps up, yelling, and thrusts a fist in the air, cheering to our Japanese waitresses . . .*

WE'RE HAVING A BABY!!

Arthur had waited his whole life for this day. We proudly wore our smiles and tears, and enjoyed our meal, with no tuna tataki, chattering about possibilities.

October 2, 2012

Jackson started his grade 5 year late, after returning from a fabulous trip to Scotland with Iain. He was put in a Grade 4/5 split class. While I trusted that his teacher could handle the challenge, she wasn't able to change the fact that he had almost no friends in the room, or that he would be spending half his time reviewing content he had learned the year before. Jackson also had a personality conflict with an old-school style teacher who would be teaching him a few core subjects.

I methodically investigated possibilities. Moving him to the other grade 5 class wasn't going to happen. Staying where he was seemed unfair to Jackson; although I didn't believe his grade 5 teacher would be the sole determining factor of his entire education, it still left me unsettled. Home school? Not a chance—I had no patience and I would risk Jackson hating me forever. Specialized program? Sports Academy!

There were some significant drawbacks to this plan: Sports Academy school wouldn't bus Jackson to school, which meant driving to and from school (or, in my case, being a working parent, this meant begging friends, hiring taxis, and using public transit), it was expensive (not only the program fees, but also trying to keep up with the Jones' and all their hockey sticks that equated to mortgage payments), and Jackson was understandably hesitant to leave his friends behind.

Despite the hurdles, we made the switch and the results were better than we could have hoped for. In addition to skating with ex-NHL coaches twice a week, he participated in water polo, ju-jitsu, golf, and all sorts of cool sports. His academics skyrocketed—engage a child their way and they become more able and willing to learn. Jackson also now had something special, for just him.

I had become the hockey mom I swore I would never be. I liked it, but didn't often admit it.

October 3, 2012

Most mothers of special needs children only describe their biggest fears for their children at very vulnerable moments, and with tears in their eyes. Mostly, we stand strong behind masks and toe the party line necessary to get support, funding, and maintain our sanity.

"He is doing so well at school, thanks to the support of our aide, he hasn't bolted onto the road at recess in almost two weeks!"

"We have some issues at home, but we are working on the fecal smearing with the Behavioral Interventionist."

"We are *FINE*. He had a mostly successful playdate last week with a nice little girl—only had two or three meltdowns before we were asked to leave."

Bullying scared me. Not having friends scared me. A child feeling rejected is painful for a mom. I reached out to someone much more in tune with millennial teens than I was—his teacher, Ellen.

e-mail Me: Hi Ellen—

Eliot arrived home tonight without his backpack. He had left it on the seat behind him and Eric. Jonah had moved up towards the front of the bus taunting Eliot (repeatedly calling them nasty names) and when the pack fell into the aisle, Jonah took it. Eliot didn't want to make a big scene in front of all the kids on the bus, so now he is home without textbooks or homework.

Eliot was upset about it, not wanting to make things worse, but quite worried and full of anxiety about Jonah and his "looks", and now about further incidents on the bus and at school. He and Jonah had a tumultuous relationship at summer camp last year involving some "gay" derogatory slurs and revenge with a bug-sprayed pillow.

Eliot is going to talk to the bus driver tomorrow morning after all the other kids have gotten off. Hopefully the pack will have been left on the bus by Jonah . . .

Thanks for your help—

Carla

eEllen: Good Morning!
I will get to the bottom of this and I will let you know how this plays out. This is totally unacceptable behaviour and this youth could lose his bus privileges, at the very least.

elain: Thanks. It's a long school year—this incident is very definitely a step in the wrong direction, and we need to re-establish a comfortable atmosphere on that bus, one that lasts. Let us know if there's anything we can do. We appreciate you getting on top of it, and I'm sure you'll find the right track.

Ellen met with the boys and they were forced to come up with a working plan on a tolerable relationship with each other. Eliot would not antagonize Jonah and his friends, and Jonah would steer clear of Eliot. No taunting, no teasing, just living their own paths with the understanding that not everyone would like everyone else. It was an important lesson to learn—don't knowingly harm people, emotionally or physically, along your life path.

The Jonah situation faded away, but my own fear of all the Jonahs in the world was smoldering.

October 4, 2012

iMe: Eliot told me this morning gender reassignment surgery is covered by Alberta Health & Wellness . . .

iArthur: WTF!!!??!!

I had known, deep down, for a decade that someday we would hit a rainbow-coloured door.

Eliot later shared with me that some of his friends knew about his gender dysphoria (previously known as gender identity disorder) before I did. It hurt my feelings. They weren't the ones who were going to have to deal with this . . . the protective bubbles I felt a need to inflate, the friends and family I was going to have to spend time and energy explaining this to, the healthcare workers I would need to engage. Why did his friends get to know first?

Apparently, I was not alone in this situation. Many kids come out regarding their sexuality or gender identity to friends, a confidante, or online, long (months or even years) before they tell their parents. Maybe it was to protect their parents' feelings? Maybe it was to avoid the burden of being "the cause" of shattered expectations? Maybe it was the fear of being abandoned or disowned? Often, even when they do come out with regards to sexual orientation, it's as bisexual— testing the waters of being a sexual minority, while still leaving a glimmer of hope that they're still partially "straight".

I hope I reacted the "right" way to his news. The lead up in a child's mind to disclosing this news to their parents is life-changingly huge. A negative reaction, even if it stems from surprise instead of disapproval, can be scarring. I Googled a bit and came across this article:

Transgender Youth and Their Parents

We need to better understand transgender people and their families.

If you thought it might be hard for a parent to hear that a child is gay or lesbian, imagine what it must be like to hear that your son feels he was born into the wrong body and is really a woman or that your daughter is certain she was meant to be a man. Parents, like most people in our society, are uncomfortable with cross-gendered behavior, especially in their children. So, it must be especially difficult for a parent to adjust to the news that their children felt as if their psychological gender is at odds with the bodies they were born into. The few experts there are in this area describe how deeply distressing such a disclosure can be for parents and how children coming out as transgender can be wounded by parental reactions and are at great risk for being thrown out of their homes.[2]

I overstepped by sharing the news with Arthur and Iain without Eliot's explicit consent to do so. Maybe he wasn't ready, but *I needed them to know*, to share in the craziness of this with me. If I were to do this again, I would have waited until Eliot initiated further disclosures. No one walks this path without hitting a few of the potholes.

October 5, 2012

I resented Alcoholics Anonymous. I believed it to be a cult. I had not sobered up to spend my life in dingy church basements with aging men who had nothing better to do than talk about the old "drinking days".

I was wrong. For me, it opened doors to other avenues of healthy living and introduced me to loving others and living fully . . .

"We admitted we were powerless over alcohol—that our lives had become unmanageable."

I dug into this Step 1 with my Serenity Sisters, a group of women from all walks of life and from all varieties of 12 step programs who met weekly on Thursday nights. We were patient supporters, quiet listeners, and kindred spirits.

2   LaSala, Michael C. (2011, February 7). Transgender Youth and Their Parents [Web log comment]. Retrieved from https://www.psychologytoday.com/blog/gay-and-lesbian-well-being/201102/transgender-youth-and-their-parents

We started late, talked too long and cried just enough. I did a painful search through my list of *Feeling Words*[3] to try to describe where I was at during check-in. At 37, this still wasn't an easy task, since "good", "fine", and "okay" were banned words.

My counsellor at Provincial Addiction Services in 2008 must have seen my familiar façade before. I arrogantly thought I was unique and special, but I was just like every other girl with an addiction. We talked about my stresses at work, at home, and in life in general. I told her about my potential plans to get well . . . Maybe attend a day program? Maybe go to some 12-step meetings when I could secure child care? I had quit cold turkey before and I could do it again.

> Counsellor: Have you ever considered a residential treatment program?
> Me: Never.
> Counsellor: How do you feel about attending one now?
> Me: I don't need that. I'm not THAT bad.
> Rehab? What would I do with my kids? What about my job? How would I pay my bills?
> Straight to logistics, things my logical brain can handle.
> Counsellor: I am concerned about how you will fare in recovery at home. Your kids don't have any more than a shell of you now. You're disengaged, emotionally unavailable, and not able to share in any of their joys.

I sat in my car in the parkade. The belly sobs I had been stuffing down for months and years came out in waves. She wasn't wrong, and I wasn't angry with her honesty. The only time I recalled a similar feeling was the first time someone mentioned having Eliot "assessed". It was overwhelming relief and gratitude for someone else noticing how hard I was struggling.

I headed to the liquor store with my car on auto-pilot, and then home alone to break my 27 days of sobriety. I drank and drank and drank. I downed a handful of pills to forget the pain and overwhelming despair that crushed me. I didn't intend on not living, I just needed a break. Life just felt too big.

3   Alcoholics Anonymous. (2001). Alcoholics Anonymous, 4th Edition. New York: A.A. World Services. Attached as Appendix A, in case anyone else needs one ☺

*By the grace of the universe, and the boyfriend who slung me over
his shoulder and took me to the hospital, I survived the night. I was
discharged from the emergency room into his care. I finally woke from a
fog with my mom caring for me several nights later. Three days of my life
had vanished from my memory. The blessing and hazard of retrograde
amnesia associated with benzodiazepines.*

 *At some point during the hazy weeks, I sat, committed in the psych
ward, in a small white room with white doors and white chairs, making
a phone call.*

 Me: There is a crazy guy looking in the window at me.
 There is a guy looking through the window at a crazy girl.

*My mom stayed to help me detox and mind the boys while I was
attending an addictions day program. I was waiting for a placement at
a women's treatment centre. I was off work and willing to shell a lot of
money to get my life back on track. I had humbled myself to ask Iain to
stay at The Gemstone and care for the boys while I healed.*

 *Powerlessness had become a relief . . . I could throw my hands up and
say, "I give up, I give in." I had not done it gracefully, though. I did it
kicking and screaming after years and years of "managing just fine" . . .*

 I had fallen to my knees.

October 6, 2012

 We stopped at A&W for burgers en route to our annual family
Cookie Day gathering. Dozens of shortbread cookies (36 dozen or
less, depending on how much dough I ate) hand-mixed, decorated,
and baked by all available extended family members.

 Me: So, kids, we have some news for you . . .
 Jackson: What?
 Me: We are going to have a baby!
 Silence. A degree of subtle disappointment. Curiosity.
 Eliot: You're not even going to be able to wear heels.
 Disgust.
 Me: Eliot! I never wear heels now . . .
 Eliot: And HOW are you going to lose all that baby fat??
 *Elderly couple in the booth next to us glance over in disbelief, jaws
drop.*

Jackson: If it's a boy, can I teach him hockey?
Eliot: If it's a girl, can I put her in pageants?
Arthur and I each took a deep breath.

October 10, 2012

I was becoming more and more frustrated with Eliot's behaviours. This typically meant one of two things: I need to get him more help, or I need to increase my own medications. Since I seemed to be almost coping with, and enjoying in a pregnant kind of way, most of the other craziness that was my life, I started rallying the troops to deal with Eliot.

eMe: Iain—

I would like to ask our family doctor to refer us back to a Youth Psychiatrist, as well as seeing the Family Psychologist, after your upcoming China trip. Partially for gender issues, but also because his obsessing over thoughts and ideas is becoming more pronounced and disruptive. Most recently is a Mac book, (though not new) he seems totally unable to focus on anything else. It comes across as begging and complaining and bad attitude, but I'm wondering if it's more obsessive type thoughts he truly can't let go of? She would be able to help sort it out. You okay with that? Will likely be a long wait anyways . . .

elain: Carla,

I don't like the idea of pursuing another "diagnosis" to hang on Eliot, not one bit, so don't book anything until we discuss this.

I had learned down the path to the Autism Spectrum Disorder (ASD) diagnosis that Eliot already had labels, just not ones from the Diagnostic and Statistical Manual of Mental Disorders (DSM-V). He was "difficult" and "challenging" and "spirited" and "defiant" and "headstrong" and "unmanageable". The problem with these labels was they didn't point us in a direction of assistance. They didn't offer us professional support, funding, or appropriate educational materials and strategies.

I had no fear of "diagnoses", knowing they were simply ways for humans to try to categorize each other. That didn't matter to me. What mattered to me was getting the help we needed.

I also wondered how much of the current escalation in behaviours was tied directly to having opened the gender can of worms?

October 11, 2012

In another musty room with strangers, I "came to believe that a Power greater than ourselves could restore us to sanity." This was Step 3.

I imagine this was the step many people hear in a 12-step program just before turning and walking out. Wounded by religious tenants and church figures and airy-fairy ideas of anything godly helping us out with real life problems, wars over human interpretations of deities erupt all over the world. I held deeply onto the tenant that "AA is not allied with any sect, denomination, politics, organization or institution; does not wish to engage in any controversy; neither endorses nor opposes any causes."[4] I could be spiritual there—my own kind of connection to any Higher Power that worked for me.

I kind of liked Step 3, except the part where we had to admit we were insane. Maybe a spiritual program was an answer to the chaos I had created with my addictive personality? And as corny as it may have sounded for a cerebral person, my connectedness was found in earthy stones and gems, in the thundering of drums in a circle, and in the colours and energies flowing. My Higher Power was not found in a book. Not in a church. It was only for me.

October 13, 2012

I loved my blue truck—it somehow gave me the freedom to do the jobs I need done without waiting for a "man" to assist. My dad, who we called Papa, was proud to have a daughter who had a truck.

I loaded up the back with construction debris and tarped it tightly. I stuffed the extra bags of garbage in the back seat, hoping the Eco Station worker wouldn't see them and charge me extra. Monty joined me because they always had doggy treats at the pay station.

4   Alcoholics Anonymous. (2001). *Alcoholics Anonymous*, 4th Edition. New York: A.A. World Services.

I backed up to the giant bin and started throwing the bags out of the back seat, freeing up room so I could un-tarp the back.

Life slowed to snail speed as I left my body and distanced myself from the chaos . . .

Monty leaped out of the backseat . . . frolicking, free, frenzied!

The mutt headed directly towards the space between the two giant garbage containers. All eyes deduce the reason there was a missing bin is because a new concrete pad was being poured.

Frantic crazy screaming lady (me) tried to coax the dog back out of the six inches of wet concrete. Too late. He was already three full leaps in. Concrete up to his belly.

Thick accents from construction workers screamed "You owe me five hundred dolla'" while waving trowels at the crazy lady and swearing in their mother tongues.

Suctioning sounds echoed as dog was plucked from caustic mixture. Ill-prepared dog owner did not have a leash and then tried to un-tarp the truck with one hand to use it to protect the interior of the cab, to sequester the mangy, hardening dog.

Dog, then contained, all but destroyed the interior of the truck. Lady worked at warp speed to empty the back of the truck while no-one, NO ONE, came to help her . . . perhaps they thought stupidity was contagious.

#ilovemydog #montyruinsmylifeagain #muttmayham

October 15, 2012

After the initial panicked phone calls to make appointments for Eliot to dig into some "gender issues" in a supportive way, the general topic of discussion had been largely absent—at least at home.

I was summoned into school to "check in" about Eliot's grade 7 year. Ellen, the astute teacher, gently prodded into whether Eliot's feminine behaviours were autistically-inappropriate cries for attention. I alluded to the fact we were seeking some help in gender identity and expression; my knee-jerk reaction was to find a way to "tone it down" to alleviate everyone else's discomfort.

Eliot didn't understand my "lingo", so I attempted to explain the concept in terms of colours.

> Me: In some situations, people are expected to act Baby Blue. Like in a library, or visiting someone in a hospital. If you come in acting Cobalt Blue, you will draw attention to yourself.
> Eliot: I like attention.
> Me: But this is the wrong kind of attention. It's more like people notice what you are doing and have negative thoughts about you.
> Eliot: I don't care what they think of me.
> Me: Sometimes it matters what they think of you.
> *I envision Eliot being fired from his 57th job, still living at home.*
> Like the person interviewing you for a job you really want at the Apple® factory, or a person you have a crush on, or other people trying to get their work done at school . . .
> Eliot: Oh, yeah.
> Can I think of . . . like . . . a faded blush pink and a vibrant fuchsia?

October 22, 2012

I was tired. I started bleeding. The threat of miscarriage was present with my other pregnancies. The core of me was terrified I might lose this blastocyst. I was worried I would run out of eggs.

> Me: I hate to call you at home. And hate sharing my news like this even more. But I'm pregnant and I'm bleeding and I need to go to the hospital.
> My boss: I'm on my way in.

Blood work and an ultrasound could not confirm a heartbeat, so Arthur and I waited another stressful 10 days to verify the viability of the pregnancy.

The bleeding continued. My light was dim.

October 24, 2012

It was Eliot's turn for a solo adventure with his dad. He was invited to spend time in China with Iain on a business trip. A dream trip come true for this worldly child. I relished a few weeks with one less child at home.

elain: Carla—

Can provide summary of Boy performance in China later—the good and the bad.

The "Hat Odyssey" was particularly unenjoyable.

Conclusion—will re-evaluate further consult with Dr. whomever. Am not prepared to turn them loose on him but am not entirely certain the right person might not be able to reach him.

Bottom line—China was very good for him, but it wasn't long before it became an extension of "The Eliot Show."

eMe: Iain—

Nothing has improved on this home front. The 48 hours since his return have been particularly hellish. It's been days of saucy, defiant, whiny, self-entitled, never-ending stream of shit coming out of his mouth. I've stopped engaging him completely. Schoolwork and behave or time-out.

Everyone is sick of it . . . Jackson, Arthur, dogs, teachers, and me. Disrespect, blame, laziness. It's been quite unbearable. He is frustrated with me trying to crack down, and he says he wants to live with you.

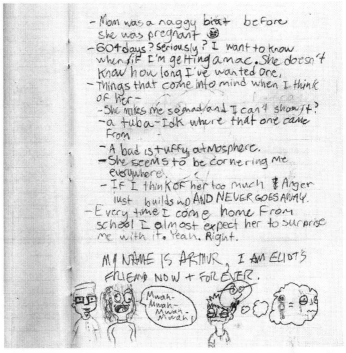

Thanks for reconsidering the psych evaluations. He really is out of control, obsessive, rigid . . . frustrating. He doesn't want to be in Academics Challenge Curriculum anymore, figuring the reason his marks are poor is because he is in a difficult program, and not that he isn't doing an ounce of work. We are spending HOURS at the table doing his assignments together (many of which he doesn't even know exist until we check online). He truly needs some one-on-one guidance to figure out what is being asked of him. He has lost his phone privilege and computer (except for school related stuff).

I will not tolerate the "it's your fault my marks aren't good," and my favorites "you just wait until I really make you suffer," or "I'm working on the list of things you can buy me to make my life more bearable." The autistic lack of ability to connect his own behaviour back to the real cause of the consequence is obvious.

C

October 25, 2012

I tried to warm my bones over a cup of decaf. My Auntie Laurelie and Claire had taken time to join me to watch Jackson's game—the Predators vs. the Pylons. We cheered loudly and I enjoyed a few minutes of letting my voice be heard. My throat chakra had been muted for too long. At the rink was one place I found I could yell and cheer and complain loudly and no one seemed to mind, mostly drowned out by overzealous hockey moms with blow horns.

Auntie Laurelie and Claire had been married in a small ceremony in their home a few years back. It was an honour to be able to share in the celebration of two souls who love one another—a union legal across Canada since 2005—the fourth country in the world, and the first outside Europe, to take such commendable action. It had given our family a gentle entry into the Lesbian-Gay-Bisexual-Transgender-Queer/Questioning (LGBTQ) world years before we knew how much we would tap into the same community again.

They shared their iPhone videos of their recent drag show fundraiser with me, and asked all about our most recent life events.

> Me: I think my son might be a lesbian.
> Aunties: Yeah, one more for the team!

I had never considered the difference between gender and sexuality. I had many gay and lesbian friends, but no gender minorities—at least not known to me. I had never had a need to examine it before.

My Aunties had a sexual (physical + mental) attraction to females; what they identified as gay, or lesbian.

My son may, or may not, have had a sexual preference at 12 years old . . . but gender was different. He related *inside* to being more female. Gender was in the mind, not between the legs. How Eliot expressed himself to the world was rooted in gender, and had nothing to do with sex.

November 2, 2012

> Jackson: Me, I don't think Dad is going to be very happy about this baby.

Me: Why? Your dad likes babies a lot.

Jackson: I don't think he's going to want to look after that baby every second week.

And he's NOT going to be happy about paying for it.

Me: Oh, sweetie, this baby is going to stay here with Arthur and me!

Logical question.

November 12, 2012

I was not at all surprised that shoes had become a contentious issue. Looking back, they always had been. I had read a small study done years earlier with some special needs children. They took three groups of young people and asked them to identify Barbie and Ken toys as boy or girl. Then, they swapped the toy's heads and repeated the questions. The neurotypical group followed the head, as did the group with Down Syndrome. The group with Autism Spectrum Disorders (ASD) gendered them based on their shoes.

3-year-old Eliot:
- Parents and teachers and aides wrote social stories, drew pictures on story boards, and produced rewards of car toys and fans to get him through the boot room without stealing all the other kids' shoes, typically pink and frilly.

4-year-old Eliot:
- Very public melt down in a shoe store because the pink sandals were not an appropriate choice for him. Shoe store employee tried to assist with consolation stickers, but we were already past logic into autistic overload . . .

5-year-old Eliot:
- Entered a mall. We held open the door for a bank executive in an average skirt suit, nylons, low heels and an up-do. Eliot looked her up and down from head to toes and said, in the cutest little voice ever, "You are the most beautiful woman I have ever seen." She cried.

6-year-old Eliot:
- Stopped me in my tracks in a clothing store. "Shhh, can you hear it?" I heard nothing. But Eliot fixated on the sounds of clicking heels in the next aisle.

7-year-old Eliot:
- "The shoes must be all black. No colours. They must not have laces nor Velcro. They must have tall soles because I feel lengthened and more elegant."

Present: 12-year-old Eliot:
- Demanding high heel shoes. He presented us with the following proposal. I spared you the Appendices.

MY PROPOSAL
Eliot Grant

As you probably already know, I have developed a desire to wear high heels to school before the end of the 2012-2013 school year. These have stirred a panic in me, due to the repeated declines, overwhelming, all-encompassing stress, and the fact that school is over in, and I'm here to tell you why, why you should fix it, and what you can do to fix it. Please read thoroughly, and feel free to ask me any questions.

Why I want to wear high heels to school

It seems to you that I want to wear these shoes to attract attention. This is completely false; they aren't to impress anyone. If they like it, good for them. If they don't like them, that's their issue. Your most used point against me is because that i haven't transitioned and that I'm not a girl yet, that I can't wear high heels to school. These shoes aren't related to my transition in any way. If it were, i would also be wearing dresses and handbags to school. As I said, these shoes are for me. The end. These shoes aren't too over the top, or too distracting. You are always pushing me to drop my materialistic mannerisms and to be less trendy and normal, but when i do something that is different and makes me feel better, you smash me back down into the ground. It takes a lot of courage to do something different than the crowd, especially in junior high when everyone is trying so hard to fit in.

CONTENTS

Why you should let me wear high heels to school
These shoes make me feel more comfortable. Lots of kids in junior high are still figuring out who they are, as well as coming to terms with themselves. I am not saying this is the prime purpose of junior high school. These shoes make me feel better, like I feel happier and that I'm okay with myself, and that there's nothing I need to change (there is lots to change, however (example my transition.)) They make me feel confident, but this confidence is not coming from the height that they give me. Another benefit of letting me wear them is that it will alleviate some of my stress. I panic over not being to wear high heels to school at least once or twice a day. I'll go to bed thinking that tomorrow is another day, and maybe, just maybe, I'll be able to wear my shoes to school. I fall asleep bursting at the seams with hope and optimism. I will wake up that morning all smiley and nice, and when you say no, all that hope comes crashing down from Cloud Nine all the way to the ground. I am sad, irritated, angry, and in a nervous panic for the rest of the day. I have many other things to worry about, such as my play, my exams, and my transition. I do not need the overwhelming stress this delivers me 24/7. Letting me wear them doesn't affect you at all. I understand your concern, but i don't feel that need it or want it. I feel confident and comfortable with myself when i wear these shoes, but then you just cut me down to be like everybody else. I would rather get beat up and teased because I'm wearing these shoes then to be sad and safe because I'm not wearing them. I know what the social and societal consequences are, but I just don't care about them. I understand that you are doing this because you love me and you are trying to protect me, but it comes across as the exact opposite. You have told me this, but nothing has changed. In fact, I was doing some internet surfing the other day.

I clicked on a question that someone was asking if they should let their son wear high heels, and I found this quote: "Encourage him. Respect his fashion preference. It's easy to follow the crowd, but takes courage to do something different. And high heels have been worn by men as well, especially in the past, so they are not necessarily women's shoes. I think a son like that should be admired." I understand that you are not them, and they are not my parents. I would rather you treat my shoe preference with indifference than the downright distaste, disgust, and opposition I feel you are showing me now. Of course, encouragement is best, but I feel that that is never, ever going to happen on the topic of me wearing high heels to school in Grade 7. Time is ticking!

It is crucial that you understand that me wearing high heels to school is not, in any way, related to my transition from male to female. I want to wear high heels because i enjoy wearing high heels, as both a boy and a girl. They add a unique twist to my fashion as a boy, and a nice addition as a girl. I plan to continue my transition as planned, after school ends and over the summer. These are Eliot's shoes, not Ella's (yet.) You have no problem with me wearing perfume, concealer, hairspray, among other girly things, and these shoes shouldn't be treated any differently. People notice my perfume, concealer, and hairspray, and often they don't have a problem with it. Neither should you.

My Proposal

I have come up with several possible plans on how to approach this.

Proposal A I wear them for the 8.5 school days from my birthday (June 17th is on a monday this year, going from my mom's house to my dad's house) to the last day of school (June 28th) (I may or may not receive these on or before my birthday.)

Proposal B I wear these shoes on a limited number of days per week (ex-3/5 school days in a week.)

Proposal C I have these shoes to wear every day as a privilege, and can be taken away due to bad behavior just like my computer.

If you let me wear these shoes to school, i might buy them with my own money (with the possible exception of proposals A and B, which they may come as a birthday gift, or with proposal

C as a gift in general.) If a teacher asks me to take them off, i will take them off and not wear them to school, or that class again. Keep in mind that I would wear these shoes like I would wear any other shoes. I would take them off and replace them with my runners in phys ed, like I would with any other shoe. I will withstand the teasing easily. You say that I can't because I've never been teased or antagonized in anyway. This is not true. There have always been people that hate my personality, every day and everywhere, but I don't let them bother me or change anything about me. I have never let them pressure me into changing. If they don't like me, that's their issue. If i do change anything about me, I do it on my own accord, and my reasons come from inside and not outside.

My Conclusion

I would rather learn this "lesson" the hard way and take the risk of getting teased, hurt, or even getting beat up because of wearing those shoes over playing it safe and being bland and normal and not wearing these shoes. They may laugh at me for being different, but I laugh at them because they're all the same.

Please try to understand this from my eyes and at least consider how i feel.

~Eliot Grant

PS I would appreciate that we (Mom, Dad, me, and possibly Arthur) get together to review my proposal as soon as possible. It is important that I am present for the meeting because reasons . . .

Things were changing and it was becoming increasingly evident that Eliot was an uncommon girl.

November 16, 2012

I loved our Family Psychologist. It was always very different to sit in a room as a third party than to directly engage with Eliot. She asked her questions in a different way. Eliot wasn't as defensive. I could really *hear* things. Like the majority of our appointments, I attended this one with Eliot solo. I recounted the visit to Iain and Arthur in a lengthy e-mail exchange:

eMe: We started with an overview of changes for Eliot—of which there have been many . . . Arthur moving in, dogs, renos, junior high school (change of friends again), gender issues, etc. Lots going on for him . . .

We discussed the different parts of the brain, and the different functions they have regarding emotions and problem solving. As I understand it, the limbic system is the BIG, usually fast, emotional response centre—the fight or flight response, intense emotions, physical sensations that accompany them (nausea, tense muscles, etc.) This is the first reaction we have in response to a situation and we need to CALM ourselves to move into the cortex to process the reaction we had.

When we calm down, we move into the cortex (and *only* when we are calm) which sorts out emotions, patterns, visual, and creativity and then we move to the areas where we process language and logic. This is when we overlay words onto our emotions (name them) and try to explain what happened.

The "top of the brain" is where problem solving, organizing, planning, and emotional control (by changing thoughts) happens. But sometimes we get STUCK moving between the areas of the cortex and never get to solving problems. Eliot's brain remains in the simplistic "I felt mad when you did _____" and he can only see one solution to a problem "_____ needs to change their mind and give me what I want." He is never getting to the place where he can develop solutions. We need to help him "get to the top of his brain." Eliot has a hard time connecting the end (him being mad) to the original problem (complaining). We talked about a few examples of how changing the behaviour changes things for HIM at the end of the line (in a positive way). Writing it out and referring to it often seemed to help keep him focused on solutions. We talked about how changing your thought is sometimes the only way to better a situation.

Theory of Mind[5] is lingering here too. Remember that idea of his neurons not being connected to understand that other people are having independent thoughts? Let alone not being able to hold two perspectives at once to reason things out based on what the other person "might" be thinking. In kindergarten it was easy to

---

5   Theory of Mind: refers to the notion that many autistic individuals do not understand that other people have their own plans, thoughts, and points of view

see the fallout of Eliot marching to the front of the line because *he wanted to*, unaware the other children had differing thoughts, and then not comprehending why they were upset . . . It's more socially complicated now.

Lastly, she did mention to me at the end of the session that she noted a definite change in him since the last time we met (about a year ago) in terms of not being able to stay on topic, being "stuck" on thoughts and not being able to let it go. She thought a referral back to the Youth Psychiatrist would be a good idea, IF we can get in (she is not taking new patients apparently, so we may have to try to pull a few strings). Sometimes the exacerbation in pervasive or obsessive thinking at this age is related more to chemical and hormone changes than just neuro structure.

Next visit I'll broach the excessive femininity . . . she did suggest we pursue a referral to a "Gender Clinic" because the wait times can be long.

elain: What happened to the autism part, i.e. I can't let go of the Mac idea because in my mind it's already happened?
I do sincerely hope this is not leading up to someone suggesting drugs for him.

eMe: The "stuck" thinking is absolutely his autistic brain at work. The difference is the intensity and frequency of the thoughts. He used to be able to "put them on the back burner" to focus on the task at hand (i.e. schoolwork or house stuff) but now he is having big troubles. He self admittedly "CAN'T stop thinking about it."

A psychiatrist may suggest meds to tweak his serotonin levels . . . which are somewhat responsible for getting people stuck in the emotional cortex instead of the problem-solving brain. But that would only be after a thorough assessment of where he's at. Hopefully, you'll be around to go and get the information first hand.

I certainly know what it's like to battle your own brain chemistry . . . please don't rule out possibilities of things which may help him before you have all the information. I'm not advocating meds, but we are not talking tranquilizers.

elain: Neither you, the psychiatrist or I will ever, EVER have "all the information." The best you will ever be able to do is say, "Let's try this and see how it goes."

I would advocate a psychologist first. Psychiatrists go to the drugs too easily and too often, and we have no evidence whatsoever that this is chemical, nor do we have evidence that his issues cannot be addressed by other means. I have no faith in the drug industry, any of it, and I am not in favour of drugging him.

He is twelve years old. I do buy the hormonal arguments and even the changes arguments, though from what Eliot tells me he has no problem with Arthur moving in, or the dogs, or the new school, but I'd like to have a long talk with him about all this. We touched on the gender stuff in China but didn't really get into it.

eMe: All I know is that we have a twelve-year-old boy who is struggling. He is not engaged or succeeding at school (teachers are concerned about his "over the top" behavior), is consumed most of his waking hours by negative or anxiety provoking thoughts, not sleeping well, having nausea and stomach issues, is making life miserable for those around him . . .

I'll remind you that I am a pharmacist and well acquainted with the drug industry—pros and cons.

I'm trying to find him some help because I am concerned.

We ARE seeing the psychologist and will continue to do that, regardless of all other options we have.

How, as parents, do we ever really know what the "right" thing to do for our children is? We don't. We just make the next best decision based on the information we have at the time, and then another, then another. If it's not a definite yes, it's a no.

November 18, 2012

I was really struggling. This cliché popped up in my Facebook feed and struck a chord.

"Depression is not a sign of weakness.
It is a sign that you have been too strong for too long."

Maybe I was feeling sorry for myself—the pregnant, stressed-out mother? My own brain chemicals seemed to be failing me, on top of some of the more in-your-face stressors in my life. Eliot. The struggling baby in my belly. New relationship. Renovations. The list was long.

For someone who was more focused on getting the Gold Star of Excellence★ than on *basking in the journey of parenthood*, being a mom was an arduous job. There was no one saying "Wow, you did a really great job of brushing their teeth a few times this month!" or "It's so fabulous that you didn't even kill one of them today!" Mothering, for me, was really a daily grind of tasks and responsibilities that offered no reprieve from my title—not even when I was sleeping, not even when they were in someone else's care. The enormity of forever conjured up bleak feelings for me; exhaustion before the days even started. Of course, there were rewarding moments that trumped the slogging a million times over, but it took a real effort for me to step back and recognize that the stormy sea of emotions, the rolling ups and downs, *were* the best part.

November 20, 2012

I drank less water than I had been instructed to. I knew it took quite a bit less than the "required amount" of fluid to have a full enough bladder for an ultrasound and not have a catastrophic urine incident.

The technician put her screen view up on a wall monitor quickly, sensing our anxiety, and I saw the tiny flicker that was the heartbeat. If I was a crier, this would have been an appropriate time to squeeze out a tear. I don't even think I sighed with relief. I had been holding my breath for so long I had forgotten how to breathe—probably for the entire 12 years since my pregnancy with Eliot . . .

Iain and I had not been together long, were not living in the same city, and were not even getting along. We were a drunken weekend couple. We were undeniably smitten, and I was taken with his witty banter and worldliness. I called him with the news and was met with a positive, if hesitantly optimistic, response. Though not planned, the pregnancy was a blessing.

I was in the middle of a challenging pharmacy hospital residency program and now had a baby on the way. This medical emergency overtook the emotional emergencies of a relationship that challenged my readiness to be in one, an overwhelming and intense professional program and, in retrospect, a blossoming problem with alcohol.

One morning, I peed while sweeping the deck. The nurse on the phone convinced me to come get checked out and the result was a royal blue coloured test stick, indicating amniotic fluid. The weeks before had been full of extra ultrasounds for measuring large, along with other inconclusive but concerning test results. Now, still six weeks early, I was destined to deliver.

What followed were 24 hours of unpleasant medical interventions: an IV line started hastily that punctured my radial nerve, antibiotics that made me sick and sore, an oxytocin drip that dropped the baby's heart rate.

Me: In the bathroom watching blood gush into the water, and I can't remember the nurse's name. I don't want to be rude.
Excuse me?
Ummm, excuse me . . .
IAIN!!

Nurse: Let's get you back into bed, I'm paging the doctor.

The doctor was a confident, reserved, elderly man. He sat in a chair in the corner and assessed the situation, drumming his fingers knowingly on his knee. Premature rupture of membrane. Painless hemorrhaging. Fetal distress.

Doctor: It's time to get this baby out.

Within minutes, I was prepped and strapped down to the operating table, which felt much like a crucifixion. My body was cut open. A baby was extracted. The residents show me an unusual looking placenta—an undiagnosed vasa previa. The tiny preemie was taken away . . . Iain and my parents saw him, but I did not.

A full 12 hours later, I held my beautiful boy for the first time. He was lying in an incubator with IV lines and tubes when I first saw him. He was healthy, but small, and hadn't yet figured out how to breathe and swallow. A few weeks of hospital beds, breast pumps, medical poking and prodding, and we were all discharged healthy and ready to take on the world.

Eliot was a fighter, right from day one.

I continued to bleed, some days quite frighteningly. There is no other option besides trusting that, like Eliot, this baby would hold on.

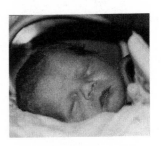

November 23, 2012

> iEliot: When is the next time we're seeing the Family Psychologist? Soon?
> iMe: She is away for the month of Jan . . . next appt is in Feb . . . I will book an appt for you and me to see the family doctor for a referral to the Gender Clinic, if you still want to go—
> iEliot: I think you can get a referral from the walk-in doctor
> iMe: I'll make an appt with the family doc. He needs to know what is going on as well—the family doctor is like the central coordinator of this stuff
> iEliot: k . . . whenabouts would that be?
> iMe: Next week, but the wait for the clinic could be years long by the sounds of it . . .

November 29, 2012

Eliot and I arrived early for an appointment with our family doctor and, as usual, waited an almost inexcusable amount of time. Eliot was anxious beyond the ability to have a calm conversation and begged me to lead the discussion.

> Dr: What can I do for you today?
> Me: Eliot wants to live his life as a girl.
> Dr: I don't think there is much we can do about that.
> Me: *Clueless.*
> I'll expect an urgent referral to the Gender Clinic, given his age.
> Dr: I didn't know there was such a thing.
> Me: Here is the psychiatrist's name and contact information. And thank you.

Our family physician was borderline acceptable at best. My own medical background and no-bullshit attitude was the only reason he sufficed. I knew from previous encounters that he was happy to make referrals when things were even slightly beyond his own scope, and this clearly was.

From that sentence forward, he wouldn't look directly at Eliot. Though he made the referral as requested, his discomfort had been impossible to miss and stuck to Eliot. Was this what we were to expect from the medical community?

Eliot: Good thing I'm not sick often. That man hates who I am.

December 15, 2012

Having survived the six weeks of prickly bitchiness following the discontinuation of my antidepressants in anticipation of carrying a baby, considering a return to the realm of the chemically-medicated reeked of personal failure. This was my third attempt to stop the anti-depressants I had been on for almost 10 years.

Me: I can't get out of bed.
I can barely care for the children I have.
I'm not concentrating at work.
There really is no joy—over something I have wanted for a very long time.
Baby Doctor: Why are you opposed to going back on medications? This level of depression causes more harm to the baby than adverse effects of the medications we can use. You *know* this.
Me: I worry about the effects of altering serotonin levels on a developing brain, just 12 weeks small . . .
Baby Doctor: How many people in your family are on medications for mental health issues?
Me: Every. Single. One.
Baby Doctor: What makes you think this baby will escape your genetics?
She's right. I'm not the boss of my brain chemicals.
Baby Doctor: Carla, this is not defeat. This is survival. You are too headstrong for your own good. Humble yourself. Allow yourself to be helped. You are powerless over brain chemicals.

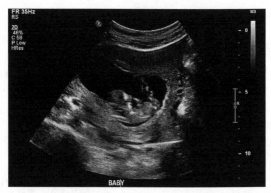

The Baby Doctor had so accurately gauged the depth of my struggles with sobriety, past abuse, and deep depression. She saw my pain and pushed me right through it when I needed it the most.

Depression, to me, was like swimming in a dark lake. I was at the centre. The water was deep and I couldn't touch the bottom to regroup. I struggled, gasping at the surface. I took on moisture and felt the onset of fatigue in my limbs. I felt the dampness in my being. This was the state when motivation had abandoned me and even the desire to feel well was abstract at best.

Medication—the right one at the right dose—was my lifejacket. Pharmaceuticals floated me up to the surface, so I was no longer drowning. All my best efforts alone were simply not enough.

I needed, more than ever, to do the work to be well—the counselling, the sharing, the meditating, and the introspection—the kicking got me from the centre of the dark lake back to the shore where I could stand and ground myself once again.

December 18, 2012

> Rosie: Beep beep BEEP! Error. Please move Roomba® to a new location.
> *My new friend calls for help in the middle of the night.*

Arthur had a cleaning obsession: cleaning products by the dozen, five Dysons®. Yet still he complained bitterly about the messes everyone else left "disrespectfully in the common areas."

Most girls would have been *thrilled* to have this predicament. But he doesn't clean like I do—he'll dust all but the bottom shelf, he'll vacuum his own areas daily but never bother to do the stairs where all the gunge is visibly ground into the only carpet in the house.

When Arthur arrived home with a Roomba®, I was less than impressed. It was a vacuum worth more than my entire wardrobe. The embodiment of lazy—a machine that sweeps up after you. We hid her from Eliot for months until he stumbled on her cleaning in the middle of the night.

Eliot: What is *THAT?*
Me: Rosie, the Roomba®. Named after the robot maid in the Jetsons.
Eliot: No more chores!
Me: Oh no, no. Rosie is MY friend, not yours.

We bonded, Rosie and me. I affectionately cleaned her gears and emptied her bin so she could continue picking up the piles of schmutz from every surface on the main floor. Sometimes I had to chase her out from under the couch so I could turn her off, at times too loud for me to hold a phone conversation.

#firstworldproblem

December 21, 2012

ilain: Battle goes poorly—down 5—0. But the Predators get a penalty shot and guess who BURIES it with a bullet wrist shot and considerable aplomb!
And another!
iMe: Fabulous!!!
Not about the score, but he'll be so pleased!!
Tell Jackson the puppies and I are VERY excited for him ☺?
iEliot: *Disgruntled about the mandatory attendance at a "Neanderthal" hockey event.*
This is a pretty little town. I could move here and open a cupcake store.

December 22, 2012

Berkley, the handyman, finished installing the cork flooring in the basement the day before my parents arrived to enjoy Christmas with us. I was pleased that although I was swimming in my line of credit, having paid for Berkley's supplies and labour for almost six full months, the house no longer looked like a construction zone. Not once did I say, "Watch your feet for nails," or "Don't be alarmed by . . ." for the entire Christmas holiday. There would always be evidence of little imperfections smattered throughout the Gemstone, but they were things only noticeable when you really paid attention . . .

In the upstairs bathroom, there is a 12-panel tile mosaic in the tub surround. It's not my style, but I have always tolerated it because it reminded me of an East Coast village. I don't know if it was an old farmer-husband's prank on his wife, or a genuine flub, but one tile is upside down. It's not ruined or broken or dysfunctional, it's just quirky. I believe it was the same spicy soul who planted the dated Playboy magazines and old coins in the basement ceiling, to be discovered years and years later.

The floors are not level, balls and beads all roll to the same corner of the kitchen when dropped. The walls are not true or plum. The basement staircase was slanted slightly downwards. It was obvious that faults had been covered up by quick-fixes in the decades of homeowners simply trying their best. I'm sure, in places, I have also contributed to the renovation nightmare that will some day be another owner's problem.

Despite the defects, the Gemstone was strong and solid. It *was* me—quirky and uniquely awesome from the inside out.

I had been spending most of this day binge-watching *Breaking Bad* hidden under puffy blankets with my faithful canines, waiting for a serotonin boost from my recently resumed antidepressants.

December 25, 2012

I took a stroll down the memory lane of Eliot's Christmas wish lists and letters . . .

Eliot's Christmas List—Age 4

We enrolled Eliot in a ballet class to see if it would help abate his spinning obsession. There was no difference in behaviours, but what I did discover was the mothers of 3 and 4-year-old ballerinas do not appreciate little boys with autism prancing around trying to steal their tutus. I caught on very early that they believed our participation in the class was ruining their chances of being the parent of a prima ballerina.

- Tutu
- Pink shoes
- Jeep

Jeep toys were a no brainer . . . we had purchased both the one he wanted from Superstore and a few we had found at the mall. Eliot would be pleased with the additions to his now wheel-less car collection, (he had chewed them all off). As for the other items on his list, they weren't quite so easy.

Iain: Not a chance.
Me: Are you really going to break his little heart and not have a tutu under the tree?
Iain: I don't think it's healthy.
Me: It can go in the dress-up box with all his other gowns and costumes . . .

We located a gymnastics supply store in search of a man-tutu. Christmas Eve we agreed on a compromise: a black body suit leotard and black ballet slippers.

He wore the slippers every day until the straps cut into his feet. The spandex suit was often worn underneath his clothing long into grade school, perhaps for deep sensory pressure, but perhaps also for the enjoyment of his feminine attire.

Eliot's Christmas List—Age 8

1. ~~Victorian dollhouse~~
1. Victorian dollhouse
2. Wensday Addams halloween costume
3. Karuockie macine
4. Rock tumbeler
5. Electric Manorah
6. a little bit of Christmas town.
7. accordian
8. bagpipes
9. cello
10. Wax seal
11. ink pens with ink well
12. magic hat

Eliot's Christmas List—Age 11

I could do with these
- Old coins
- Tea (Indian spice, lemon ginger, peach, mint, sleepytime throat tamer, surprise me ☺)
- The Sims 3 Late Night

Preferred
- Lindt Dark Chocolate Bars—70% Cocoa, Ecuador, Sea Salt, Citrus, and Chili
- Cash. Lots of it.
- A bathrobe (preferably a white fuzzy one)
- Animation book

REALLY, REALLY WANT THESE!
- 2011 to present 13-inch MacBook Pro or a 2010 to present 11 or 13 inch MacBook Air
- Hair Iron—just like mom's!
- IPOD NANO PLEAAAAAAAAAAAAAAASE!!!!!!!!!!
- Zones of Exclusion Book—Pripyat and Chernobyl
- Realistic Stuffed Cat—Orange Tabby

Personal Things I Have Wanted to have for a very long time
Dad—Consider Family Guy PLEASE ☺
Mom—Consider Facebook PLEASE ☺

Jackson's Christmas List—Age 9

1. R.C. car
2. Lego [sith fury class interceptor, malevolence, republic striker class Starfighter]
3. Fuzzy slippers
4. Snowboard

January 4, 2013

The first week in January was the Atom Hockey Christmas Classic. The moms sat huddled in the bleachers together complaining about why the crap heaters weren't working. We had finally (mostly) learned which number was which kid, and to which parents he belonged.

> Mom #1: Ethan looks so sluggish this morning. I wonder what he ate for breakfast.
> Mom #2: Coke and fruit loops. He'll perk up for the second period.
> Dads: **Ice it.**
> Mom #3: 2 hands on your stick, Jacob! 2 hands!
> Mom #2: Icing? For real? I think that ref had too many wobbly pops last night . . .
> Mom #3: Not as many as I did . . . I loathe early morning games.
> Mom #2: We are going to an all-inclusive in Mexico next week, and I was trying to get back in the game!
> Mom #1: Ouch! That was a nasty hit . . . not nice! What did his mother teach him?!
> Dads: **Solid.**
> Mom #3: 2 hands Jacob! 2 hands . . .
> Mom #1: Faster, sweetie! Skate as best as you can!
> Dads: **Harder. Connect that pass!**
> Me: Jackson is working so hard today . . . Arthur told him he would give him $100 for his first hat trick.
> Mom #1: **PASS IT TO JACKSON.**
> Mom #2: **GO, JACKSON, GO!!**
> Mom #3: Jacob! 2 hands on your stick!!
> *Jackson scores. Twice. And after an end to end rush, in Bobby Orr fashion, he snipes his hat trick goal! He throws his arms up then drops to his knees for a well-earned "cele". I am the proudest mom ever.*

Mom #1: **YEAH, JACKSON!! YIIIPPPPEEEE!!!**
Mom #3: **WOOOOO HOOOOO!!**
Me: Thank you guys so much for your support, you rock.
Mom #2: Are you kidding? He's taking us all out for breakfast!

January 5, 2013

Me: Mark your calendars . . .
Tuesday, March 26th. 10:45. The Gender Clinic.
His wait list is over 2 years, and I'm very grateful we were fast
tracked . . .
Eliot: This year?
Me: Yes, this year!
Eliot: EEEEE!!!!
  Shrill ear-piercing squeal.

It was confirmation of the first appointment to have "permission"
for him to be a girl.

I was not normally one to ask for help, but a *LONG* series of
behind-the-scenes phone calls to people who *can* help from people
you *know* propelled us to the top of the pile with red ink on the cover
of the file.

January 20, 2013

Next to childcare, transportation of children was second on my
list of anxiety provoking struggles with parenting. I usually had
somewhere for them to go, but no way to get them there.

Jackson needed rides to hockey academy each morning and to be picked up after school at the most inconvenient times possible for parents who work 9-5. Luckily, Arthur had taken on the morning drop-off routine, saving my pregnant nose from the nauseating hockey bag stench at 7 a.m.

As much as I hated to do it, I caved and begged friends for the occasional after-school pick up. That, interspersed with a few stale-smelling smoky cab rides and a few extra late shifts for me, covered the week.

January in Alberta is cold. Stupid cold. And dark. Stupid dark. I'm talking -35°C and pitch black at 4:00 p.m. The journey—scrape off the car, dig it out from under the snow, skid and slide on winter tires to the school, wait for the mass of kids scrambling with hockey bags to disembark, white-knuckle drive home again—the drive is just long enough for the car to finally be toasty warm. Jackson and I pulled into the driveway and turned off the car engine. We just sat. In silence. No music. No traffic. No dogs barking. No Eliot making demands. No cell phone calls or text bleeps. No dinner preparations. Just for a few minutes. I cherished the blips of time which allowed the world to just melt away with my Jackson.

January 23, 2013

We hadn't seen the Youth Psychiatrist since grade 1. At the time, Eliot's new school division required an updated diagnosis of ASD to continue support and funding. I resisted the urge to challenge them with "Do you require confirmation of a diagnosis like Diabetes?" Autism doesn't go away.

On this occasion, they had been asked to unravel what they could with regards to the blossoming gender concerns. Eliot spent almost three hours with two psychiatrists and then he, the experts and I met to discuss their conclusions.

Psychiatrist #1: The word we use for youth like Eliot is COMPLEX.
Me: That's much politer than the words I use some days . . .
Psychiatrist #2: The ASD obsessions and pervasive thinking are still very evident, although masked under very sophisticated language. He is frequently "stuck" on ideas and I had trouble keeping him on topic, when the topics are not of his preferred interest.
Me: I agree—homework is a nightmare.
Psychiatrist #1: If gender dysphoria was a fixable issue, we would have you leave, fix it, and return to address the distractible thinking and pervasive thoughts, perhaps even with medications. But, it's not possible to unravel it out of the fabric that makes up Eliot. We'd like you to come back after you visit the Gender Clinic, as it will be interesting to see what Dr. Gender has to say and we can go from there.
Psychiatrist #2: The difficult behaviours that are challenging for you at home, the lack of perspective taking, the "not having a clue" façade, are the products of ASD. That IS his autism. That is WHY he has a diagnosis. My only suggestion for help is to return to your strategies of changing his behaviors away from punitive and back to a place of teaching a socially odd child.
Me: Right . . .
Psychiatrist #1: Eliot, if you had a magic wand and could have three wishes granted right now, what would they be?
Eliot: I would go to the Arts School.
I would fast forward my life to when I'm 21, and am living as a woman.

I would ask for three more wishes.

January 24, 2013

I had not yet mentioned anything on Facebook about our induction into the LGBTQ community. Eliot had requested, though, I delete all photos of him from my feed. I complied, reluctantly. It was troubling to me that I was required to "hide" photographic evidence of such special times that now somehow had an ugly secretive filter on them.

There did come a point, years into acceptance, when those photos resurfaced in Eliot's own Facebook feed.

#allinduetime

February 2, 2013

20 weeks pregnant. You know who your true friends are when cupcakes show up at your door.

> iMe: I'm glad Jackson greeted you. You'd run screaming from Eliot these days . . .
> iLisa: Oh dear. Sorry Eliot is still giving you grief. I should have left extra cupcakes.
> iMe: Haha. Having a bigger ass will not help Eliot's behaviors . . .
> iLisa: True, but it might be fun, in the short term ;)

February 3, 2013

Discussions in our home about a new name were lengthy. They involved baby name books and Google searches. I preferred names beginning with E so his initials wouldn't change, and old artwork signed EG would remain accurate, never requiring an explanation.

We voted, but I retained veto power.

In the end, Ella was a classic choice for him. Elegant, with an old-school feel, just like my blossoming daughter.

> iMe: What do you think about Margaret for a middle name?
> iGramma: I would be honoured. And Great Grandma Mac would be proud, too.

I was the fourth generation "Margaret", and Ella would be the fifth. Sentimentally, it was a significant move. A bold message to our immediate family that we would tolerate nothing short of **absolute acceptance.**

Gramma had made a point of saying, in a pointed conversation, she and Papa were "really okay with *this*." I knew in my heart they would be, but of course it was reassuring to hear the confirmation.

I had an ancient scene etched into my mind . . .

My brother had come over for "Gramma-Day", and the cousins played and played and played. When Jeff could finally drag his girls away from their dress-up buddy, Eliot, it was well into the evening and my parents were well into their wine. Eliot pranced across the kitchen floor in a white chiffon gown, black wig to his waist, and every necklace he could find draped around his neck. We were too drunk to adhere to his bedtime routine.

Papa: He is so girly.
Did I give him the gay gene?

The gears were turning madly in his head—Papa had a gay brother and a gay sister, and now a flamboyant grandson. He did not say it to be unkind, just as an uninhibited concern for the well-being of his family. His family of origin was not a place of love and acceptance for the LGBTQ population and Papa was just finding a place to start thinking differently for the generations who would follow.

February 8, 2013
Jackson would agree that one of the benefits of having a pregnant mother was the increasing ratio of yummy treats to healthy food choices. Buy One Get One Blizzard® ice cream treats were heavenly. BOGO meant one for an evening treat, and a free decadent delight for the morning-after breakfast in bed.

#bestmomever #pregnancycravings

February 14, 2013
I was still (barely) able to stuff my belly into my normal work pants, but I felt immense relief when I succumbed to the elastic fronts of my maternity pants. My lab coat didn't close completely—when I tried, the fabric stretched ridiculously tightly over my ass. My shifts were long at work, but I enjoyed my customers and my colleagues.

I started gently broaching the topic of Eliot's gender with them, testing the waters. I was a public person, and I needed to be able to bounce ideas and questions off others. I could not live in isolation.

Me: We finally got an appointment for Eliot to see a new psychiatrist.
Kristi: Oh, that's good. He's really struggling, eh?
Me: Yeah, junior high, autistic behaviours, being a teenager! This appointment is at the Gender Clinic.
Kristi: I didn't even know there was one . . .
Me: Eliot wants to be a girl.

Kristi: Wow.

Really.

Huh.

He is very feminine . . .

Silence. I had methodically chosen to mention this in the first few
hours of the shift so she had time to process . . .

Hours passed. We are happily busy and distracted with work.

Kristi: What are you going to do about Eliot? He's so young! Is this
new?

How do you feel about it? Iain and Arthur must be freaking out.

How do you *DO* that? Oh my. If that was my son . . .

I was *real* with her. And I was ready for her *real* in return, whatever
that was. And it was okay. I suppose this was like a "coming out of
the closet" type of hard conversation. I'm no good at living in closets.

The more times I "came out", the more I realized what I was doing
was "inviting in". We had nothing to be ashamed of—no reason to
be in a closet. I was inviting people I loved and trusted to have an
opportunity to support us as our family trudged forward down a
difficult path of living authentically.

February 21, 2013

The open house at the Arts School was a much-anticipated evening
event. This was the creative school known for having a very diverse
student population, where we thought Eliot might fit in better. We
arrived early to get the lay of the land, listened to the administration
sell their elite programming to eager parents, and tried to assess the
culture of the school. I waddled around, exhausted and headachy,
scoping out the best person to spring my hard questions on.

The father of a child with Down Syndrome and I cornered some
important looking administrators trying to escape the auditorium.

Father: Do you think you'd be able to support a special needs
child?

Principal: We have hired an inclusion coordinator to ensure all
our students are supported. That said, this school focuses on
academics in an International Baccalaureate environment, and the
arts.

Father: I see. And how competitive is the application process?
Me: *Waiting my turn.*
Disheartened—Eliot is not yet outstanding in any art, despite his aptitude and creativeness, AND has Asperger's.
Me: What about sexual minorities?
Principal: We have many students who have identified as gay or lesbian, and we have counsellors trained in the area and have an active GSA.
I Googled GSA—Gay-Straight Alliance.
Me: What about students who are *"transgendered"*?
Father leaves. Clearly uncomfortable with how I hijacked the conversation.
Principal: We have many of them, as well. At all grade levels.
Inclusion Lady: I can help to answer any support questions you may have.
Me: That's great, because this school might not know what hit them when they get Eliot!

February 24, 2013

Eliot had been begging me to drive to Dorothy for years. The abandoned farm town in the south of the province was miles from anywhere I would ever need to go, ripe with vacant churches, schoolhouses, and homes. Short of flying Eliot to Pripyat to see the ruins of Chernobyl, this was his dream trip, and since I had no intention of going to Ukraine any time soon, this would be the consolation trip.

My belly, Eliot, and I took the bucket list drive on a cold winter morning. We stopped at every old barn and decrepit house we saw on the way. It was an unbothered day—just us and our cameras. Eliot's unique and strange perspective was once again amusing to me as my serotonin levels had started to recalibrate, six weeks after resigning to be among the medicated.

This is the last known photo of the child I named Eliot, framed among other remnants of the past.

February 27, 2013

The application letter to the Arts School was signed and sent.

My love of the arts, the personality I express, and the areas I would like to further develop myself are the reasons I would like to attend the Arts School.

I have an adventurous spirit. Last year, I took a trip to China, and this trip gave me a chance to experience a world very different from the one I live in. I didn't speak any Chinese, so I had to express myself in ways other than words to communicate with the people I met. My adventurous nature makes me a better actor because I'm not afraid to take a chance. If something goes wrong in a play, I improvise and keep the play going. Once upon a time, I played Prince Charming, and Cinderella forgot to leave her slipper at the ball. The king forgot his lines, so I created dialogue on the spot and kept the flow of the play going. I even picked up an invisible slipper, and the play ended happily ever after.

My inquisitive personality gives me a thirst for knowledge. When I became interested in stop motion, I researched the topic and taught myself all about it. I then created many stop motion shorts and shared them with family and friends. I didn't write dialogue for these shorts, but instead I used music and action to convey the mood and tell the story. My favourite director is Alfred Hitchcock. I have studied his style, read about him, and watched nearly all his films, and produced my own films in his style. I even creeped out my babysitter with my shower scene re-enactment!

I would like to further develop my ability to express emotion through art. I create drawings that show the function and image of an object, but at the Arts School, I hope to learn to show more emotion in my artwork. I think I will learn this from the Arts School because of the emphasis the school places on emotional and spiritual well-being and balance. I hope to be given time for reflection and skill-building that will teach me how to do this better. I think I will also have a chance to learn from my peers and not just my teachers.

Attending the open house made me feel like I was "at home" and in awe at the same time. I was excited about the possibility that I would be able to explore the arts in a fabulous facility. I suspect the curriculum would be like the Academic Challenge program I am already in, so the transition would be a good one instead of a confusing one. I think the school itself is a lot like me, full of quirky stuff that makes life interesting, and I can hardly wait to start.

Looking forward to my career at the Arts School,
Eliot Grant

The complexity of decisions seems to increase the further down the gender road we travel. Eliot's application to the Arts School was submitted and we had a date for the group interview. There was a fair amount of pressure for him to do well at the interview because not being accepted to the Arts School not only changed schooling plans, but also life plans.

I spoke at length to the inclusion coordinator at the school about Eliot's transition plan, and we discussed who should attend the interview; Eliot or Ella. I didn't trust that he had enough practice being Ella to not spend the whole interview over-acting.

iMe: Arthur will be taking you, as a boy. I have already spoken with the staff and they know you intend to come in September as a girl (IF you are accepted and IF Dr. Gender agrees), but we agreed they could better assess you as a "student" and as an "artist" if you come the way you are.

iEliot: It's about my comfort. If I show up here as a guy, then go as a girl, people are going to notice. And I noticed you said, "if you come the way you are." Does that mean I have a choice?

February 28, 2013

Jackson had lived with Eliot for all his 11 years and knew all the quirks, the behaviours, the oddities. He had been present for many conversations and was aware of all the appointments and planning going on . . .

> Me: Jackson, Eliot wants to live his life as a girl.
> Jackson: What the fuck?
> Does that mean I have a sister now?
> Me: Firstly, watch your mouth.
> Secondly, how long have you known Eliot was a girl?
> Jackson: Forever.

The rest of Jackson's questions were very logistical and practical. When a friend calls and asks for Eliot, what do I say? What kind of person would girl Eliot marry? Does he need a surgery to do that? Jackson was the first to jump on board with testing out new pronouns. Although he struggled with the hours of primping and fluffing of hair, teenage girl to the extreme, from his new sister, he called Eliot his sister and was not embarrassed to be with her. I'm sure he fielded questions and ignored insults from his friends, but he rarely mentioned it and he never complained.

March 5, 2013

> iMe: Yesterday was a long, stressful day . . . all of us are tired out and really trying to deal with a lot of shit. 💩 Appointment with the Family Psychologist itself was good . . . just SO much to deal with. Mostly we dealt with "limit" setting.
> iGramma: That sounds good. Did Jackson get a chance to be heard?
> iMe: Yes . . . he voiced frustration about Eliot "beautifying" all the time and walking around on his tip toes . . . we made a code word (turtle) that signals E needs to go primp in private if he can't just stop . . .
> iMe: I'm just sick of the whole thing.
> iGramma: Were Iain and Arthur there?
> iMe: Yes. All 5 of us . . .
> iGramma: Oh my . . . xox

March 6, 2013

My struggles with Eliot came up in conversations with my regular customers at the pharmacy. I was becoming bolder. My comfort levels with the topic were increasing.

> Me: I am pulling my hair out with Eliot. Autistic teenagers are what nightmares are made of. I'm worn out and pregnant! And on top of that, there are gender issues . . .
> Customer: Gender issues?
> Me: *She works with foster children and seems like a kindred spirit. I blurt it out . . .*
> He is probably "transgendered". He wants to live as a girl.
> Customer: My niece—er nephew, is just transitioning. Have you been to PFLAG?
> Me: *When the student is ready, the teacher appears.*
> Customer: It's a support group for **us**. I go with my sister once a month.

I suck up her information. Phone numbers. Dates. I learned that PFLAG—an outdated acronym for the "Parents and Friends of Lesbians and Gays"—was an organization that supports, educates, and provides resources for anyone with questions or concerns about sexual orientation, gender expression, or gender identity. For me, PFLAG turned into a monthly escape.

March 7, 2013

> iMe: What is your gut instinct on Eliot truly wanting to be a woman forever, as opposed to this being a passing obsession like molecular gastronomy or Apple® products?
> iGramma: We watched a talk show on gender this aft and have been chatting about it since. My gut tells me the essence of him is female . . . xox
> And I read someone's blog that discussed males with Autism who have female role models, thus they equate femininity with social confidence. The blogger's take was that transgenderism is an escape from "themselves"
> iMe: Eliot was a "girl" long before he knew about fitting in or escaping from himself . . .

It would be easier for ME if he was an effeminate man . . . he has his interview at the Arts School on Tuesday . . . and then an appointment at the Gender Clinic.
I bought him makeup this weekend. Like when you took me to Merle Norman for my grade 9 grad makeup purchase . . .
iGramma: Where did you shop? Was he happy?
iMe: I brought him to the drugstore where I work. He was over-the-moon happy . . .
Timing is urgent for him . . . he is madly obsessed with all of it
iGramma: It's biologically urgent, also, if you decide to use puberty blockers . . .
iMe: Very true. Luckily, he doesn't have a mustache yet! Ugh
iGramma: Ugh?
iMe: It's all very tiring . . .
iGramma: Yes, it is. It's also 11p.m. on a work night, and the kids will be up early, and no wonder you feel tired!! Book yourself a prenatal massage!
iMe: I might do just that.

March 8, 2013
  Is this going to go away?

iMe: We had a BIG talk with E last night . . . he really is oblivious to, and does not care about, the safety concerns. I think since none of them have happened to him yet, he believes they won't. My other concern was the "false sense of popularity" he gets from the girls who are interested in the girly things he engages in (makeup, perfume, shoes) . . . and for the first time, I wondered how much of that is fueling the current intensity of the gender issue.
iGramma: There is more going on than just one disorder or the other, for sure. Start your question list!
iMe: Question list:
1) If I ignore this, will it go away?
2) If Eliot gets a boob job, can I have a discount on mine?
3) Will I make enough money on a book about my life to pay for my own psychologists forever?!?
iGramma: Good questions! My answers would be no, no, and possibly maybe!? You can't make this shit up!

March 9, 2013

I needed background information. In addition to some books on the topics of interest today, I also ordered a few etiquette books for girls, and Googled "finishing schools" to see if they still exist. I anticipated that Eliot was going to need as much help as possible on this path he was forging.

iMe: I have a few LGBTQ books on order . . . since those topics don't seem to be covered in "What to Expect" . . .
iGramma: LGBTQ?
iMe: Lesbian—Gay—Bisexual—Transgender—Queer/Questioning
iGramma: Oh! I would have been awhile figuring that one out! #LGBTTIQQ2SA[6]

March 10, 2013

iMe: Jackson scored the game winning goal with 7 seconds left in the 3rd period today . . . Ridiculously exciting. Semi-final game is Tuesday evening.
iAASponsor: Awwww!! Soooo proud of him . . . he must be PUMPED!!!

March 15, 2013

I had hand-picked the Baby Doctor to deliver my precious bundle. She had founded and ran a Centering Clinic, which was conceptually a combined pre-natal class with direct physician involvement. It was a monthly, then bi-weekly 2-hour meeting, during which all six ladies had their "checks" and engaged in discussions ranging from pre-natal food choices, to birth strategies and pain management, to post-natal care.

We ranged from first-time young moms to third-time matriarchs. The interactions were uplifting, and I suspected the level of post-

6   Lesbian – Gay – Bisexual – Transsexual – Transgender – Intersex – Queer – Questioning – 2-Spirit – Asexual

partum depression and isolation was significantly less than with
the typical system of 1-on-1 prenatal care. The Baby Doctor, a wise
and experienced woman, likely knew all too well the benefit of
connectedness—or rather, the dire consequences of being alone.

On that particular day, I was feeling particularly edgy and
pregnant. Arthur and I listened to the swish-swish of baby's heartbeat.

> Me: I'm struggling at work. Not as much physically as just a
> creeping sensation that I need to be home with my big kids. Some
> stuff going on.
> Baby Doctor: Then you need to be home. You're 30 weeks, I'm
> taking you off work.
> Me: Then I had better order myself some Cervidil® now, in case I
> need it to induce myself in a few months . . .
>   *Only half joking.*
> Baby Doctor: Carla! Don't. You. Dare.
> She *got* me. Like only she could have.

March 26, 2013

The waiting room of any psychiatry clinic is a great place to
people watch. Especially one that houses a Gender Clinic! I carefully
surveyed everyone sitting there, scripting their stories in my head.
They were probably doing the same about me.

Dr. Gender was a wise, insightful, gentle man. He reported:

> Thank you very much for referring Eliot Grant. The patient was
> accompanied by his mother and father. The patient is currently 12
> years old, turning 13 in June. He attends Suburbia Junior High and
> is in grade 7. He is described as healthy. His parents are bringing
> the patient to me because of some concerns over gender identity.

Eliot sat at the front edge of his chair, lips pursed, eager to have Dr. Gender tell us to plow forward, full speed, with transition.

The report stated:

The patient was born from a pregnancy that was terminated at 34 weeks with an emergency caesarean section because of vasa previa. There was a threatened miscarriage also earlier on in the pregnancy. He weighed 5 pounds 10 ounces at birth, and spent a week in pediatric intensive care, but otherwise went home healthy. His milestones for the most part were normal, although he was diagnosed as having some form of autism at the age of 3 ½, which was revamped to Asperger's. Consequently, he has had several one-to-one aids in playschool, kindergarten, and in his earlier years of school, but now is doing well. Apparently, he is academically very bright and is in an Academic Challenge program. He still exhibits some problems to do with Asperger's, in that he has black or white thinking. Often, he becomes preoccupied with topics and gets stuck on them for lengthy periods of time. He behaves in a somewhat socially inappropriate manner, although this has markedly improved. He does have several friends at school, and they are mostly female and often artsy in nature, which is probably a reflection of the gender issue

The parents state that the patient has always been very feminine. He apparently was caught stealing his mother's clothing at the age of 2 or 3, to dress up as a female. He would also wear t-shirts in a manner that would mimic female hair. He was always attracted to things such as jewelry and makeup. He really exhibited no male typical activities when younger, shunning contact sports and rough-and-tumble play and things of this nature. Because of this gender atypically exhibiting itself when he was in kindergarten, the parents took the patient to see a Child Psychiatrist, who has some expertise in gender. She helped the parents come to an agreement to allow the patient to express himself in the female gender role at home if he wished, but not outside the home.

This past year, the patient apparently came up with his own announcement to his mother that he knew gender reassignment surgery was once again paid provincially funded. It was at this point that the parents realized what they had been observing up to this point needed to be dealt with further. The patient has been seeing a Family Psychologist, who has been helpful in sorting out matters for the patient.

At the present time, it is the gender issue that is the main concern that the parents have, and they had a lot of questions regarding puberty-delaying hormones and whether to allow their child to transition, et cetera. The obsession with female clothing and makeup is tiresome for the parents, but no more so when the patient was stuck on other topics in the past. He would like to dress as a female outside of the home; however, this has not been allowed except on a couple of shopping excursions when the patient was with his mother. The patient has chosen a female name, but does not use it beyond the home.

Regarding other activities that the patient is involved in, he often has friends over and they make movies with video cameras, and the patient always plays the female role. He always expresses himself as a female in computer games, and in his art. He has acquired some female accoutrements, such as perfume and some jewelry.

The mother and father are divorced. They were married five years and then separated at the time when the patient was just going into kindergarten. There is one other sibling from that relationship, a younger brother. The mother is in a new relationship and pregnant from that relationship. The father has not re-engaged. The mother is a pharmacist who works full-time, and the biological father is a policy analyst for the government.

With regards to family history, the mother states she has problems with depression and has been hospitalized a couple of times for the same. She has had problems with alcohol. Apparently, alcoholism and depression occur in many of her first-degree relatives. On her father's side, he has 2 siblings who are gay. On the father's side, there is no diagnosed psychiatric illness. With regards to the parents' feelings, both said they were totally fine with the gender issue and what should be, would be, and they plan to be very supportive of their son. The mother states that she tires of the obsessiveness. The father is equally supportive, although he has some concerns about where all this will lead and whether the path will be safe for the patient.

The patient presented in the office as a young boy, looking his stated age of 12, probably just on the cusp of going into puberty. He certainly was very outspoken about his gender issues, which probably reflected the Asperger's. He also had a number of feminine mannerisms and his voice certainly had a very feminine quality to it.

Iain: What is the percentage chance that if he transitions he will hate it and *go back*?
How can we be *sure* this is not just an autistic obsession with girl accoutrements?
What *causes* this?
He is *young*. Surely, there is no harm in waiting?
Dr: In literature, you will see quoted rates of people who question, transition, and then revert to the gender assigned at birth. Most of those publications have since been refuted. I have only had 1 patient in my 35 years of practice "go back" temporarily, and that was because of a physical disability that prevented her from accessing a safe washroom in a particular institution.
If you set out on a path and it turns out to not have been the best decision, then you simply make another decision.

There are no diagnostic tests one can do to determine transgenderism. Previous studies on effeminate boys have shown that the clear majority of them turn out to be homosexual, in terms of sexual orientation, and lose a lot of their feminine qualities. A small number go on to be heterosexual, in terms of orientation, and within all the studies there are probably a few who are transgender. However, these statistics are older, and at that time, transgenderism was not identified as such.

At this point in time, I think it is prudent to make a referral to an Endocrinologist. The patient could be assessed as for his stage of puberty, and puberty-delaying blockers can be evoked if appropriate, to buy more time to allow the patient's gender identity to solidify. The family also planned to move the patient to the Arts School in the fall, and the question is whether they should allow him to go as his female name or to remain as his male name. Today, I was unable to say definitively about this, however, I plan to see them again a few more times and work through some type of satisfactory solution with them.

I also sent a referral to the Gender Psychologist, who specializes in seeing younger people who have gender issues and runs a group to that effect.

Thank you again for the referral.

We left the office with a carry letter in hand. That was the piece of paper giving him permission to be a girl.

To whom it may concern:

Under psychiatric/medical supervision, this individual is going through a transformation from being a male to a female. As part of the accepted "standards of care", it is a necessity for this individual to dress and be seen in public in the female gender role full-time, known as the one year "real life experience".

Please extend to this individual all the courtesies that you would extend to any other female.

Dr. Gender

March 27, 2013

"Isn't he too YOUNG to be making such big decisions?!?"
"He doesn't even KNOW who he is yet."

He *was* young, but he could legally begin driving in two years, and would be of legal age in just over five.

I was someone who worked with medications daily, and even I had limited knowledge of the options available to those transitioning. In my crash course, I learned we were *not* talking about a "sex-change operation". What even was that? Top surgery? Bottom surgery? Vocal cord surgery to change the pitch of the voice? Facial contouring? Hair removal?

What we *were* talking about was a referral to another professional, the Endocrinologist, who knew and could commence, pharmaceutical options. Some of the options could preserve his choices later, and prevent some of the traumatic and irreversible physical changes that would be brought on by testosterone.

What we *were* talking about was a desire to start the expensive, painful injections of leuprolide (Lupron®), which would lead to a blockade of testosterone and estrogen. The monthly shot would delay of the onset of puberty; halting the masculinising the skeleton, deepening of the voice, facial and body hair, among others. It would leave Eliot's body in a more mouldable slate, waiting for an age-appropriate decision to be made about more invasive and long-term treatments, like hormone replacement therapy to feminize the body, and surgeries. They would also give him the opportunity to enjoy his days as a young girl, instead of dreading each day as his physical body continued to diverge from his spirit through puberty.

If **Project Ella**, as Iain called it, was a failure, and Eliot determined he was destined to live as a man, the injections would be stopped and the postponed puberty would resume.

March 28, 2013

Fears and raw emotions spilled out of people in tears, mopped up by Kleenex, at PFLAG. The biggest common fear of the children, friends, parents, grandparents, aunts, and uncles at this meeting is overwhelming fear for the safety of those they love in the LGBTQ community.

We awful-ized them being jumped on the streets, beaten and tormented in both public and private, enduring verbal abuse, and all levels of inhumanity. This paralyzing fear trumped the fears that they would never be loved or accepted, never succeed professionally, and never realize the full potential of what they "could have been".

I had a hard time even capturing in words the depth of this fear. I could feel the lump in my throat—the one that squeezed the words so tightly I could barely even utter them. How could I allow a child to live a life with such high stakes attached? At the same time, how could I stop him?

Let me digress into the world of the known facts; the world where my brain is the most comfortable. I chose to be armed with evidence about the realities of life for the transgender population. They are not positive statistics, but they are accurate. YouTube, Facebook, and most news sites are filled with the sensational, ratings-focused stories, but don't paint the whole story.

In 2011, the National Center for Transgender Equality and National Gay and Lesbian Task Force published *Injustice at Every Turn: A Report of the National Transgender Discrimination Survey.*[7] The data was compiled from a survey of 6,450 transgender and gender non-conforming people across all the United States.

They reported:

- A staggering **41% of respondents reported attempting suicide compared to 1.6% of the general population**, with rates rising for those who lost a job due to bias (**55%**), were harassed/bullied in school (**51%**), had low household income, or were the victim of physical assault (**61%**) or sexual assault (**64%**).
- People of color, in general, fare worse than white participants across the board, with **African American transgender respondents faring worse** than all others in many areas examined.
- Those who expressed a transgender identity or gender non-conformity while in **grades K-12** reported alarming rates of **harassment (78%), physical assault (35%),** and **sexual violence (12%)**; harassment was so severe that it led almost **one-sixth (15%) to leave a school** in K-12 settings or in higher education.
- **Fifty-three percent (53%)** of respondents reported being **verbally harassed or disrespected** in public places, including hotels, restaurants, airports, and government agencies.
- Of those who have transitioned, **only one-fifth (21%) have been able to update all their IDs and records** with their new gender.
- **57% experienced significant family rejection.**

Are there not laws to protect the rights of *all* people? Not everywhere, it seemed.

I'll throw this second set of numbers at you; I chose to hang onto these ones from a 2009 survey of 224 LGB youth aged 21-25.[8]

- Lesbian, gay, and bisexual young adults who reported higher levels of family rejection during adolescence were (compared

7   Grant, Jaime M., Lisa A. Mottet, Justin Tanis, Jack Harrison, Jody L. Herman, and Mara Keisling. (2011). Injustice at Every Turn: A Report of the National Transgender Discrimination Survey. Washington: National Center for Transgender Equality and National Gay and Lesbian Task Force.
8   Ryan, C., Huebner, D., Diaz, RM., & Sanchez, J. (2009). Family Rejection as a Predictor of Negative Health Outcomes in White and Latino Lesbian, Gay, and Bisexual Young Adults. Pediatrics, 123(1), 346-52.

with peers from families that reported no or low levels of family rejection):

- 8.4 times more likely to report having attempted suicide
- 5.9 times more likely to report high levels of depression
- 3.4 times more likely to use illegal drugs
- 3.4 times more likely to report having engaged in unprotected sexual intercourse

Youth who are **accepted by family** have **better health outcomes**. They are 8.4 times *less* likely to attempt suicide, 5.9 times *less* likely to struggle with depression, and 3.4 times *less* likely to use drugs or engage in risky sexual behaviours.

Love. Accept. Advocate.

March 29, 2013

The Easter Bunny brought Eliot a bag full of makeup, and Jackson an iTunes card. They were both thrilled. Eliot organized his goodies into piles . . . eye shadows, lipsticks, foundation and concealing products, mascaras. He showed it all off to his female cousins and my brother, Jeff, when they arrived for dinner. They thought it odd that Eliot had makeup, especially considering they were not allowed to wear any themselves, although they were similar ages.

And later . . . the family fallout.

> iJeff: My girls were asking their mother about why Eliot had makeup.
> iMe: *No point in lying.*
> The makeup . . . we are in the process of supporting Eliot through a big life change. He *wants and needs* to live his life as a girl. The makeup was a gift of acceptance, to allow him to start exploring safely at home . . .
> iJeff: Oh. Wow.
> *Surprised, but not really.*

March 31, 2013

I turned 38.

I treated myself to some small baby purchases.

Arthur: Why do we need receiving blankets?
Isn't the doctor going to catch the baby?

April 3, 2013

iMe: Decision from the "Summit Meeting" with Iain and Arthur . . .
Eliot will be going to the Arts School as Ella. He will transition over
the summer, but Arthur and I oversee the shopping. We are all
going to try to help him distinguish the line between the feminine
"core" of Ella and the vain obsession parts . . .
iGramma: You must be exhausted. Now that a decision has been
made, you can put that turmoil behind you and work towards making
it happen. I will try and help however I possibly can, so let me know
what you think will be appropriate. I love you all so much . . . xox
iMe: Ugh. I don't even know where to start really . . . the more I do
right now in terms of shopping, the more anxious it makes Eliot
to want to wear it all!! I'll call the Arts School today and accept the
position and . . . then maybe go back to bed.
iGramma: Go back to bed! Can lots of that shopping wait till
summer? He's going to grow before then anyway . . . 5 months till
new school!
iMe: Yes . . . all the clothing will wait until then. I'm thinking
more "discrete" things we'll have to order or hunt for . . . the trans
underwear and silicone bra cups he is obsessing over etc . . . but
you're right. For now, he just needs to do some math!

Even the dogs are stressed.

April 7, 2013

I am grateful for friends who respond to S.O.S. texts.

iMe: Lots to talk about . . . my little Eliot is going to be attending
the Arts School in September as Ella . . .

iLisa: Wow!! I admire his (her?) confidence. I imagine it must be very stressful for you though, hard to let Eliot go in the world as Ella where others are not so kind . . .
iMe: Would be nice to change the world . . . I actually think changing everyone else might be easier than dealing with Ella! lol
iLisa: Lots of changes for sure . . .
I will make a big cake

April 11, 2013

Me: I am a ray of fucking sunshine.
Says the pregnant mother of a hockey fanatic, an autistic transgender teen, and three rescue dogs.

The only thing that pulled me out of bed was the magnetic sunrise pouring in the window. I sat outside with a cup of decaf and ruminated.

The exterior of the Gemstone was an eclectic mixture of rough-edged stones and glimmering gems. The hardened façade is an envelope of security around a vulnerable inner core . . . not unlike me. From a distance, the siding resembles that of the builder-beige stucco of sprawling sub-divisions, but up close it was nothing like it. Even the unpolished rocks were individual shades of browns and pinks that comprised the "sunset mix" rock purchased decades ago to throw into hand-trowelled concrete. Ironically, broken beer and wine bottles (and 7-up green glass, and some type of glass that looks like purple amethyst) were mixed in for pizazz. Until sunbeams caught them at just the right angles, they stayed camouflaged; every so often they reflected their beauty in stunning rainbows of light.

There was a small spot on one of the street-facing corners where the siding finally fell off; it had finally given way to the demands of holding in the years of stories, just as I had given way to years of stuffing all emotions. It was tricky to find a person skilled enough to be able to match the stone, and skill needed to repair it. The patch remains visible to someone who cares enough to really look.

April 15, 2013

By this time, Eliot was all but demanding he be allowed to dress as he wanted to during evenings and weekends. The moment he stepped inside the door after school, he transformed into a feminine version of himself. I insisted he change back when people were over—especially Jackson's friends—I wasn't prepared to answer the questions yet. He had become very adept, with the help of the cosmeticians and YouTube, at facial contouring, highlighting, and application of various feminine products.

Iain, on the other hand, was profoundly uncomfortable with him in anything but jeans and a t-shirt. He refused to take him out in public. He lamented sardonically about being "stepped on by his son's high heels". Eliot was not equipped to deal with the obvious disconnect between the "accepting father" he claimed to be, and every gesture that did not support transition.

I was not especially patient with Iain, either. In retrospect, his path to acceptance just took longer. I was quickly on-board with the logistics surrounding what I thought we needed to do, but Iain was more cautious and questioning. There was no right speed. He was grieving the perceived loss of his first-born son, dealing with fears in his own way, challenging beliefs he had about "trannies". There was never a question of love, but Eliot really began to question the "unconditional" part.

"He's known this for a LONG time, just like you have, Mom. If you're not surprised, why doesn't Dad get it?"

April 16, 2013

Fiona, my fiery friend and doula, met with Arthur and me for the first of three planned visits; I was 32 weeks large. I begged her to be my birth coach years earlier—before I met Arthur. Women with Alzheimer's may not recall their husband's name, but many can tell you about the births of their babies . . . it's too profound to not give it effort and preparation.

The session took a few hours and included discussion about what my previous births were like, and how I envisioned this one.

Fiona: When the nurse asks you if you want something for pain, what are you going to say?
Me: I got this.

My pregnancy with Jackson in 2002 had been planned and uneventful. There was some frightening bleeding at the beginning, and aches and pains, but I was young and working in a local pharmacy. I had one trip-and-fall-on-my-belly while carrying donuts to a friend's house to help her move, but the contractions were short-lived.

I started bleeding on a Saturday morning. After setting plans in place for Eliot's care, we headed into the hospital. Watching and waiting . . . I was not in active labour, so they put me in a recovery room for the night with a mom and her new baby. My contractions were strong and regular, and I did my best to stay mouse-quiet out of respect to my new-mom neighbour. The machine to monitor contractions was, apparently, broken. The nurses confirmed I was NOT in labour each few hours when they came in, although my body told me I certainly was!

A young doctor came to check me in the morning and assessed I was 4cm. He offered a C-section (because of my previous surgery), or to break my water to move things along.

Me: It doesn't matter, as long as I have this baby before midnight. Canada Day, July 1st, is a good birthday.

I was moved to a delivery room overlooking the city. My water was broken, IV started, contraction monitoring machine strapped on, internal monitor screwed into my baby's skull, and waiting for the anaesthesiologist to puncture my spine with an epidural. This was a far cry from the book I had read on natural childbirth, where you go off into the woods like a primal mammal and just breathe heavily. But the western medicine machine had been set in motion, and I didn't even know there were other options.

I rested, and laboured, with Iain and my parents at my side. The doctors told me it was time to push . . . even though I couldn't feel a damn thing. I pushed, and pushed, and pushed. For hours, I pushed, until it felt like my asshole had fallen out of my body. The nurses felt it necessary to ask the doctor, who had a hand in my vagina trying to spin a turned baby, about his Thai dinner take-out order. Obviously, it was just another day for them.

Finally, a vacuum was assembled. Broken suction attempts, a doctor using all his physical might to pull a baby down a canal that wasn't ready yet, and an epidural that numbed all sensation except everything

*that hurt, and finally, 15 people in the room for the moment when . . . a
beautiful boy with a tennis ball sized protrusion from the vacuum on his
head entered our world.*

*Fireworks celebrated the day we met Jackson Stuart Grant. I opted out
of his first bath, too tired and drugged to care. I discharged myself early
the next morning and we headed home—to heal and bond.*

Me: I am *not* doing that again. I want
to experience a baby being born,
instead of just needle pokes and
prods. I want my body to be the
boss of this, not a doctor on a time-
line. I want to *birth* a baby, not just
have a baby medically sucked out of
me. I want this birth to be the one I
remember and smile about.
Fiona: Then let's do just that. This will
be your ultimate test in letting go of
control. You can't have a baby like this
(tightly clenching her fists) . . .

April 17, 2013

eMe: Youth Psychiatrist today . . . trying to separate the Asperger's
obsessions from other core issues:

She described the obsessions as pervasive topics of interests
that limit his ability to engage in "normal" conversations with
other people about less preferred topics and consumed much
free mental space, as we know. The current interest in shoes,
makeup, etc. is being amplified by the Asperger's. Likely those
interests would be evident if he wasn't on the spectrum—but the
Asperger's is making it much more obvious and "in your face". The
difference with him is that typically the obsessions don't change
your "being". i.e. kids that love Thomas the Tank Engine don't want
to BE Thomas, or an engineer, or drive trains . . . they just want to
be mentally engaged by him.

Support at home(s):

Eliot is still expressing strong resistance to being at your house and a profound displeasure with the way you are handling the whole gender issue. The Youth Psychiatrist spent a lot of time last session talking about how some people respond to change differently—some love it and latch on, some need more time to adjust to new ideas. She also tried to describe how people react differently to the same situation—but those feelings are THEIRS, and we don't need to internalize them.

I'm not sure where to go with this one. Eliot is hurting and not capable of understanding the depth of core issues of adults. Your feelings and opinions are yours to keep and deal with. The bigger the wedge between you guys, the more difficult it will be to seal that gap later. He is scared to be Ella with you, thinks you hate him, can't stand to look at him. That environment can't help with what is already a difficult transition. What Eliot is doing is not wrong, his personality and style is not for us to dictate (within set "reasonable" parameters of course . . . *NOT* Lady Gaga). Are you just holding out your support until someone tells you this is 100% the right way to go? Or is there room for you to move from where you're at to a supportive position?

elain: If we say Asperger's does not shift him from liking Thomas to wanting to be Thomas, why do we say it shifts him from liking effeminacy to wanting to be a girl? In other words, I'm still waiting for someone to give me a convincing argument that this is anything less than obsession; that the affinity for things feminine is equivalent to the sort of burning need to be a girl that we have seen in neurotypical kids.

I KNOW the feminine streak is there, but what makes me hesitate is the form it's taking. Ok, Asperger's amplifies it, but what's driving it? Why are we discarding the autism argument that this is a cry for social acceptance from the group he normally identifies with, using the most effective tools available: teenage girl cattiness over brand names and cliques? Superficial and vain. These are not traits I want to encourage.

I would shove my hesitation aside if I believed which way this should go. You know me well enough for that, so let's not turn this into "his father is unsupportive". Rephrased, I have doubts and wonder if endorsement could do more harm than good.

I'm pretty sure my motives are pure here, and I have faith in Eliot's core good nature, so I'm not worried about a wedge. At the centre, my connection to Eliot is very strong and I could use some help reminding him of that.

It is not easy to look at him when he's dressed like a girl. It is not easy at all. It would be so much easier without all the destructive accoutrements. It's not about "wrong" or "not wrong". It is about honesty. And I'm not convinced this is honest. If it is not, are we doing him a favour by saying go nuts?

As for dictating style, yes, of course it's mine to dictate. I might not succeed, but I'm obligated to try. I'm not talking about clothes or colours or hair. I'm talking about teaching him to relate to and respect others, Asperger's or not, I must try to teach him these things. I am going to structure my parenting on the belief that ethics can't be sloughed off because they don't fit with some other issue you have, or because they're inconvenient. The cattiness, the vanity, the self-obsession, the superficiality . . . I absolutely 100% disagree that these are off-limits—it is most certainly a parental responsibility to instill ethics of respect in their children, and these traits run counter to the ones that Eliot is making the core of his being. I am trying to teach respect, humility, and citizenship. If this means discouraging the Tao of Snooki, then I'll accept that.

I don't know why you would characterize my position as unsupportive. If he came home with a joint and said pot makes him feel good, and I ruled it out, I'd not be "unsupportive," I'd be nixing behaviour I believed to be harmful, or at the very least was preaching hesitation while I analyzed and learned and reflected toward some sort of position. I sure wouldn't respond when someone snapped their fingers and said "decide".'

For the record—I agreed from the start that the hormone blocking therapy would buy time, and it was my idea to get him to the Arts School because it stood the best chance of being a safe environment—that it turned out to be the most supportive environment we could find is a bonus. I am not opposed to Eliot living as a woman eventually, because we have the right to choose[9] these things. But the "proof" we're seeing now—every

---

9   See my grimacing face here

single recent manifestation of his effeminacy—doesn't seem like it comes from a deep need to be female. It seems like a recently discovered thrill of "fitting in" because he's found a forum where his autistic talent for research and detail is meshing with a phase that most girls seem to go through.

To be even more clear . . . I will come to the next support event and try to learn something. If you could tell me when and where. THIS IS NOT FUCKING EASY.

April 18, 2013

Gramma was visiting to lend a much-needed hand to the "sort out the mound of baby clothes donations" project. I was very large and a bit overwhelmed most days. I could play Tic Tac Toe in the swelling of my ankles and my ribs continued to dislocate, popping over each other when I laid down.

Gramma happily ventured out on her first public outing with Ella, while Jackson and I completed our errands. Then, we all enjoyed a sushi dinner together.

> Ella: Can I have a new bathing suit?
> Me: Swimming might be one of those activities you might not be able to do for a while . . . like kids with tubes in their ears . . . they just don't go.
> *Were there even safe options for trans people to swim?*
> Ella: Maybe I can wear some gaff underwear, and a tight suit to hold in the cups?
> *I Googled gaff: underwear made of tensile material to hold the male "package" tucked in place.*
> Gramma: I agree that bathing suits might not be enough clothing to hide your male body under.
> Ella: But I *LIKE* swimming. And what about "dampolining"?
> *Fond memories of a sprinkler under the trampoline drenching the summer heat.*
> Jackson: Maybe you could get a tan?

If it were only that simple. We roared with laughter. The innocence of kids.

April 19, 2013

After the excitement of acceptance to the Arts School faded, I launched directly into logistics. We arranged a meeting with the administration at the new school.

> Principal: The students here will hold Ella in check. They don't tolerate anything but genuine.
> Iain: I'm glad to hear that. This is the first time I have heard anyone comment on the importance of not over-acting.
> Ella: *Sits, as a proper queen would, completely over-acting the new role.*
> Me: We have a lot of work to do on the subtle actions and attitudes of females.
> We went out for supper last night, and I noticed that even picking up a dropped fork will require practice to train those knees to stay closed!
> Ella: Won't some man do that for me?
> *Hysterical laughter from all educated, administrative feminists in the room.*

We rounded out the discussion with practicalities. They couldn't change his name in the computer system to Ella without a legal name change, so there was a possibility someone could get it wrong. Were we planning on legally changing his name? Ella had the option of which bathroom he chose to use: Men's? Women's? Staff? Thank goodness: in many schools in the city, and far more in the Catholic system, the washroom privilege had not yet been extended across genders.

Should the teachers have been made aware of his gender dysphoria?

The verdicts:

I would investigate a legal name change.

Ella would use the women's washrooms.

The teachers would know so they could be the undercover police.

April 20, 2013

The behind-the-scenes work to setting Eliot up for possible social situations was a bit mind boggling. There was no possible way we could teach him responses for every possible scenario he might encounter, and luckily for us, he was bright and articulate enough to dig himself out of some of the unusual conversations on his own.

I also couldn't keep him home in a protective bubble forever, so he had started setting out on a few solo mall excursions. I suggested to him some "script" responses might be beneficial. I'm unsure which part of the brain is responsible for anticipating if someone might question why Eliot would be trying on ladies' size 10 red platform heels, but we clearly had some hurdles ahead . . .

> Me: What would you say if you run into a classmate at the mall today?
> Eliot: Maybe "I was born Eliot, but there was a little mix up and we're going to get *that* fixed later . . ."
> Me: Hmmm . . . that could use some work.
> Eliot: How about "I was just having fun . . . looking at shoes at Ardene, which is, by the way, my favorite store, and I absolutely love their spring line up of crop tees and printed leggings, and then I saw . . . and, um, hmm . . . yep. I need some scripted answers!"

So, we did just that. We compiled a list of the most commonly asked questions he might encounter and an idea of how to respond, being mindful of his own right to privacy, and their need to be respected, despite the often-inappropriate questions.

April 21, 2013

I spent the night pondering common questions I had been asked recently, heard others complain about, read articles where they were discussed at length.

The answers to these questions for each trans person would be unique and not neatly categorized. As a cisgender person (someone whose gender matches their biological sex at birth), I once tried to define the trans-identified community in a similarly concise manner. The fundamental flaw in this is that the task itself is impossible— humans are anything but simple.

TRANS TIPS 101: *Things you've always wanted to know, but*
***SHOULDN'T** ask!*

1. Have you had / when are you having "the operation"?
2. Which bathroom do you use?
3. How do you have sex?
4. Are you a drag queen?
5. Are you sure you aren't "just" gay?
6. Can I see a picture of you *before*?
7. Can I feel your boobs?
8. I can't even tell that you used to be a man/woman. For real?
9. Do you ever think you'll go back?
10. What's your *real* name?

If you are concerned about these things, Google them. Keep your mind open and your mouth closed. It is NOT okay to ask intimate questions about people's private lives, just as it would be inappropriate to ask a stranger or a colleague about their sex life. I would hope that you would honour and respect personal boundaries for a trans person, just the same as you would for any other person.

There *is* a difference between wanting to educate yourself and asking ignorant questions because you're curious about what is in someone else's pants. There *is* an appropriate time and way to ask respectful questions of someone with whom you have a personal relationship, and it's not approaching an acquaintance prying for juicy gossip. Even assuming we are entitled to this information stems from being the cisgender *normal* majority of the population, looming over an *abnormal* deviant sector.

"All people are equal, regardless of the alignment between their brain and their genitals."[10] ~ Deen

April 22, 2013

I had been thinking of excuses to try to make this day not happen for weeks; I had managed to postpone it once, but the momentum was bigger than me. My Al-Anon group had decided it would be "helpful" for me if they came over to have a "work-bee", and help me catch up with my runaway house.

I was comfortable with my gunge, but I was not so fond of my friends seeing all of it. The thought of getting ready for them to come was just about enough to send me over my breaking point, but instead, I thought of it as an exercise in simply accepting help gratefully, and gracefully.

Sponsor: Where are your rags?
Me: Here, under the kitchen sink.
Sponsor: *Opens the cupboard to an unorganized array of Arthur's stockpile of cleaning products, rags, soaps, who knows what else . . . Clearly unacceptable, but she tried to downplay her own neurosis.*
Can I start in here?
It's BAD when the cleaning starts with the cleaning cupboard.

There were ladies painting, vacuuming screens, washing out hutches, scrubbing toilets . . . some attempted to engage Eliot in some cleaning. However, it was clear he pictured himself as a trophy wife, more than a housewife.

Eliot: Mom, which one of your support groups is this?!?

Al-Anon, AA, PFLAG, quirky moms . . . whatever gets me through!
The result, after just a few hours, was a wonderfully fresh start. I was blown away by the infusion of fresh positive energy into our living space, and I was so grateful for all the fabulous, uncommon women in my life.

---

10   Deen. (2015). An astute and wise-beyond-his-years trans man who has awarded me the honor and privilege of insight over the years.

April 23, 2013

I can see, in retrospect, the very different paths that Iain and I walked when adjusting to some major parenting curve balls. We had a diagnosis of autism. We had a transgender child. I made appointments, formed teams, researched and got connected, likely as an unconscious strategy of keeping "busy" to avoid my emotions. Iain sat with the information, letting it settle where it needed to for him. My path was one of a gung-ho parental advocate. His path, from the outside, looked like a hesitant one—maybe even a non-supportive one. Months and years later, we have arrived at similar places of acceptance of the children as they are. If there were a test to compare, though, I'd bet he has done a better job of really dealing with his shit along the way.

I have not researched grief; I can't name all the stages, and I offer no examples of healthy ways to cope with it. I have been in situations where I have watched people receive troubling news. Some people seem to jump into action mode, and some people demonstrate a need to be immersed in the emotional realms. Some attend a vigil to honor memories of a lost loved one, while others get busy and organize the sandwiches. Neither is better, neither is right.

PFLAG mom: If I allow myself to cry, I may never stop.

That's not me, but I love that it is them. I rarely cry, and never for long. I'm destined to be among the people who stay more comfortably in active logistical support.

April 24, 2013

Since **Project Ella** had been set into motion, things could not happen fast enough. It was agonizing listening to Eliot's voice dropping. It was crushing for me to accept that neither of us were the one pulling the strings on the puppets that were acting out this show.

PFLAG friends voiced frustrations on all sorts of fronts. Waiting for their loved one to be ready to come out of the closet, waiting for medical appointments and referrals, waiting for everyone to catch up emotionally to where we have been for what feels like forever. And then when the waiting is over and a step forward is taken, how it sometimes feels like we have walked right into a brick wall . . .

Rare is the time that the parents, the child, and the system are in alignment. One is ahead, pulling the others along behind them, or one is in the rear, holding the forerunners back. I think the trick is to try to have some constant pressure—but not so much that the tie between the various participants snaps back and stings like a giant emotional elastic band. Snap.

May 6, 2013

I enjoyed my last few weeks of pregnancy. I was physically unwell, but I had a few pre-natal massages and acupuncture treatments to prepare my body and mind, and it felt good to get some pampering. I took the last of my belly photos in my homemade photography studio, complete with teenagers mocking me, hysterical about the set continually falling down around my (mostly) naked body.

Jackson was the most active of all of us, and was keen to join me for any adventure. Being pregnant had given the two of us some sacred private time. We walked to Safeway together to get junk food— taking full advantage of every pregnancy excuse. We delighted in Frappy-Days at Starbucks and basked in the sun shine after a long, cold winter. We bounced on the trampoline together . . . drop, baby, drop! He was also eager to try out the baby wraps and carriers on Benny, our smallest dog. I tried not to be neurotic about their being covered in dog hair before they were covered in baby spit!

May 13, 2013

While I understood being on the receiving end of parents frustrated by time lags in the health care system, I couldn't help but become the persistent parent on the phone with the Endocrinologist's office. The squeaky wheel got the grease . . .

Me: Could you PLEASE check your faxes again? I have called the
Gender Clinic every two days for the past few weeks trying to get
them to send the referral. They have switched computer systems,
and it is now affecting the *future of my child*.
Gatekeeper: I have checked again. It's not here. Maybe try their
office again?
Me: *Sigh of exasperation.*

I know this is just another referral to you, but for us, starting the
hormone blockers could mean the prevention of thousands
of hours and pain of hair removal, surgery to raise his already-
changing voice, and the chance of maintaining a somewhat
feminine body. I don't know what else to do.
Gatekeeper: Give me your phone number again, and I'll call you
when I see it . . .

I make more calls to the Gender Clinic and am told, like each
time before, they have a large stack and they are months behind. I,
again, offer to come and type it up myself. I will hand-deliver Dr.
Gender's handwritten notes to the Endocrinologist if it would help
things along.

May 14, 2013

iGramma: Your horoscope today says you feel the need to
contemplate your navel (ha!). You will be surprised to see how old
habits are still controlling your present behaviour. Hmmmm . . .
iMe: Yep . . . control, control, control. Obsess over what everyone
else is doing instead of focusing on what I am feeling!
iGramma: And what ARE you feeling? (Aside from fat!)
iMe: Impatient. Frustrated with Eliot. Maybe a bit useless now that
some of the big projects are done . . . Broke
iGramma: You are busy producing the biggest project of all! How
about spending some time feeling contented about that . . . you are
SO your Papa . . . xox
iMe: I am very much Papa
iGramma: No wonder I love you so much!

I loved science fair; the towering trifold cardboard display of perfectly stenciled lettering, measured and mounted hypotheses, materials and methodical procedures. The data was always solid, and the conclusions were logical (other than the one sad year of the snail ecosystem calamity). Papa regularly volunteered to judge the event at school, from elementary all the way through my high school years.

He never judged my project; it wasn't about having an advantage—I don't even remember if I won top prizes or not. Science fair was such a great event because Papa and I worked together on a level I understood. We didn't talk about his obvious stress, trying to recover financially from a bankrupt business while building his own professional corporation . . . we just measured, and calculated, and made logical deductions during a special time set aside for just us. He was proud of me, and that meant the absolute world. This realms of logic and accomplishment were where I felt my most comfortable connections with Papa. It still is.

May 23, 2013
Arthur and I attended our prenatal Centering Class on Thursday mornings. I had been brewing something wicked in my chest for days; I was having problems deciding moment-to-moment whether to hold my ribs so they didn't crack when I coughed, or to hold my crotch so I didn't pee my pants.

The Baby Doctor asked us to stay afterwards because she wanted to review some test results. I was spilling protein into my urine. My blood pressure was sky high. My lungs were full of crackles, likely pneumonia. My ankles were crazy swollen. I had super jumpy reflexes. My ultrasound showed litres of extra fluid in my baby belly. We were sent to the hospital for more testing.

Arthur and I enjoyed lunch out, tended to the dogs, and meandered over to the hospital, where we were greeted with "grab your bags, we are going to induce you." I had no bag, even though on every level I knew we weren't going to be leaving the hospital without a baby in our arms.

> Ob-Gyn: We can't induce you with drugs because of your previous C-section.
> Me: Even just a half dose? I DO NOT WANT another section.

Ob-Gyn: No drugs. You have never seen people run faster than
when a uterus explodes.
I'm not interested in doing that today.

We opted for a Foley catheter induction, which involved multiple
speculum attempts to insert a catheter through the cervix. Arthur was
traumatized, and labour hadn't even begun yet. We waited to see if
my body would understand what we were asking it to do . . . to open,
to relax, to deliver. I laboured gently overnight, pestering friends on
Facebook to send me more lives on Candy Crush™ to pass the time.

Baby Doctor: You are 4 cm. Just give me a minute here . . .
Painful pressure and gross sensations.
Baby Doctor: Now you are 6 cm. I just broke the scar tissues on
your cervix.
My hidden wounds from Jackson's delivery, no doubt.

My water broke in spectacular fashion, four litres of fluids spilling
onto the floor. It was exactly at this moment that the appointment
reminder chimed on Arthur's cell phone. Months earlier, I had told
him to put it in his calendar on the full moon nearest to my due date:
May 24, 2013—Carla thinks we are having a baby.

Fiona arrived exactly when she should have. The weight of the
room lifted, and everyone exhaled a sigh of relief. Gramma sat quietly
supportive in the corner.

I didn't know how to get on top of the intensity. I couldn't manage
the "out of controlness", and seriously doubted my decision to not
have had a section just a day earlier. And yet, in her expert doula
way, following her expert doula instincts, Fiona helped me into the
shower, where the baby spiralled out of its backwards presentation,
corkscrewing down and pressing hard against my tailbone. I simply
attempted to survive the next minute. The Baby Doctor—monitoring
nearby—respected my wishes, and in her own empowering way,
allowed me to labour how my body laboured.

A fire alarm went off while I was in the soothing shower water
. . . the hospital could have burnt down around me for all I cared.
Nurses and doctors piled medical equipment into my room, though I
remained mostly oblivious to the emergency.

Baby Doctor: Carla, you are minutes away from this baby being born, but his heart rate has fallen and we don't have minutes... So. You are going to push. I am going to pull with the vacuum. We are going to have a baby...NOW.

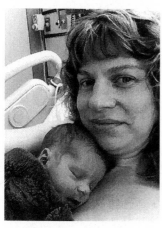

A grey infant lay listless on the bed beside me for only a moment before he was swept away to be monitored. Arthur attended to him, speaking gentle words of encouragement. The walls and bed were sprayed with blood, and the room resembled a trauma bay. When the eternity of 10 minutes finally passed, Arthur and I finally cherished this little one, skin to skin, as he gently woke from his shock. I was in awe and overwhelmed at the wonder of life and the connection of motherhood.

Welcome earthside, our sweet baby Jet.

May 27, 2013

Dear Ella,

Congratulations! Based upon your application package, we would like to offer you a spot to attend Camp fYrefly "Littles Day" in July!

The age limit to attend the entire Camp fYrefly as a camper is 14 to 24. We are offering a special portion of camp for our "Littles" between the ages of 10 and 13. This year's applicant pool was extremely competitive, as we had more youth apply than we could accommodate. We hope you are excited for Camp this summer!

Cheers"

Camp fYrefly was "Canada's only national leadership retreat for lesbian, gay, bisexual, trans-identified, two-spirited, intersexed, queer, questioning, and allied youth. The Camp is designed to help youth develop the leadership skills and personal resiliency necessary for them to become agents for positive change in their schools, families, and communities."[11]

That sounded like a great place to start. From all accounts, it was an incredible camp where if a youth could be persuaded to walk in the door, would never want to leave.

May 30, 2013

Thunder boomed and the skies opened, dumping enormous raindrops and pea-sized hail. While the rest of the family watched out the windows, Jackson took the opportunity to strip down and run wild into the backyard. He bounced on the trampoline, and the gathering hail exploded around him. I was slightly concerned about the lightning strikes—but not enough to quash his pure delight.

May 31, 2013

Like father like son?

Do we still get to use gender-binary clichés?

June 11, 2013

Grammas are the best. She helped with the 14-day-old baby as we attempted to arrive at the long-awaited appointment with the Endocrinologist on time. Strollers, nursing pads, receiving blankets, trying to sit comfortably myself, and a highly anxious teenager. His

11   University of Alberta. (2015). Welcome to Camp fYrefly. Retrieved from http://www.fYrefly.ualberta.ca/

support staff were empathetic and welcoming—being mindful of names and being careful not to misgender.

Dr: So, you prefer to go by Ella?
Ella: Yes.
Dr: I'm going to ask your parents a bit about your history, do a physical exam, and then we'll talk about a plan. Is that okay?
Ella: Sure.

HISTORY:
The parents report that Ella was very feminine from at least 2 years of age. When in kindergarten, they were seen by a psychiatrist regarding gender identity. At that time, Ella was insistent on wearing female clothing. Ella has always preferred female friends. About 1 year ago, Ella became very definite about wanting to live as a female. Currently, Ella is attending school in grade 7 as a boy and has mainly female friends who accept Ella as-is. Starting next September, Ella will be attending the Arts School as a female.

PHYSICAL EXAM:
Dr: I'll have you slip on this blue gown and be back in a minute.
All males exit room.
Ella: Mom, can you help?
Me: *Notices the 5 pairs of underwear Ella is sporting, a few of which she has her stomach through the leg holes, deeply cutting into her thighs, obviously affecting circulation.*
What are you doing?? Let's sort this out before the doctor comes back.
Ella: Just one pair doesn't work well enough.
To hide his maleness.
Dr: *Enters room.*
Examines head, chest, neck, extremities . . . and then down below . . .
Do you have pubic hair?
Ella: No, I shave it.
I had never considered that she may have done this.
Dr: But there was hair down here?
Ella: Not anymore.
Dr: When did you start to see hair down here growing?
Ella: There is no hair.

Me: Ella, was the hair like peach fuzz or rough and curly?
Ella: It was nasty.
Dr: I think we have established there was some hair down here, at some point.
Ella came to the clinic dressed completely as a female, including makeup and purple high-heel shoes. Height was 159.3cm and weight was 58.8kg. Extremities were normal, and there was no back tenderness or deformity. Head and neck examination were normal. Chest and cardiovascular examinations were normal. Neurological examination was normal. There was Tanner 3[12] genital development and shaved Tanner 3 pubic hair.

ASSESSMENT:
At this point, Ella is quite adamant that she would like to live as a female. I discussed with Ella and her parents the hormonal intervention and the baseline investigations prior to commencing. They have agreed to proceed, and will return in July for the commencement of Lupron® suppression therapy.
I did inform them quite clearly, and they were all in agreement, the opposite sex hormone will not be introduced until 15 or 16 years of age.

We had the necessary bone density scan and bloodwork completed, and we anxiously awaited the first injection . . . witnessing his body beginning to masculinize, his voice dropping, his feet growing, and praying a beard and chest hair wouldn't appear overnight.

June 14, 2013
The Quirky Moms started meeting every few months, years ago . . . initially it was
    "Coffee with the Autism Moms", then;
    "Wine with Moms of those with Special Needs", then;
    "Quirky Kid's Mom's Night Out", then;
    "The Quirky Mom's Whine and Wine"!
We all know the apple doesn't fall far from the tree.

---

12   The Tanner Scale is used to assess physical development based on external sex characteristics, such as the size of the breasts, genitals, and the development of pubic hair. Hormone suppression therapy is ideally initiated at Tanner 2 or 3.

We laughed about our childrens' inappropriate behaviour in inappropriate places—things we couldn't laugh about at the time because they were typically very stressful public situations. Like 12-year-olds tearing pads out of their underwear and yelling "NO MENSTRUATION" in Costco, and pulling fire alarms at school. We strategized about how to best support our children in life, whom to ask for, and how it works. It's an expansive web that supports special children.

They arrived this night bearing blue gifts for my babe. They cuddled and ogled and sniffed his intoxicating newborn smell. I didn't turn my nose up at the gender binary gifts, but was acutely aware of how we slot babies into two neat silos, pink and blue. My friends had likely never felt the need to examine it before. Statistically, I suppose that makes sense, but it sets up society for those that diverge from these roles to be the "abnormal" ones.

That evening, we spent some time reflecting on everyone's birth and child-rearing stories. There is always a sliver of resolution missing for a mom who wonders why her child has autism. There was conflicting research, a multitude of theories, and no simple answer.

I reflect on the list—some with no "definitive causal link" but enough to warrant more investigation. Ultrasounds (and in my case, fetal distress), high-fructose corn syrup, oxytocin, C-section, vaccines, acetaminophen, fluoride, mercury in fish, the list goes on and on. I also fed him a lot of tofu—and now he was a girl. Bad parent? Guilt-ridden? Nope. I made the best decisions I could, based on the information I had at the time. Simply the best I, or any other parent, was capable of doing.

June 15, 2013

June 17, 2013

Eliot turned 13. His birthday "want" list was short:

- Estrogen
- A new 17" MacBook-airsoft-retina-mac-attack-super-pro-Mac-Pac laptop
- A sweater

Unfortunately, some were not possible.

I opted to reminisce on his list of past obsessions to satisfy the teen wonder child. And by obsessions, I do not mean an area of interest—I mean pervasive all-encompassing thoughts and actions all day, every day. That child could think of nothing else, speak of nothing else, and would be satisfied with nothing less. It made gift-giving easy, and staying sane challenging. This was a day I missed my quirky *little* Eliot.

18 months: Tupperware, with which he had become very proficient at spinning, and as well as recognition of numbers and letters (lower and upper case) including obsessing over the dot on top of the lowercase i

2.5 years: Sparkly girl shoes and all the dresses in my closet. He had a meltdown every time we passed a woman in heels in the mall and attempted to steal them right off any child who happened to be wearing "fancy" shoes. This was also the start of the ballet and tutu obsessions.

3 years: Naming all the countries in the world, along with their
capital city and flag. I'd never seen anything as impressive as a
knee-height child schooling me on Uzbekistan and locating the
island of Vanuatu on a globe. He would occasionally try to catch
Iain and I out and ask, "What's the capital of Monaco?"

3.5 years: Fans, fans everywhere—in the produce department
at the grocery store, at the front of the library bus, on top of the
building next to the daycare in the a/c unit. He slept with a small
one he named "Mary", after my grandmother.

4 years: Cars. Not playing with them—categorizing them, by
colour, make and model, and logo. The parkade of a department
store was an amusement park for him. Dinky cars sufficed because
he could take the tires off and spin them on his tongue. We had
a Tupperware container full of little tires that satisfied some oral
sensory fixation.

5 years: Antiques and shiny things: replica spinning wheels and old
china tea sets.

6 years: Architecture.

Child: Oh, look at that beautiful bi-level split-entry with the
Victorian bannister and post-modern influence!

Me: Oh, that brown one?

7 years: Titanic. Probably my favorite obsession of all. He knew
everything—which of the smoke stacks was just for decoration,
who designed it, who built it, every little detail. He made
handwritten books about it. Every art project at school depicted it
somewhere . . . even studying the Inuit people of Canada.

We watched the movie Titanic. He went to bed in tears. Had I
crossed the line for age-appropriate movie selections?
Me: I know it's sad so many people died.
Eliot: No, it's not that. It's the beautiful staircase still at the bottom
of the ocean and no one has brought it up to restore it!
8 years: We read Romeo and Juliet together. The original version,
because Eliot would accept nothing less.

Clocks. All sorts. Clock doctors
(clocktors!), Big Ben, and grandfather
clocks . . .
9 years: The periodic table of the
elements—uranium in particular.
And molecular gastronomy. I know;
what the hell is that? It is chemistry
and food combined. Using reagents
to turn tomato soup into spaghetti-
like noodles, and mint syrup into tiny
minty tapioca-like balls. For me, it was
dishes that were impossibly hard to
clean.

10 years: Chernobyl. Pripyat.
Abandoned buildings. Ad nauseam.
11 years: Apple products, operating systems, the sound that plays
when you load each version of windows OS . . .
12 years: Makeup, perfume, Christian Louboutin shoes. Not just
liking them—knowing ALL about them, stopping in at the shoe
repair store weekly to see if they had some in that she could just
touch . . .
13 years: All things girl—sounds normal enough? Right?!?

June 20, 2013

I stopped at a high-end baby store to get some wooden letters to use in some baby photos. On a stand at the till, they had a lanyard for a soother. I chose a pride rainbow. Baby Jet will never know his oldest brother, only his elder sister.

It reminded me of a poster hanging on the wall at the Gender Clinic. It was a newborn baby with a hospital bracelet that says, "presumed heterosexual". How true that is. When you deliver a penis, you expect to raise a boy.

One of my personal catchphrases had always been "I'd rather raise a hockey team than have one teenage girl". Wasn't it a given that, after delivering three boys, I was off the hook? Apparently not.

The loved ones of transgender youth mourn their loss. For me, this grieving was not so much for the loss of my child. I didn't feel like I was "losing my son"; my intuition had been hinting about this for years already. What I did grieve though, was the loss of the potential that my expectations would be fulfilled. The career and relationship paths that one assumes a biological male will follow—gone. I felt the crushing loss of the fantasy life I had created for Eliot in my head.

In reality, we had lost nothing tangible.

June 22, 2013

We deliberated about how best to share what was going on inside our family with those beyond our walls. My parents needed a way to communicate the information to people they didn't see often, but who we felt were important people to include from the onset. Extended family—it would only be a few months before they met Ella, and we didn't want them to feel a need to keep secrets from each other. Old family friends, still very much connected, we wanted to share our journey with at once. We did not want a group who *knew* and a group who *didn't*.

We crafted a letter. This would give people a chance to digest the information in private before anyone was required to respond. Time and space are necessary to process, especially on a topic many of them had probably never heard of before, let alone be knowingly exposed to on a personal level.

And it was sent.

Dear Family and Friends —

We have some important news we would like to share with you. Eliot has confided in us that he wishes to live as a girl. Few of you will find this surprising. We don't either, but this observation is no longer abstract—it is a reality and we find ourselves with decisions to make. Through lengthy discussions, professional assessments, and much consultation and thought, we are moving forward, accepting this very special and gifted young person. We are doing what we can to support an individual whose inner core is, and always has been, female.

She has chosen the name Ella, and over the summer will be making the transition to living as a girl. Ella has been accepted to a fabulous arts program in the city, where she will get a fresh start for grade 8 in September. The school will allow her to explore film, photography, and media arts in an environment which actively supports both artistic individuality and gender minorities. She is very excited about this, and we are proud of her for having the courage to live in a way that reflects her true self. As parents, we have concerns about safety, societal intolerance, and social acceptance—we are doing our best to build support networks, to discuss it with those we can, and to set Ella up for success.

You are an important part of our lives, and we understand this may be very confusing. Please understand that it is not our intention to alarm or shock you. There is a lot of information available about transgender people, and about gender dysphoria. We have found many informative websites, well-researched books, and some television shows to be great places to start. We also encourage you to ask us any questions you may have— this complex subject is still foreign to us, and we are having to undertake a crash course (most of it under the demanding watch of a highly internet-capable and far-too-articulate 13-year-old attorney), but we are happy to share what we've learned. While this is a private matter, and we are telling you in confidence, it is not a secret.

We love and support Ella in her journey, just as we always have Eliot, and we have every confidence that you will, too.

Love,

Us

June 23, 2013

The dogs (affectionately named poopies to reflect the amount of pick-up that is required) reacted to the arrival of baby Jet in ways that were as different as their personalities.

Angie was his nursemaid. She awoke at every peep and coo. She would not go outside to pee until she had checked to make sure the baby was safe. She cleaned off his face, and we safely guarded all diapers at the risk of finding disgusting piles of digested absorbent material all over the yard!

Monty was aloof. He jumped on my lap, not even noticing the baby was nursing. He refused to let the intrusion of this little person impact his life in any way.

Benny was a nervous wreck. He had lost ¼ of his body weight with projectile diarrhea and nervous panting. He required veterinary attention and was the reminder that, really, there was a LOT going on at the Gemstone.

I can equate their reactions on a similar level to the people we know and the "arrival" of Ella. Some are lovers, some are indifferent, and some are so uncomfortable that they disappear, unable to control their own bodily response.

June 24, 2013

> **"It was lack of REM sleep that killed Michael Jackson, not propofol".**
> **~ Arthur, father of a 4-week-old baby**

June 26, 2013

Official Full-Time Transition Day! I learned about and embraced the Transgender Pride flag.

We were about to launch into months of intense Ella-ness.

Change

June 29, 2013

Ella was on Facebook. "Eliot's" profile was deleted. All previous photos vanished, all former acquaintances unfriended. She wanted to never speak of it again—to move forward boldly as Ella.

June 30, 2013

> iGramma: Will E be Ella at Iain's next week?
> iMe: E will be here, I think. Iain insisted he take "Eliot" to the birthday movie tonight . . . much to Ella's dismay
> iGramma: Has he taken Ella anywhere publicly yet?
> iMe: I don't think so

July 2, 2013

What emerged when the traditional binary gender rules placed on "Eliot" at birth were softened was a simplistic construct of what a child with autism would see as feminine. Though she hadn't been able to identify with the feminine world for long, she had been mentally preparing for years.

Not all trans women are comfortable, nor have a desire, to present themselves in a stereotypically feminine fashion. They don't want pink, fancy shoes, or manicures. I fall into that category, even as a cisgender woman who is comfortable with my femininity. For some newly introduced to the concept of gender not being the traditional binary of "F" or "M", any rejection a well-intentioned "girly" gift can sting, like the rejection of a peace palm.

Ella, on the other hand, bought into every facet of toxic beauty culture. She swung to the very extreme edges of vanity. She longed to be the female in every airbrushed image and to comply with the sexist standards of the day. I wondered how long it would take for her to feel as disappointed as most other girls are when comparing her own body to the "western standard" of the perfect body.

Her every photo had a sex-bomb, lip-pursed face. Playing with newfound girlfriends led to a photoshoot in a pink dress and stilettos, sitting in provocative poses on ladders and rooftops in selfies on Facebook, which I had a problem with on a whole bunch of levels, none of which had anything to do with gender. So, this was what parenting a teenage girl felt like.

Overnight, she had become a cross between a Hitchcock leading lady and a hooker, with ambitions of being a "made up" housewife (but one who does no housework). She was becoming a poster child for media's messaging of all the superficial things a woman is "supposed" to be. It was a sad reflection of society. We

nicknamed this persona "Betty-Sue", to use as a quick cue to remind Ella about unhealthy self-expression.

It reminded me of a craft that had come home from daycare when she was seven or eight. I had kept it all these years knowing, somehow, it was telling of things to come . . .

July 3, 2013

eMe: Iain—Couple things for your consideration:

1. I'd like to let her get her ears pierced. Any objections? I don't know very many 13-year-old girls who don't have them done, and they will grow over if she doesn't want them later.
2. I spoke with the coordinator of the College Film Camp about E attending as Ella. E is adamant about it. They stay in groups of 4 in residence, but each has a bedroom with a room that locks, and 2 share a bathroom (also locking). She had no problem with E attending as Ella, only asking we let her know ASAP so she can let the teachers and supervisors know to watch for issues, to assign her to the appropriate room, and to change her name on the roster. It was a positive response, and I would be comfortable sending Ella. She wanted E to be comfortable, so she could get the most out of Film Camp.
3. Legally changing her name. The process is: fingerprints, a "Change of Legal Name" form signed by both legal guardians, and $$ taken to a registry office. Approximately 6 weeks later, we receive a certificate of name change in the mail (it will not change the sex marker—will still say Male). We then use that certificate to change the name with Alberta Education, Alberta Health and Wellness, etc., if/when we choose.
4. I booked some appointments for Ella and Jackson with the Family Psychologist over the summer. These are big changes and I want to know they are both doing okay . . . they are both so frustrated with each other (having way more to do with ASD, teenager attitude, and tempers, than gender!).
Thoughts?

  c

July 4, 2013

Gramma was visiting to help give baby snuggles and big kid lovin'. Jackson was frustrated with "maybe laters" and crying babies. I couldn't join him for a jump outside because my undercarriage was still recovering slowly . . .

Jackson: Come ON Ella . . . come on the trampoline with me!
Ella: It's too hard to undo my shoes, and I don't want to change out of this dress.
Jackson: Ella! I'll wait. PLEASE!
Ella: Ugh, no. My makeup might smudge, and I'm tired.
Jackson: Well, then, can ELIOT come out to play??

July 5, 2013

Ella arrived in the back yard on her way to, or from, something in an ultra-short, pink polka-dot halter dress, ruby red lipstick, 5-inch pink stilettos, and gaudy sunglasses. She stuck her bum out one direction and bust out the other and spewed arrogant, self-entitled lines about her big evening plans. She exited in the same arrogant way she had arrived, and I composed this e-mail to my 12-year-old-son turned 13-year-old-bitch-daughter, currently at Iain's house, and elicited responses from the other parental units.

I felt as if I was a mother to two newborns—one two months and adjusting to life on the outside, and one 13 years old but in the infancy of her female life.

eMe: Ella—
Your attire and attitude today, for the 10 minutes I witnessed, was completely unacceptable. Choosing to act and dress in a manner you KNOW is over the top (we have discussed what is appropriate many times) proves to me you are NOT CAPABLE of or WILLING to make good decisions.
Because of this, I suggest implementing the following guidelines—Iain and Arthur can comment as needed . . .
Observation #1: The lipstick/eye shadow colors were outrageous.
Consequence: The neutral gloss and other natural-colored lipsticks/shadows will be the ONLY colors you may wear, unless given permission to wear something else for a special occasion.
Observation #2: The shoes are inappropriate for a 13-year-old girl (and most other women, for that matter).
Consequence: You may only wear flats or wide heels with less than a 1.5-inch height, and heels over this height are forbidden, without express permission on special occasions.
Observation #3: Way too much perfume being applied too often.

Consequence: 1 spray on each wrist ONCE a day, and 1 spray on the neck ONCE a day. More than this will result in ALL perfumes being taken away and no more trips to the department store for samples.

Observation #4: There is lipstick on the roof of my car.

Consequence: NO makeup to be opened or applied in vehicles. This also includes nail polish and perfume.

Observation #5: Terrible saucy attitude, with know-it-all statements. Arguing with every comment. Answering questions with questions. Expecting your way all the time.

Consequence: Back to childish time-outs for acting like a 3-year-old. Any disrespectful talk to/or about other people (parents, Arthur, Jackson, others) will NOT be tolerated.

Observation #6: Excessive time on the computer. Refusing to turn it off when requested.

Consequence: At the Gemstone, you may ONLY be on the computer from 7-9 a.m. and 4-5 p.m. No exceptions, but if we aren't home at those times, you may have your hour later.

We all support and love you, Ella. Some of your choices have not been good ones, and for you to have a successful entry at the Arts School, and a successful life later, you MUST make some changes and trust we are helping you along.

Love you -

Mom xox

eElla: 1: The lipstick was understandable, but the eyeshadow was the brown Maybelline one I always wear . . . Also, when I asked, you said the lipstick was inappropriate for school (a while ago when you had your friend over [the one whose son was allergic to dogs]) although it was on me nowhere near school. AND WHAT ABOUT MY CORAL GLOSS? ☹

2: Unless we find some like, blister covers, shoes with backs really hurt, and flip flops look awful on everyone.

3: Understandable.

4: Understandable as well.

5: What's wrong with answering a question with a question?

6: Nothing yet.

For the most part, it isn't apparent that Iain is trying to help me. For example, Iain (mostly in the past 2 days or whenever I go out as *ME*) says I am overdressed and need to wear neutral clothes. He says eventually, he is trying to help me, but it just comes across that he wants me to look boring all the time. And I am NOT a neutral person—those clothes are NOT for me, and the only time I'd wear something neutral is when I'm A—doing lawn work, B—shovelling snow, or C—raking leaves.

I would much rather stay at your house, where your dress codes make sense and you are SUPPORTIVE, as opposed to Iain, who thought a tank top, shorts, a cardigan, and flats was overdressing. I have tried, and failed, to believe that the joint custody agreement was made in my best interests. It's unbearable.

Reply soon! I'm lonely over here!

LOVE YOU SO MUCH!

XOXOXOXOXOXOXOXOXOXOXOXOXOXOXOXOXOXOXOXOXOXOXOXOXO ELLA ❤

P.S.—Shoes with backs really irritate my blisters, so could you please try to find some blister covers?

P.P.S.- I have NO clue what goes on in Iain's mind, aside from him ALWAYS dresscoding me [fun fact: he asks me if I have anything that disguises the fact I don't have boobs, then I put them on and he gets all mad at me] and getting mad over everything I do. He says I'm not even allowed to wear heels inside ON THE CARPET.

P.P.P.S.—Come get me out of here, pleasssssseeeeee.

elain: The rules at Iain's house will be the same, with additions:

A. Internet research on high heeled shoes is now banned—it has become vain obsession, and as your mum points out, these shoes are not only blatantly inappropriate for a young teenager, they'd be inappropriate by most women, unless they were attending a banquet, a wedding, or other very formal occasion. To wear them otherwise would be seen as very, very tacky.

B. We will be meeting with the Family Psychologist in an attempt to teach you the perils of vanity, of trying too hard to "make an impression," or to be too desperate for compliments on your appearance and/or attire from other people. Vanity is a terrible trait, and I am very worried about your lack of awareness on this point.

C. I will relax the Internet time limits on days this summer when you are in the house without me because I'm stuck at work. Specs on a case by case basis. But the high heel embargo remains.

D. Fully agree with your mum that the constant arguing with adults is ludicrous. I do not see this as the natural effort of a young teen to exert a bit of independence—in your case, you extend it to telling me "how the world is". And that, given the gap in our ages, is preposterous.

E. Your mother will be taking you shopping for appropriate casual clothing that is not designed to say, "Hey everyone, look at MEEEEE!" Neutral colours, plain shorts, t-shirts. You know, like the other girls in Suburbia. And everywhere else.

Prove to us you can make this transition like a responsible young adult, and we will support you. But continue this path and the rules will tighten, and force us to reconsider whether something else—not honest awareness of gender dysphoria—is driving all of this. It does not seem terribly natural to me right now—it seems vain, forced, and more than a bit phony, Ella. If you want us to believe you, start listening to us, and we can help you to make this transition safely, properly, and appropriately. And respectfully of the people around you. No one likes a diva.

Finally—your frustrations on these points do NOT entitle you to be mean to Jackson. You are the elder sibling, and it is your responsibility to be encouraging and respectful of his feelings, and to help him build confidence instead of running him down.

Love,

Iain

eArthur: My Ella:

Would be a stylish, demure young lady.

Would be an active participant in the family and household.

Would be open and willing to learn from her guardians/mentors.

Would strive to be the best she can in all her challenges.

I love the Ella that we have and wish that she were willing to relish her place in her age group and enjoy growing into a young woman.

Arthur

eGramma: Next time I ask you how you are and how it's going, just slap me upside the head.

July 6, 2013

I started paying closer attention to some articles popping up on some of my news feeds. As a rule, I try to ignore most of them. There is too much sadness and trauma for me to process, so I tended to stay somewhat clueless about many current events. This caught my eye, though, because of my astonishment that gender was not explicitly protected in the Canadian Human Rights Act or by the Criminal Code of Canada. That was CRAZY to me!

Bid to Pass Transgender Rights 'Bathroom Bill' Suffers Setback after Senate Fails to Vote

OTTAWA—An eight-year bid to include transgender rights in Canadian anti-discrimination and hate laws is likely to suffer another legislative setback, despite support from a majority in both chambers of Parliament.

The proposed legislation appeared poised to pass the Senate but did not make it to a final vote before the summer recess began last week.

"The Senate should have passed this, and it's disappointing that the transgender community is going to have to wait months again now unnecessarily for them to do this, but I still expect them to pass the bill," said the bill's sponsor, New Democrat MP Randall Garrison.

Bill C-279 would protect transgender Canadians against discrimination in the Canadian Human Rights Act and prohibit the promotion of hatred or the incitement of genocide on the basis of gender identity in the Criminal Code.[13]

July 8, 2013

Rosie the Roomba® was struggling. The dog hair. The piles of baby paraphernalia. The suffocation by all things Ella.

She sent me a clear message that she was at the end of her rope when she threw herself down the stairs this morning into a telling pile of atrocious heels . . .

#vacuumsuicide

---

13   Ditchburn, J. (2013, July 4). Bid to pass transgender rights 'bathroom bill' suffers setback after Senate fails to vote – nationalpost.com. Retrieved July 6, 2013.

July 10, 2013

> iArthur: I lost my job 3 days ago
> iMe: Tell me more
> *Fuck.*
> iArthur: There was a difference of opinion and I was escorted out of the building
> iMe: Where have you been going for the past 3 days?
> iArthur: I couldn't tell you
> I am an earner—I will sort this out
> I'm so sorry

I was understandably taken aback by the unexpected announcement from someone who spoke nothing of troubles at work. I was also understandably shaken about the financial impact of the only working adult in the home with 3 kids and 3 dogs no longer being employed.

July 13, 2013

Gramma, Jet, Ella, and I departed for an extended weekend trip to my hometown. The purpose of the trip was twofold: for the extended family to meet our baby Jet, and to call in the big guns—my most awesome girly BFFs—to help tone down "Betty-Sue".

Learning how to be a young lady

1.   Have your mother write a clothing manual so you have an idea of what is appropriate for where/when. In addition to the basics—formality, appropriate skin coverage (no boobs, no belly, no butt), weather and season considerations—have her include things such as:

- Why you shouldn't wear a prom dress to coffee
- Why you shouldn't wear white kitten heels in the city in December
- Why you shouldn't wear a shirt that reveals your entire back and some torso to your grandfather's house

2.   Book an afternoon with a good-spirited esthetician so you don't spend all your money, forever, on someone else doing your nails:

- Don't show up with your nails coloured black with permanent marker or you may give your lovely esthetician a heart attack
- Don't make excuses like "it hurts to bend over to my toes," as all women have experienced and overcome this pain, including your 6-week post-partum mother
- Make a special effort to thank someone who has gone out of their way to help a girl out

3.   Have coffee with the most classy, stylish, trendy women you know. Be very sure they have a sense of humour:

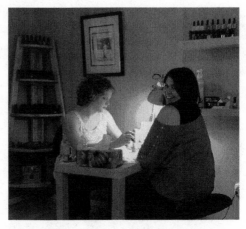

- Don't show up to a table of four women with one brownie and one fork. You need four brownies, or four forks
- Don't spend more than 36 seconds showing them photos

of yourself on your phone. They are sitting with you—they know what you look like. (Exceptions are for selected special occasions in life [new love interests, vacation photos that make the people at the table eating the brownies look skinnier than yourself, and so forth])

- When the conversation drifts into a topic you aren't particularly interested in, watching videos on YouTube on your phone is disrespectful
4. Start listening to other ladies . . . they have learned the "rules":
  - Ladies think everyone under five years old is cute (even if it's not)
  - Babies, or photographs of babies, or stories of babies are ALWAYS cute, beautiful and funny respectively (likewise for pets)
  - Ladies don't fart. Or burp. They turn on blow dryers when they enter a bathroom to hide the sounds that bodies make in bathrooms. They pass enormous wads of toilet paper to each other under the stall dividers when they are out.
  I also took this opportunity to explain why girls even wipe at all— she was confused by the physical difference between the sexes!
  - Ladies HATE pictures of themselves that are not flattering, even if they're making a funny face

Every day, every situation, was a new lesson for someone who didn't get to practice being a 4-year-old girl, or a 7-year-old girl, or even a 12-year-old girl. There is a LOT to learn about being "feminine". Especially for an autistic someone who has no innate ability to know the nuances or even care that rules exist!

And then, when we learn the rules, we break them. The stereotypical "female" gender role is quickly becoming passé as some millennials attempt to overthrow the gender binary.

July 20, 2013

It was about this time that Jackson was willing to jump back on a bike. He felt more comfortable in a full-face helmet. I was glad he was back in the saddle.

July 22, 2013

How do I connect with a child who is socially isolated? This is the consummate struggle for autism moms who nurture children often lacking stereotypical outward signs of affection. It's the lack of hugs and lack of closeness, and the lack of them *wanting* to share joyous moments. In retrospect, I clearly see that void with "Eliot". He never ran into the kitchen exclaiming "Mommy, look, come see . . ." like Jackson did so naturally. Instead, I found "Eliot" engulfed in "his" own joy and I joined "him" there.

I read *The 5 Love Languages*[14] eons ago, and recall clearly seeing us in it. I give love in acts of service. I recall madly painting a wall blue, from green. Seething out of my pores came "Of course I fucking love you—can't you see I painted this whole room because you hate green?" while Iain was cowering in the kitchen witnessing the madness and silently screaming out in his language "*TOUCH ME*" just a month before our separation. I receive in acts of service as well. This was likely learned by watching Papa bring Gramma a coffee every single morning as a small tangible gesture of his love. She longed for him to just sit and enjoy it with her . . . quality time.

Jackson was a quality time guy. A Frappuccino date at Starbucks went a long way to reconnecting with him. Ella was a receiver of gifts. She often said, "I know you love me because you bought me . . ." It was not surprising that someone without a strong inherent desire for social closeness would resonate with this Love Language— words of affirmation or physical touch were likely hard to interpret and uncomfortable. How, as a parent, did I reconcile the faux pas of *spoiling* her with outpouring my love in a way she could accept? I just did. The nooks, crannies, and secret spaces of the Gemstone filled up with love gifts, small and large, without further guilt attached.

Arthur needs words of affirmation and I suck at giving them. That's my work to do.

I told you I loved you once, and nothing has changed. Why would I need to say it again?

---

14   Chapman, G. D. (1995). The five love languages: How to express heartfelt commitment to your mate. Chicago: Northfield Pub.

July 24, 2013

The social worker had arrived at the house to review Ella's funding agreement for "disabled" children. We had been fortunate enough to qualify for some financial support to cover the extra cost of adult kid-sitters and special camps because Ella wasn't appropriate "material" for many typical childcare scenarios. Anyone other than an adult person being paid an adult person's wage wouldn't have tolerated the expenditure of energy, nor had the skill required to mind my children.

The annual meeting was always anxiety evoking because, although you never wish for your child to have a bad day, there was a requirement to convince the worker of *need*. Only now can I admit to hiding oscillating fans and cars with no wheels which were guaranteed to set her off, and feeding her Coke for breakfast for such assessments when she was young. On this day, I had copies of all the most recent diagnoses (no one should need to know the plural of diagnosis) and report cards to defend my position.

Ella sat at the table, rude, catty, and demanding. She constantly interrupted, and her attempts to derail the entire conversation were almost successful. Arthur had retreated to our room upstairs—headphones on, watching literally thousands of dollars' worth of downloaded iTunes shows, door closed.

> Ella: It not a universal LAW[15] that girls dress prudishly like you.
> I got more likes on that rooftop stiletto picture than you've had in your life.
> Is this going to take long? Because I need you to take me back to Value Village . . .
> *Social worker is visibly affected by Ella's crazy energy, speaking at a just-louder-than-the-newborn-baby-screaming-volume.*
> Social worker: I think we should increase your respite and community aide funding.
> Is there *ANYTHING* else that could help support you at this point?
> Me: I don't even know.
> *I may have squeezed out a tear.*

15   When Ella was young, we broke down rules according to severity of the consequences of breaking them to delineate consequences for the autistic mind. Mama Laws were ones that Ella could expect to be different from house to house and the consequences had some wiggle room – like bedtime. Hard Laws were ones with severe consequences that should be strictly followed – like at airports or border crossings. Universal Laws were ones where natural forces would dictate the consequences – like sliding down a snow hill on a toboggan towards a road or farting loudly in an elevator.

His acknowledgement of my difficult reality was what I needed. Perspective, from someone who has not become immune to life at the Gemstone, brought me back to the reality that this is not everyone's normal. That was enough reinforcement to continue.

As the universe would have it, the social worker's daughter's girlfriend was a pharmacy acquaintance of mine when they were embarking on their own journey of raising a little girl together. He was an ally in disguise.

July 27, 2013

ATTEMPT #326 TO TONE DOWN "BETTY-SUE"

It was finally time for fYrefly! I dropped off a very eager Ella. We were early, but she was scooped up by the camp facilitators, and she quickly went on her way with a smile that engulfed her whole face. They disappeared into a bright room with obvious rainbow paraphernalia, filled with youth in small groups and happy photographs pinned on the walls.

Arthur opted for pick-up duty. He texted me for directions to find Ella. I was in bed with Jet on my boob.

The evening had ended with a mock fashion show, where Ella was chosen as emcee. The flat-out encouragement of this group of youths was for them to "Just be yourself," and "Don't pay attention to anyone else, set your own style!" was taken to heart by our young lady. For nearly all participants, fYrefly was a powerful place where deep-seated positive ideas were planted and genuine self-acceptance was fostered. Without the understanding that the camp was a closed, safe environment for these youths and not typical of the outside world, Ella had learned some dangerous lessons.

> iArthur: Did you drop her off in a long lace dress and tall heels?
> iMe: I did not.
> iArthur: I found her. In a black slip dress and 4-inch tan peep toe shoes.
> It's so over the fucking top that I don't have words.
> This child is the only prostitute here.

I'm waiting outside while the Queen makes her farewells. This is not cool.

iMe: I can't fix it . . .

iArthur: Ella is confusing looking mature with being mature. Quote me on this one.

I am not asking you to fix anything.

I'm observing that we have a serious problem. Very, very serious. This youth will get in trouble well beyond her ability to understand or deal with.

This is not good.

I cannot endorse the continued public release of Ella without supervision.

I'm serious Carla; this is not in any fashion acceptable or safe behavior.

iMe: I agree.

iArthur: This will end badly if allowed to continue unabated. Ella needs to act like a 13-year-old and heed her mentors' guidance. If there is no compliance, then I will have no choice but to withdraw my support of Ella's transition.

I'd rather be the stepfather of a very unhappy "Eliot" than a brain damaged or crippled Ella.

The incident broke my heart and brought down the hammer. **Project Ella** was in danger. I organized more meetings. I begged for focus group discussions. It was the first time I was genuinely concerned this whole gender escapade was truly an elaborate rendition of an Asperger's obsession, and we had all been led horribly astray by a very clever 13-year-old.

July 31, 2013

The pronouns were hard. Very, very hard.

It was kind of like trying to stop biting your nails . . . before you even know it, you've ripped that strip of white you've been pampering for a month right off Peter Pointer.

"Eliot", "boys", or "he" slipped off my tongue before I could even stop them. Often in public. Luckily, Ella was gentle with me as I broke a language habit as old as she. "Pssst" was our code word. A gentle reminder to me that I had misgendered her in public without having to make a scene about it. Eventually, the neurons dug a new path to fire down in my brain and I got it right more often than not.

The last frontier to be crossed was when speaking of the small child I knew as only "Eliot". I would switch to "male" pronouns about that infant—not able, yet, to see that being as Ella as well. This, too, changed over time. And I recognize the child I knew as "Eliot" was Ella all along, referred to with a different name.

I consider myself fortunate to have not been asked to wrap my head around a more gender-neutral pronoun like zhe (or ze, hir, hirs) or to a singular plural they (them, theirs)! I would have done it, but it would have been a mental challenge. Just a year earlier, like many, I hadn't even known such things existed.

I was equally relieved that Ella identified as the traditional binary "female" (meaning the traditional concept of only two genders: boy or girl), only because explaining the *spectrums of gender and sexuality* to people who have never contemplated the concept was an arduous task. Again, I would have honoured any identity out of respect to Ella if she had identified otherwise, but I was fortunate that she was on a path that was more traditionally understood.

In a Canadian survey of those whose birth sex does not match how they feel, more than ⅓ identified as something outside the boy/girl binary.[16]

- 8% did not identify as transgender
- 40% identified as transgender and identified as a boy/man
- 16% identified as transgender and identified as a girl/woman
- 26% identified in some other way

Refusing to honour someone's preferred pronouns tells that person that you value your own opinion of who you think they are more than who that person really is. It repeatedly hurts them and feeds into them not feeling safe or respected. Take a moment to consider how it must feel to have someone demonstrate to you that your identity isn't valid, simply by refusing to change salutations.

---

16   Veale J, Saewyc E, Frohard-Dourlent H, Dobson S, Clark B & the Canadian Trans Youth Health Survey Research Group (2015). Being Safe, Being Me: Results of the Canadian Trans Youth Health Survey. Vancouver, BC: Stigma and Resilience Among Vulnerable Youth Centre, School of Nursing, University of British Columbia.

August 1, 2013

I dug into my recovery program. "Sought through prayer and meditation to improve our conscious contact with God *as we understood Him*, praying only for His knowledge of His will for us and the power to carry that out".[17] It was the only thing I could think of that might bring me out of the crazy of the last month.

"For the LOVE OF GAWD!!" is probably not the prayer they were thinking of.

The Big Book of Alcoholics Anonymous speaks of a God of our understanding. I don't call my Higher Power "God" because, for me, the word reeks of organized religion. AA is a fellowship that encouraged me to be spiritually connected to my Higher Power without any affiliation, sect, or denomination. I did not, nor would I, bow to an ideology or obey certain religious "rules" in fear of some divine punishment. Spirituality sets me free—to follow my heart, to learn my own path, and to feel connected in a way that is just right for just me.

Praying is talking. Meditating is hearing. Doing it is more difficult.

My practice of meditation has been a bit different. In "awareness" classes, yoga retreats, or solstice celebrations, I have taken opportunities to try calming my mind which were always met by an arsenal of a million squirrels on a million typewriters.

I tried . . .

Teacher: *Relaxing breathing exercises, progressive muscle relaxation.*
Be the watcher.
Watch your mind.
What will your next thought be?
Just wait, and watch, and observe.
Me: *I wonder what my next thought will be?*
Was that it?!?
I wonder if wondering what the thought will be counts as a thought?
If that's the best thought my brain comes up with, that's lame.
Stop judging. It's just a thought. Just like this one.
I wonder how many thoughts that was.
I fail at thinking. Or do I fail at not thinking?
I tried again . . .

17   Alcoholics Anonymous. (2001). Alcoholics Anonymous, 4th Edition. New York: A.A. World Services.

Friend: I often use a river, a stream of consciousness, as a visual for meditations. I am at the bottom of the river, watching the thoughts float by in boats. I just watch them float by, and don't swim to the surface to get into the boat with the thought. If I notice that I have, I get out and swim back down.

Me: *I see the rippling blue water with a glimmer of sunshine illuminating the scene.*

I must have a respirator and goggles, or I would never be able to do this.

Watch for boats, Carla! BOATS!

I see the bottom of canoes, but not thoughts . . .

I wonder how long I can stay here with this tank of air that I am not supposed to be thinking about . . . suffocating . . . slowly . . .

Clearly, not thinking, for a mind like mine, is not the way to listen and hear. I have had more success with guided meditations and focussed breathing exercises so I don't run away with my train of thoughts.

August 5, 2013

We arrived at the police station on time and approached the officer sitting on the other side of a bullet proof glass wall.

Me: We're here for fingerprinting.

Officer: Why?

Me: For a legal name change.

Officer: Why?

Me: Eliot is transgender.

Officer: Pardon?

Me: Eliot is transgender.

Is there no privacy in this fucking place?

Officer: Uh. I'll get the printin' officer.

Peering awkwardly over the rims of his oil-covered bifocals

We had waited weeks for the appointment to have Ella's fingerprints taken. They were necessary to accompany the 16-page Legal Name Change application form, which also required signatures of both legal guardians and $200. Our family was easily able to jump through these hoops, but the impossibility of doing so for many transgender youths struck me. How may would not have the funds, nor the required consent, to complete this task?

We were lead into a dim hallway, like uncommon criminals, to the printing station located adjacent to three vacant incarceration cells. Though the officer was pleasant enough, the experience reeked of shame and violation of civilian code. It was almost like my irrational dream of being framed come true.

August 6, 2013

We had invited Ella's friend Sage over for the afternoon. They were inseparable at one point when they were young. Common interests in drama, films, and creative arts have ties that run deep. Sage was aware of Ella's transition because I was good friends with his mom. They hadn't seen each other in about a year.

He was a guinea pig of sorts. A kind-spirited good sport with an artistic flare. We watched for the classic suburban minivan to arrive and I greeted them in the driveway.

> Ella: *Struts onto the scene in a yellow sun dress, overdone makeup, and pink stilettos.*
> Sage: Hey . . . s'up?
> Ella: Not much.
> *Prancing around uncomfortably. Overacting the feminine role, with wrists cocked and chest pressed forward.*
> Sage: Cool. Are you excited to go to the Arts School?
> Ella: Totally!
> *Breaks into some uncomfortable song and silly dance, during which she bends forward and to her horror, one of her silicone breast cups falls to the concrete and lay there, jiggling . . .*
> Me: Awkward. We were just having a discussion this morning about double sided tape.
> Sage: *Blushes. Disbelief. Utters a stifled laugh.*

And the ice was broken. We all laughed. We all understood.

It was mere hours later that infectious laughter was heard from the backyard. The kids were dampolining—Jackson with his bronzed body and agile moves, Sage in his t-shirt and surf shorts, and Ella in my one-piece bathing suit with four obvious pairs of underwear shoved up her ass crack and slippery boobs threatened to jump out again on every bound . . . And they laughed, and laughed, and laughed, and basked in the okay-ness that seemed to be pouring down from the skies above.

August 7, 2013

   Ella and I were wandering around a small lingerie store looking for prevention strategy for the "boobs falling out issue". I was praying Mad Baby Jet wouldn't wake for another few minutes. I stood next to the nursing bras hanging on the wall, ironically, next to the mastectomy bras. We were approached by a perky young sales associate.

> Me: Ella has never been fitted for a bra before. Could you maybe measure her so we know what band size to look for?
> Perky: Like, for sure.
> *Flighty head tilt.*
> Me: Ella, are you comfortable with her measuring you?
> Ella: I guess so.
> Me: *Looked around, surveying the area for other people within eavesdropping distance.*
> Ella is *"transgendered"*. She also needs some boobs to put in her bra. I was thinking maybe a mastectomy bra? Do you have forms here? How do they work?
> Perky: Uhhh . . . I'm, like, gonna' ask, uh, my boss . . .
> Boss: *Approaches with a sympathetic smile.*
> Let's get you measured up!
> Ella: Can I have C cups?!? And a bandeau?
> And it began. A mostly painless process of finding sports bras, stylish bras, youthful bras with silicone cups that wouldn't fall out. And, a nursing bra for my own leaking, saggy, floppy dogs.
> Ella was quite proud when we left with lingerie more expensive than any I had ever purchased for myself in my whole life.
> Ella: And, Mom, it's transgender, not *transgendered*. Adjective.

#schooled

August 8, 2013

We arrived for our long awaited first counselling session at the Institute for Sexual Minority Studies and Support (iSMSS). iSMSS is a research and advocacy hub for local, national, and international work on sexual and gender minority issues, which occurs in the intersection of research, policy, and practice in education and culture.[18]

The same Gender Psychologist led the PFLAG meetings, so we had met before. She was young, passionate about the issues that surround this population, and super intuitive. She had opened us up as a "family" file so some, one, or all of us could access her services.

Ella filled out a questionnaire about how supported she felt at home, at school, at work, and elsewhere. Stemming from this, we set a few goals:

- Awareness of DANGER (behaviours, attitudes, and choices)
- Decrease stress levels for everyone, including addressing the refusal to go to Iain's house
- Teach Ella the subtleties of stereotypical femininity
- Improve communication so Ella is not frustrated trying to be heard

It's interesting that the physical transition didn't even make our Top 5 when, for the public, it seemed to always be *the* first question to be uttered. Even I was only beginning to grasp how the physical body does not define gender identity or gender expression.

carla grant

I loved having a neutral third party in the room with Ella. It had always given me a chance to sit back and listen to the entirety of what she was saying, without feeling the need to explain or rebut or retaliate. Ella likely felt the same way when having a "conversation" with me.

---

18   University of Alberta. (2015). Welcome to iSMSS. Retrieved from http://www.ismss.ualberta.ca/

August 20, 2013

Ella had a cat-coughing-up-a-hairball cough that wouldn't quit. The sounds coming out of her mouth were highly masculine and very annoying. We visited the family doctor for a few reasons . . . my ulterior motive was so he could see the young lady that he hadn't seen since the referral to the Gender Clinic. He maintained a borderline professional decorum but didn't make eye contact and didn't ask her any questions directly.

Transgender people have experienced, and reported, countless cases of discrimination and demeaning treatment by health care professionals, like receptionists asking probing questions *loudly* thus breaching every facet of patient confidentiality, and ignorant physicians refusing treatment or passing off care unnecessarily. Patients in need of support are often re-victimized.

The treatment plan was an x-ray to rule out something lingering in the chest, a stomach acid suppressor to eliminate stuff coming up causing the cough, and maybe a nose spray to stop the stuff dripping down! The x-ray technician, a pleasant 50-ish woman, instructed Ella to change into a scant blue gown, but then eyed up her sundress and determined they could do the x-ray quite easily if she simply removed the bra.

I helped her undo and slip the bra off from under her dress without taking off the dress. This was a skill girls learned in the first few years of wearing one—Ella was astonished this was even possible.

> Ella was guided down a hallway towards the x-ray room but was still within ear-shot of me.
> Technician: When was your last period, dear?
> Ella: Never.
> Technician: Oh, you haven't started yet.
> Ella: No.
> *Drops her voice an octave.*
> I'm a biological male.
> Technician: Oh . . . my, my!
> Ella: Had you fooled, didn't I!
> *Girly giggle.*
> Technician: Oh . . . oh, yes! Well, come right this way, my dear.
> Me: *Well played.*

August 23, 2013

Ella's knowledge of, and interest in, makeup and style had quickly surpassed mine. She made weekly, if not daily, walks down to the mall to do whatever it was she did: checking in at the shoe repair shop to see if they had a pair of Christian Louboutin shoes in for re-soling, stopping into Claire's to say hi to the staff who had become her "mall guardians", and in keeping with her older spirit, dropping in at The Bay. I suppose I was relieved she wasn't sitting around the food court smoking and stealing things from Target.

Ella had befriended the sales associate at the Dior counter at The Bay. Patricia was an almost-retired, British, "proper lady" who had been exceptionally friendly towards Ella. She called the house when she had an old sample bottle of perfume to gift; she invited Ella and her friends to "cocktail" events with makeup artists flown in from across the country. She created opportunities for Ella to feel like a beautiful girl.

This is all very strange to me because I had never thought about shopping there once in my life, except when looking for a melon baller or some fitted sheets. I giggled to myself when The Bay came up on our call display, and I was told I had a coat on hold to come pick up.

Sometimes, connections to our special people don't come from support groups or family gatherings; they arise from a genuine common interest, which transcends age and societal gaps. Often those involved don't even know it's happening.

Thank you, Patricia. I am so very grateful that you continue to interact with my persistent and odd child in a professional and loving manner.

Please don't be offended I continually turn down offers to sign up for your cosmetics events and promotions. I haven't purchased new makeup since my wedding day and even high-end skin products cannot touch the worry wrinkles imprinted on my forehead. Your commission sales structure will be lost on me.

August 24, 2013

Jet was 3 months old. The summer had been full of orchestrating camps, child transportation, baby naps, and sordid Ella details. We desperately tried to lose all remnants of "Betty-Sue" before she hit her new city junior high, the Arts School.

> Me: Ella, I'm just packing up Jet to go pick up Jackson. Back in a bit.
> *Jet was wailing, dogs were cowering, I was scatterbrained and late.*
> Ella: I can watch Jet, you know, if you want to leave him.
> *The first inkling of interest in the baby, ever.*
> Me: That's nice of you to offer! What will you do when he cries?
> Ella: Oh, it doesn't bother me.

Pure autism-ness answer. Jet stays with me.

August 27, 2013

Today was the test run for the bus to the Arts School. Ella has never taken public transit before, and I'll admit that, other than while travelling abroad, I probably hadn't for 15 years.

> Mom: Let's take a selfie.
> Ella: Of what?

We spent time printing bus schedules, locating the best routes, and downloading the apps onto our devices, highlighting the times at each of the stops, and figured we had things sorted out. I wrapped Jet and we headed out on our big adventure.

Our best lesson of the day was taught by a 20-ish, fit, good-looking rig worker who boarded our bus at some point while we were utterly lost. He was chatty and told us all about his apprenticeship for his welding ticket and his travel plans.

Guy: I love to surf and wanna' go to Brazil. And, like, Egypt would be next on my list.

Ella: I'm pretty sure that's not the most stable place to visit right now.

Guy: Oh? What grade you going into? 11? 12?

Ella: 8.

Guy: Damn!

We get off at the next stop and I take this opportunity to use this real-life example of *DANGER*.

Me: So, that guy thought you were reasonably witty and attractive or he wouldn't have chatted at all. What would have happened if he got off the bus at the same stop as you and continued the conversation?

Ella: I'd talk to him, he was nice.

Me: What if you had a great conversation and decided to have lunch together. And, maybe, while you were talking, he finds out you are biologically female. How does he feel?

Ella: Embarrassed?

Me: For sure. You duped him! Maybe even humiliated him. What do stereotypical rig mechanics do when they are humiliated?

Ella: They beat the crap out of me?

Me: Unfortunately, that is a possibility.

She's heard our fears.

The same evening, I shared this headline with Ella. The possibility is tragically real.

Hundreds Rally in Harlem After Beating Death of Transgender Woman

Hundreds of people gathered in Harlem Tuesday night to mourn the 21-year-old transgender woman, Islan Nettles, who was beaten to death, allegedly after a group of men discovered she was born male.

Ilsan Nettles died of blunt impact injuries to the head after she was assaulted by a group of men . . . authorities say.

Nettles' mother cried as she spoke to the crowd at a rally to denounce hate crimes against the gay and transgender communities.[19]

19   Siegal, I. (2013). Hundreds rally in Harlem after beating death of transgender woman. Retrieved August 30, 2013 from http://www.nbcnewyork.com/news/local/Islan-Nettles-Harlem-Rally-Transgender-Woman-Beaten-Death-Lavergne-Cox-221415871.html

August 28, 2013

Ella liked going to the Gender Clinic. Dr. Gender was a wise man and never questioned the genuineness of her convictions. Likely, he had seen more than enough in his years that he could be comfortably quiet about his own predictions.

We give him a quick overview of the status of referrals; we had finally started the Lupron® injections, had been to see the Gender Psychologist, and she had attended camp fYrefly as a "Little".

I had pointed questions for him . . . mostly questions fed through me from Iain, who was not present.

> Me: We asked Ella what feels "different" inside now that she is Ella, and she said nothing had changed; she is still "Eliot" but different on the outside?!? Does that mean she is just "Eliot" in drag?

Dr. Gender smiled and softened his face. He went on to describe how, when people transition, they are aware of some differences of feelings inside, such as more joy, perhaps some new anxieties, but often usually they do not really change as the person they are on the inside. They were this person all along but had been seen otherwise . . . It was more correct that Ella had been *managing* as "Eliot"! My concept of drag was also corrected to be an art form of a typically gay man to create an over-the-top illusion of female beauty. I had "drag" confused with "cross-dressing"—there was so much new terminology.

> Me: It feels like Ella is spending enormous effort and time to create this "image" of a woman she wants to be . . . as if she is acting, but is missing all the subtle mannerisms and behaviours of a "girl". What do I do about that? Is this all her Asperger's shining through?

I was relieved to hear it was not uncommon. As transgender people explore their identities, they tend to exaggerate their styles; they go all out now when they *finally* can. Ella's "extra formal" clothing was probably not as outrageous as some other styles you would find on many Grade 8's elsewhere—Goth, athletic, punk, etc. He suggested we focus on identifying and avoiding the provocative styles and behaviours to err on the side of "safe" and be a little more lenient with style. Ella had a strong conscious and subconscious aversion to "boy" clothes, especially blue jeans, and we were to simply respect that.

We left the appointment a little more enlightened.

Ella: Why does it take a psychiatrist to tell you what I have been trying to tell you for months?
Me: Like?
Ella: Like . . . that I still feel the same inside, but that's not a bad thing. And that I just feel ugly and "boy" in jeans, and I *can't* do that anymore.
Me: I guess I need to listen more. I get overwhelmed.

August 31, 2013

Dad,

Okay, I'm only writing this stupid letter because Mom really wants me to—beats me why. But, Iain, if you're reading this, stop. Mom told me you wouldn't read it, and I will find out if you are. Anyways, she wants me to think of ways to improve my "improvable" relationship with you. So, here goes.

I do not understand why, when you say you've known for years that this is who I am, you are taking forever to deal with it. "I love you, but I HATE you in those clothes" is confusing. Which part is true?

Idea one—if I don't want to be around you, please don't try and "fix" my way of thinking towards you, because it is not helping. It might even be making it worse. It seems you won't let me distance myself from you when I'm mad at you. You almost seem to be more in my face then. Then I must go away from you somewhere you can't touch me, like to the mall, or Safeway, or a friend's house. I just need you to leave me alone when I don't want to be around you. Letting me cool my jets away from you might help a little bit.

Idea two—please don't ask me to do so much work. At Mom's house, I only have to do the occasional poo pickup or cleaning the bathroom, but at your house, it feels like I'm working my butt off all the time and then you criticize me for being lazy, when in reality I'm only taking a break. Please lower my workload (well, a lot.)

Idea three—When you are teasing me or yelling at me, I can tell you that it is hurting my feelings.

Thank you for reading.
ELLA

September 1, 2013

We hit the mall, yet again. Ella needed clothes for gym. This proved to be a challenge, as Ella was obsessive about keeping in line with her sense of style, even in a sweaty gymnasium, and trying to find clothing that hid her biologically male bits.

Leggings were too revealing, unless they were coupled with a longer shirt—which tended to be oversized all around, and she wouldn't go for anything that was not flattering. Loose shorts were out of the question because they reminded her of Richard Simmons. I found a tennis skort. Genius.

While I was hiding in the change room across from Ella, boobs hanging out feeding Jet, another last-minute-school-shopping mom approached me to politely ask how old Ella was. She was confused.

Lady: She talks to my girls like she is their mother, but I honestly can't tell if she is 12 or 21.
Me: We get that a lot! She is 13.
Lady: *Clearly blowing her mind, Ella is the same age as her own girls.*
Me: I think Ella knows your girls . . . through a mutual friend?
Lady: *Confirms with her girls . . . yes, they have met Ella before.*
Do you guys know Nadia and her mom, Shannon?
Me: Very well. We haven't spent much time with them in the past year, but Ella and Nadia were kindred spirits, inseparable for years and years.
Lady: I'm sorry to have to tell you this here, but Shannon was killed in a motorcycle accident.
Me: *Welling with tears.*
Thank you for telling me.

Ella insisted on wearing her sunglasses for the rest of the mall excursion to hide her tears. She unfortunately learned from me that showing emotion was somehow embarrassing or undesirable. She was a stuffer, with food or masks of being okay.

A conundrum came as we pondered our path of grieving. Most of her friends, Nadia included, didn't know that Ella had transitioned. Even if they did, they had not met this outwardly feminine version of their old friend. Funerals were certainly not the place for such announcements, and the decision was made that only Jackson and I would attend the funeral to pass on our condolences and support.

The service was tragically sad. A passionate, feisty, single mother who helped me nurture the different-ness of my own children was now gone. A bird flew in the front doors of the old cathedral during the final Amens, circling in the dome above the casket, like Shannon making her spine-tingling last goodbye. I couldn't help but spend my time sitting on the hard-wooden bench thinking not only about the changed course of Nadia's life, but also about the gaping hole that the loss of Gramma will someday leave in me.

Ella couldn't attend this event because she wore dresses and makeup. That is not what Shannon would have wanted, but it was the most "socially appropriate" course of action.

Good-bye Shannon. I miss you. Your spirit remains within us.

September 2, 2013

I had done a serious Facebook "friend" purge. Those I hadn't been able to tell personally about Ella didn't deserve to find out by random voyeuristic visits to my page or by photos popping up on their feed. My friend count dropped from over 400 to under 40.

The more positive I became with telling people about Ella's transition, the more space I allowed for them to be positive about receiving the information. It allowed them to follow me into happiness about it, instead of allowing them to be sucked into a path of fear, or dwelling on the unknown.

There were certain people we chose to tell through various media which would allow for processing the information before they were forced to utter a response. My perspective on things is often different after a good night's sleep and some time to ponder, and I believe that others are similar. An e-mail to share news from us was not a sign of distance or insincerity, it was a sign of respect for their right to space and time to process. We posted some people the letter. We invited some people out for coffee.

Casual acquaintances typically found out by happenstance. The waitress at our favorite pizza joint laughed uncontrollably before simply giving Ella a hug, unable to find any words. We ran into the administrator from my pharmacy at a Chinese buffet, and she was excited to introduce Ella to her young children; hopefully the conversation that followed at home opened their eyes to the world of gender diversity. Neighbours already knew by the time I formally told them, having seen Ella heading down to the mall in dresses. They enlisted their older children as allies and protectors, not even allowing for the possibility of them being anything less than accepting of their community members.

I was proud of who she was and I shared every chance I could get.

September 5, 2013

Some divine intervention got Ella, Jet, and I out the door on time for her first day at the Arts School. She had been planning her first-day-of-school outfit for months, lobbying for an exception to the "heels no more than twice a month to school" rule so that this day wouldn't count towards her accumulated total.

I hadn't taken the time to fathom the courage it took her to march into school in her houndstooth dress, A-line red coat, Mary Jane pumps, and retro-camera-case purse. She was as cute as a button and walked as if the world would never touch her. Maybe it wouldn't.

September 13, 2013

Me: Ella, there is a support group for youth who identify as trans at the Pride Centre, would you be interested in going?
Ella: Is it another boring social skills class?
Me: No—it's more like a supportive group for youth that have some of the same challenges as you. You might enjoy being with people outside your school that "get" you more. I always learn how

to deal with things better from people who deal with the same shit.

Thinking of resonating with Fight Club, *where Edward Norton starts faking stories to attend support groups searching for help . . .*

Does it matter to you that you are a part of the LGBTQ community? Or is it easier for you to ignore that, because being a part of it actually "outs" you?

Ella: Well, if I wear my pride-striped socks and someone asks about them, I just say that I support my friends who are LGBTQ . . .

It doesn't matter to me what orientation my friends are; I see them as just being a person.

She learned so many things before I have even clued in that there is something else to consider! I had always been very conformable with sexuality being a continuum, but gender was always two boxes—F or M. Genderfluid, agender, bigender—all new words to me. Ella's explanations, combined with those at PFLAG, totally shifted my dated beliefs. Gender and sexuality are only two axes in a fluid sphere, inside which there are infinite possibilities.

"The light in me sees the light in you" was all I needed. This was still difficult for a hard-core scientist, searching for labels, categories, and predictability where none existed.

September 14, 2013

Arthur, Jet, and I boarded a "Jet" plane for a quick vacation to see Gramma. We got *THE LOOK* that all people boarding planes with 3-month-old babies get from the entire boarding lounge. The glance of "I hope to hell I don't have to sit beside THEM". But Jet was a superstar, and we made the journey to Gramma's house without incident.

We let our guards down and enjoyed amazing meals, kite flying, sunburns on the beach, an extra set of loving Gramma hands for baby, and afternoon naps with the smell of the Jurassic rainforest blowing in the windows. Soul food.

Gramma and I got an e-mail from Ella:

eElla: Do any of you know who sings this song? I heard it at
Addition Elle™, and I recorded as much as I could . . .
<Sunshine in the rain.mp3>
eMe: I can't open the file . . . what are some of the lyrics?
And more importantly, why the hell were you in a plus-size
clothing store?!?

September 15, 2013

I sat and watched the rain falling outside the window on luscious
plants on Vancouver Island. I loved it that things grew easily there.
Alberta's growing season is barely long enough for a carrot.

*There was a day when "Eliot" and Jackson were outside, collecting
worms in Tupperware containers with plastic spoons. It was an activity
they were enjoying together—two brothers who often enjoyed activities
beside each other but for very different reasons.*

*'Eliot' counted his worms, categorized them, and drew an elaborate
picture of a house worms could live in when he came back inside. I was
instructed to wash off the sides of the container (because we hate dirt),
and store them in the fridge for further investigation.*

*Jackson entered the house with excitement and spunk in his 4-year-old
step. I had my hands full washing "Eliot's" worm house and didn't pay
much attention.*

Jackson: MOM!!!

I have a 'mergency!!

*I charged upstairs to see the pedestal sink overflowing with black earth
and water. Jackson was on his step stool, arms to the elbows in filth, trying
to fish out the worms out of their muddy slurry.*

Jackson: SAVE THEM!!

Worms coodn' swim!

While many stories are of "Eliot's" quick remarks and quirks,
it is Jackson who brings me back to the land of the children . . .
sleeping in a 'piderman costume every night, accidentally setting fire
to Gramma's bedroom, taping sticks on his back to have wings in
shadows. I love his gentle heart and puppy cuddles.

September 20, 2013

Back in Alberta once again, I returned to being strung out by long nights of breastfeeding and burping. I lived in some perpetual loop of day and night. Ella had done a miraculous job of getting herself up and out the door on time—a task that required her setting her alarm at some ungodly hour. Arthur had been doing morning transportation with Jackson to the rink, and I was often able to "sink in", Jackson's newly-coined term for hiding in bed for that extra few minutes, with Jet.

Ella arrived home from her day at school and I greeted her in the kitchen.

> Me: Ella! Where are your pants?!?
> Ella: What do you mean?
> *A saucy look completes her outfit of a longish, yellow tank-top, black nylons, bouffant up-do, and crayon lipstick.*
> Me: Those are nylons. Nylons are not pants.
> Ella: They are leggings.
> Me: No! You see the underwear section and how see-thru they are?
> Ella: Mom, they are LEGGINGS because they have feet!
> *Miscategorization of objects, rooted in autism.*
> Me: Nope. Those are nylons. Nylons are a member of the "underwear family", not a member of the "pant family".
> *It hadn't occurred to me to explain that a top needs a bottom in her clothing manual!*

The next day, she texted me a pic of her outfit at 7:07 a.m. to make sure I didn't "dress code" her when she arrived home. She was trying.

September 22, 2013

I walked down the stairs to intervene in a loud sibling dispute.

I immediately saw the cause of the disturbance. Ella's silicone boob cups were suctioned onto the den door—eye level. Like jelly tumours.

Me: JACKSON!
Jackson: Yes?
Giggling.
Me: *Making deep eye contact.*

I *know* this is funny. But, it's *not* funny.

September 24, 2013

We had another whole family meltdown at the end of a long day. This implosion involved Arthur, intending to help me out, teeing off on the kids for chores they hadn't done, and they didn't know they were supposed to do. Clearly there was work to be done on boundaries, expectations, and roles. Who parents? Who enforces? Who is the king pin of which operations? Surely every blended family combats this at some point.

In our house, it seemed amplified by adults who were traumatized as children and never developed the coping skills to even begin to deal with this. We were broken into pieces and didn't know how to put us back together because we never saw the picture of the completed puzzle to use as a guide.

Arthur had his own traumatic story to tell. Our two broken souls had found each other. Without outside help, a lot of it, we didn't have the wisdom of healed perspectives and we continued to suffer. After years of intensive recovery programs, I still barely grasp the full impact of trauma . . .

When women who had been molested, sexually violated, shared their stories, I always heard them out, and responded with the appropriate amount of sympathy and encouragement. In the back of my mind, though, a very troubling script of "Get over it; it's not that bad" was present. It wasn't until I was sitting in rooms of really broken women that I began to examine the underlying belief system.

I was admittedly uneducated about the harmful shrapnel that victims of sexual abuse deal with. Tiny pieces of implanted negativity affect the way so many natural processes happen in life. I learned it can be at the root of jaded sexual relationships, an inability to trust, poor self-esteem and self-worth, which translates into poor performance at work and in careers. It can permeate its way into our ability to enjoy fellowship with others, how we handle anxiety and how we develop coping skills for life. Depending on the age and coping mechanisms of the victim, sexual violations can halt maturity.

Rehab Counsellor: Most sexual offenders have had things done to them, or shown to them, usually at a very young age.
Me: I was highly sexualized when I was just young.
I was always the instigator of playing "doctor" or inappropriate sexual lines of friends.
An impassible lump developed in my throat. I could barely swallow.
Rehab Counsellor: How else would a child know these things?
Me: How do you know you have suppressed memories if they are suppressed?
Rehab Counsellor: The brain has a way of unlocking them exactly when you are ready.

I sought the professional guidance of an expert in the field, who helped guide me deep into the storage network of my brain. I experienced a full-body recollection of the vivid sensations of my molestation. I saw a small child, just three or four, in my bedroom with an adult male, whose identity has never been clear to me, kneeling at my bedside. I have a bird's eye view of the event and the memory stored energetically in my body tissues.

"Just get over it. It's not THAT bad. I did". I hadn't. I didn't even know I could or should. That journey began, as did a newfound sense of empathy.

September 25, 2013

I noticed I was watching a little girl walking in front of me. She had on knee-high pink boots, frilly tights, a twirly dress, matching coat, and jewelled purse. I thought of how much Ella would have LOVED to have been dressed like that at three years old. I imagined how much pleasure she would have taken in choosing out her own mismatched pink outfits, like she had when it was "dress-up" time in the safe confines of our living room. I enforced the rules under the guise of safety and normalcy.

You can't wear that outside the house because you'll get beaten up.
Instead of the coveted glitzy pink shoes and long wigs, "Eliot" strutted down the road in a button up cardigan, tweed newsboy cap, and his hard Samsonite briefcase on the way to the bus stop in grade four.

I listened to the sound of Ella heading off to her bus stop now. I envisioned a flight attendant, or a bank executive with a big smile.

Click-click Door locks.
Tap tap tap tap Her kitten heels connect with the concrete.
Rrrrr thunk rrrrr thunk Her rolling suitcase-backpack carting every worldly belonging on the sidewalk.

September 26, 2013

I read an article about the intoxicating effects of the smell of a newborn baby, especially on mothers. It apparently activates the same centers in the brain as drug addiction. Arthur has been telling me to "Stop *smelling* the baby" for months. It was my hit.

At four months, Jet was cooing and gooing and pooing. His first two teeth erupted. The dogs enjoyed the Jolly Jumper because he spun and jumped around and around, swinging by for an occasional dog sniff and lick at dog eye-level. He had learned he could touch his hands together and I often caught him in this "praying" position and wondered if that is exactly what he was doing . . . "Give me the strength to endure in this gong show!"

September 27, 2013

"Jackson's School" coming up on call display instantly stirred the same emotions as being called to the principal's office. It was either going to be really good or really bad. There was rarely a reason to call otherwise. This call followed three I had last week regarding bullying and rude behaviours, and I briefly thought that my child was starting his life of delinquency by being kicked out of grade 6.

> Geoff: Hi Carla, Geoff here. It's nothing terrible.
> Me: What's up?
> Geoff: Jackson took a puck to the heel on the ice this morning, and he is still in a lot of pain. He can bear weight, but you might want to have it checked out.
> Me: I'm on my way.

The diagnosis was usually a deep bruise, not likely broken. We both needed some "Feel Better Pho".

When I got up from resting, Jackson had his ankle taped and wrapped and up on an ice pack atop many pillows. He'd had a hard few weeks with Ella, troubles at school and home, and hockey evaluations. I'd been there.

It hurts a bit, but really, I just need some love and attention I can accept.

In 1980 Gramma was paged on the overhead speakers while grocery shopping: an urgent message. The doctor's office was tracking her down because my brother Jeff's blood work had come back showing his blood sugar levels were coma-high. He had just turned six, and I was four.

She had taken him in to see the doctor for a real failure to thrive. Ill-looking, not engaged in anything, not eating but always thirsty. The diagnosis was quick and easily made, once the doctors were convinced to investigate. He had Type 1 Juvenile Diabetes.

The situation was urgent. She scooped Jeff out of a sand box, headed straight for the hospital and left me with a babysitter. I was later collected by my Auntie Danelle to spend a month on the family farm while my parents stabilized Jeff and learned their new role as medical caregivers.

When we all finally arrived back at home, everything was different. The food was different. The attention was different. The roles were different.

I wanted what he had. I demanded needles like Jeff was getting. I was headstrong and relentless. Papa finally injected me with some saline just to shut me up! I never cried, just taped it up with cotton balls to show that I was bigger than the pain. The seed of a belief system, that being sick was rewarded with love and affection, was planted.

It has been an ongoing life struggle for me to identify what is going on internally when I have physical symptoms. Psychosomatic? How serious is this? Don't minimize in case it's real. Don't exaggerate if what I need is attention I can receive.

This day I gave Jackson a big hug and didn't question his pain further. I hope he got what he needed.

September 28, 2013

> iSponsor: Hey sugar, how are u?
> iMe: It's been a long week . . . baby Jet + a cold + immunizations + 2 teeth = cranky!!
> Arthur is on a hair trigger—stress-filled house ☹
> I've done a good job of staying in a place of compassion, though, and not from a place of arrogant knowledge or resentful passive-aggressiveness . . .
> I'm FINE!!
> iSponsor: Fucked up, insecure, neurotic, and emotional-FINE or really fine?
> iMe: Bit of both, probably!
> iSponsor: Some days the best we can hope for is the right mix of both.

September 29, 2013

I'll freely admit, though not loudly, that I did not like Ella these days. It's taboo as a mom to say such a thing but I will divulge here that she was not someone I would have chosen to hang out with. Her energy was negative. She was a consummate taker. She was egocentric and demanding. Her values sharply diverged from mine. I had felt embarrassed by her behaviours and style; I had been deceived and betrayed. *I did not like her.* Some days, I didn't like Jackson, either.

> Me: Jet is my favorite.
> Ella: Mom! You're not supposed to say things like that.
> Me: But it's true. Today.

They have all been my "favorite" at times. Sometimes for a moment and sometimes for months. I think it's time that we, as parents, give ourselves a break and accept our humanness; it's impossible to like everyone all the time or all the same, not even our own children.

I love my kids. I appreciate them. I cherish and adore them. I embrace the challenges they throw my way and can't imagine my life without them. They have been my greatest teachers and inspiration. But I don't always like them, and that's okay.

#keepitreal

October 1, 2013
06:24

> iElla: Here's the link for the tutorial to turn shoes into knock-off Laboutins.
> I watched it a few times and the clear top coat is optional.
> Did u check our spray paint to see if we have red?
> iMe: I'm still in bed.
> iElla: Oh . . .
> *This was not new. I envisioned a 5-year old child poised at the side of my bed . . . 6:02am . . .*
> *'Eliot': What is the agenda for today?*
> *Me: I don't even know yet, sweetie.*

'Eliot': Well, I am going to watch out the front picture window for the 1967 Cadillac to drive by at 6:19 on his way to work—then I will come up here for the plan.

Of course, I *got* Ella. I catered to her need for schedule and routine because on a deep level I empathized with the unnerving anxiety that was provoked in their absence. I was likely more oblivious to other people's social gestures and non-verbal language than I would ever really know. It took me a while to learn how to step back and perspective-take—a thorough task of cognitively reasoning out what *another person might be thinking,* especially in relation to me. This is my Half-Asperger's—not so extreme that it would ever be diagnosable—but certainly I identified enough traits in myself that I knew the statistics about autistic parents being secondarily diagnosed following their children were dead true. Even the crappy Facebook quiz told me I was 10% right brain and 90% left brain. Egad.

I didn't really enjoy watching movies—of course I liked the popcorn and the licorice. But I don't *connect* with the characters in the movie. I rarely cry or walk away *feeling* differently. I understand the take-home-messages, but I fail to tap into what the actors, writers and directors were likely trying to accomplish—establishing an emotional connection with the viewer.

Like this memoir, my brain is based in logistics. I assume others will relish in the details, be comforted by dates and specifics like I was. Transitions and unknowns temporarily paralyzed me some days—I needed to sleep and escape, since drinking to forget was really a bad option for me. How would Ella ever survive this? How would I?

October 2, 2013

iGramma: There was an article in the newspaper yesterday about transgender couples having children—part of a series on Pride & Joy. Remind me to show you.
The trans women had all banked sperm *before* hormone therapy.
iMe: I encouraged Ella to do the same to keep options open.
Can you honestly imagine her as a mom?!? Maybe everyone would say that about their 13-year-old teenager daughters!
iGramma: Well she's sure not the "I love kids" kind of daughter!

I engaged Ella in a private conversation about this very topic. I prefaced my questions with "You, of course, do not need to answer this question—you may not even know the answer . . ."

Ella described a complete lack of desire to have genetic offspring. She was keen to adopt an international child that needed a home—*IF* she ever had a partner that wanted a child. I was not surprised by her sentiments.

Ella: I could NEVER do *that*.

Her aversion was to the physical act of collecting sperm to bank. Her dysphoria was so deeply seeded that the collection of the sample was a psychological impossibility for her. Should I have offered to harvest and freeze my eggs for her?

I did not know, as a mother, how to encourage natural sexual exploration and development in a youth who was disconnected from her body. Ella had intense and persistent dysphoria and detested many of her physical attributes. She had shaved most strands of hair from her body. She begged to bind her feet to make them smaller. She mastered facial contouring with makeup to trim her jawline. She longed for curvy hips and an hourglass figure. How would she develop a healthy self-image when she loathed parts of her body? How she could honour natural desires when the anatomy that produced intense pleasure was that which she wished to be rid of the most?

I pressed a bit further—was there NO maternal sentiment? I realized quickly that this was *my own* desire and realization that although I now had a daughter, she wasn't one I would be supporting through a pregnancy. It was *my* disappointment that I would likely only ever be the legal grandmother of a newborn, never a maternal grandmother in a delivery room.

To fulfill this desire, I pursued birth photography . . . capturing the joy in special ways for an event that I may never witness again. Really, who's to say a daughter with a uterus would want me to be in the delivery room anyways?

October 3, 2013

Jackson was disappointed that he did not make the Pee Wee AA hockey team. The superstars he played with daily at school had been in hockey since conception; moms were at the rink before their children were potty trained. Genetics played a significant role here, too.

I felt his pain, though. I paid lip service to the "If you are trying your best, it doesn't matter how good you are," and "Playing with kids more skilled than you will help you play up to their level" arguments. Somewhere, stuffed deep inside, I didn't really believe that myself. It sucks to have your ass whipped. It sucks to not be given a Gold Star★. It sucks to have other people point out that you are not the best'.

I had a personality conflict with my teacher in first grade and spent most it with my nose in the corner behind the doors. I also had to go up to her desk and have her write on a small square of pastel colored paper how I had done each day to take home to my parents. She disguised her spirit-crushing comments with animal stamps on a rainbow ink pad.

> *Carla was very chatty today.*
> *Carla had some trouble with her attitude today.*
> *Carla didn't get her work done because she was too busy being a feisty little girl . . .*

I stuffed those notes in a glass jar at home, my mom read them but never made a big deal of it. I learned quickly that it didn't matter what REALLY happened at school, only that the note was a good one. If you got a Gold Star★, it doesn't matter what you did to get there. I pray I have not passed this philosophy on to my kids . . . Integrity lives in effort.

> Me: Do you love playing hockey? Then just do it.
> If you don't love it, or the other kids make it impossible to enjoy your time, then it's okay to choose something else.
> Jackson: Hockey.

October 4, 2013
  15:43

iJackson:

iJackson: On wrong bus
iJackson: Now heading West towards the skate park
iJackson: And I am now driving past my old school
iJackson: Jasper's house . . . Damn
iJackson: I'm pretty sure I'm not on the A9
iJackson: Near the pool . . . Heading towards Dads
iJackson: What's for dinner?
iJackson: When I get back to the bus station, maybe I'll be on the same bus as Ella
I was napping and missed all the anxiety of a lost-and-found child.
iMe: Thx for letting me know ur safe ☺
iJackson:

As much fear as I had about my babies being on a city bus, I am glad I overcame it and gave them the chance to prove they could be responsible and independent. I guess we don't know if someone can catch a ball if we aren't willing to drop it.

October 5, 2013

iElla: A sneak peek at my next stop
motion, called "Cosmetic Calamity". It's
about a house party attended by makeup
characters and a tube of lipstick dies. They
must find the culprit . . .
I'm not ready to part with my dollhouse.
iMe: Awesome idea!!
*The dollhouse was an epic project—
countless hours of tiny and finicky details.*

I had mixed feelings about it. When I looked at the dollhouse, I saw the glue on the hand-dyed shingles progressing from tidy rows to a sloppy mess. It was a visual reminder of evenings spent progressing from sober to the end of my bottles of Merlot.

iElla: I made a lipstick crime scene in the tub and it wasn't coming off so I used a towel but it got soaked and it's too heavy to get out . . . can I just leave it until u get back?

Nvm. I got the towel, but the red splotch is still there.

Ella filmed her first stop-motion film when she was just six. She used a simple point-and-shoot camera and an online photo-slide show program. Her first film went viral . . . 28 likes!

They were brilliant; truly a special gift was emerging. And in Ella style, she dove into the history, the current film selections, the makings-of, and finally demanded we make a wire-framed doll covered in Plasticine® with removable faces. My attempt at the doll creation was Frankenstein-esque, and we finally agreed on a commercially available Coraline mouldable doll.

October 6, 2013

iMe: Ella is having hot flashes . . . very funny. Probably a side effect of her shots ☺

iGramma: Ha! Funny until it's your turn! How are things? I have done NOTHING since the dinner party.

The image of my mother with her head in the freezer when I got home from school, claiming to be having a "chinook" comes rushing back to me. My mom went through menopause for about 12 years—a battle between her psyche regretting having never had more children and the body that was biologically shutting things down.

iMe: Good for you! You're long past overdue for some rest.

I'm editing some pics I took last night, folding laundry, feeding a baby, assisting in Ella's latest stop motion production (yeah!!!), and waiting for Jackson's first hockey game of the season on his new team, the Scorpions!

I'm thrilled to say that Stop-Motion-Ella appeared this week ☺. I've missed her creative escapades. Even though it's about the death of a lipstick.

iGramma: Oh good! That's one of the best parts of Ella, I agree. Can't wait to view and, truth be told, lipstick does die!

October 9, 2013

iElla: Guess what
Well this guy from Suburbia transit came to our bus and gave all the passengers a free notebook, pen, and Tim Hortons cookie. And I still feel like somebody implanted a rusty, dirty marble into my leg . . .
iMe: I know, sweetie . . . the other option is an injection every day . . .
iElla: As in I tripped and fell because it hurts so much. In a dress. On my way to the bus stop because my leg gave way . . . that actually happened multiple times before I even left the house . . .

The monthly Lupron® shot had been the best, and the worst delivery system for the hormone blocker. Other than having a teenager with menopausal symptoms, she tolerated the medication well. Facial hair had not grown or become more coarse, her Adam's apple was not prominent, and generally, she was beginning to take on a softer, rounder form with the complete suppression of testosterone.

I have heard horror stories from our neighbours across our southern border that justification of Lupron® to insurance companies can be a nightmare, and the cost without that insurance is prohibitive (it costs even more in the U.S.A.). Luckily for us, there was no special approval process and the $500 monthly syringe was a benefit. This is just the tip of the iceberg in terms of the transitioning some pursue. Laser hair removal and electrolysis, top-surgery (in this case implants), facial contouring, and shaving of the Adam's apple are expensive and painful. Not to mention the collaterals—time off work for appointments and recovery, a new wardrobe, documentation changes and fees, and on and on.

I was trained to give injections, but I hated doing it. The needle was huge, the long-acting formulation was thick and difficult to push. It often resulted in tears and Ella clamping down on a towel in her mouth while I pulled myself together, and tried to be brave, as my mom had been when she gave my brother his insulin injections.

October 11, 2013

The snow was already threatening to fall.

> iJackson: Can we go get some new winter boots? Mine are too
> small.
> iElla: If we have time, can we go to Value Village to get some winter
> boots?
> Ankle boots are more flattering on me than tall boots, and I usually
> dislike taller ones unless they have kitten heels.
> Have u found any kitten heel boots? Just askin'.
> And during the winter, am I still going to be able to wear my Mary
> Janes/kitten heels/china boots/flats/grey wedges?

October 17, 2013

Arthur was a self-proclaimed survivor. He had survived his abusive
family of origin, he had survived his unstable upbringing in Nigeria,
he had survived living far out in the bush, and he had survived the
collapse of a marriage. But I was still not convinced he could survive
our clan, let alone thrive in it.

> iMe: Same old shit here. Ella is a bitch (or an individuating,
> opinionated teen with autism if I'm in a sympathetic mood) and
> Arthur is an arrogant, lazy, glutinous, rude, selfish, lying man-child
> (or a hurting, broken soul if I'm in a sympathetic mood). Jackson is
> lovely right now. I'm failing at being a control-freak . . . just like I'm
> supposed to.
> I need a fucking drink.
> iSponsor: Nope. You need a fucking meeting.

October 18, 2013

> iGramma: Happy #%^*ing Full Moon! The only one in your sign all
> year.
> Key words: dicey, impatient, overly emotional. Chill . . . xox

October 19, 2013

I don't know when it exactly happened, but a shift has occurred in my brain.

I was the one correcting people when they said "he" instead of "she". I was the one who got my pronouns correct most of the time.

Ella came into my room wearing only underwear, still dripping from her bath. I instinctually turned away, a gut reaction to witnessing something private. I hadn't seen her flat chest in months.

Me: Ella! You need to cover up!
Ella: I am just so tired.
Me: I know, baby, but you are a lady now.

October 20, 2013

Jet learned how to spit. I was very proud. You never know when this skill will come in handy.

October 21, 2013

Halloween was not my holiday. It meant having embarrassing "fun"— everyone judging how well you had done at turning yourself into something you were not. I understood when Ella wanted to go as Clark Kent one year—the real guy, not the unrealistic Superman. Root cause analysis? Likely a small Carla greedily eating all the candy at her diabetic brother's expense, while her mom sat sadly and mourned the loss of her carefree, healthy boy.

I did my best to not pass my hatred of All Hallows Eve on to my children.

iMe: I couldn't decide . . . so we have a Tigger and a parrot costume . . .

iGramma: Papa votes for Tigger.
Do parrots spit? Do Tiggers?
iMe: Hmmm . . . I don't know! They didn't have an ostrich costume
. . . They spit!

October 24, 2013

Me: Ella, I'm having crazy anxiety about you going to the
Halloween Dance tomorrow.
What kind of mother sends her transgender daughter into a dark
gymnasium with hundreds of pubescent Neanderthals?
Ella: That makes 2 of us!
Me: The kids at your old school who know won't care, but there
are probably a few who may find out who will care . . . in the bad
way. Maybe showing up as Effie Trinket [from *The Hunger Games*]
to introduce yourself to Suburbia Junior High en masse now that
you're a girl isn't very safe?
Ella: I miss my old friends.
Me: I know, sweetie. We could contact someone and connect with
them outside of school?
Ella: Mom, I'm going to have to "come out" my entire life . . .

Action plan required. Set her up for success and let go of the
outcome. I called the school and asked to speak to anyone scheduled
for dance supervision.

Vice Principal: How is "Eliot" doing?
Me: ELLA is really doing great. SHE is exhausted and misses her
friends, but that's more a function of switching schools than the
gender issues.

Vice Principal: For sure. That's a lot for HIM.
Me: Yes—SHE is a brave soul.
SHE is coming in a female costume this
evening, but the word that SHE is living
as Ella may spread quickly. I have given
HER explicit instructions to not be alone
this evening, stay with a friend, have HER
phone, and stay with a teacher if SHE feels
threatened.
Vice Principal: Great. I'll be at the door most
of the evening and will keep my eyes on
HIM. We also have a staff supper meeting,
and I will bring it to the others' attention.
*If only I could make the bubble big enough to surround her
everywhere . . .*
Me: I truly appreciate it.

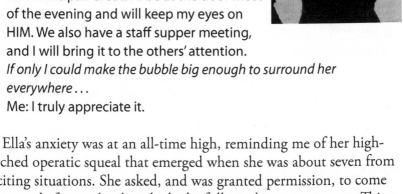

Ella's anxiety was at an all-time high, reminding me of her high-pitched operatic squeal that emerged when she was about seven from exciting situations. She asked, and was granted permission, to come home early from school so she had a full two hours to prepare. This was the finale of 11 months of obsessing over the costume; ordering clothing off eBay from China, and endless trips to various stores to collect every detail.

She asked me to work some magic with her hair—diffusers, baby powder, crazy pink streaks and helmet-hard spray. Her face was painted and powdered white, she had perfectly placed the fake eyelashes.

We pulled up in front of the school, where meandering along were kids in jeans.

Me: Are you sure this is a costume dance?
Ella: *Terror. A live version of the "naked at school" dream flashes on her face.*
Oh Gawd.
Me: I'll go in first and make sure . . . then come get you?

At the door, I saw Buffy the Vampire Slayer and "What Does the Fox Say?". We decided to walk in together, the vice principal picked her out right away, and gave me the "I got her back" nod. I heard murmurs and mutterings; my heart sunk deeply into the pit of my stomach. But Ella walked on, her runway model strut perfected, towering over me in her 3" heels.

I keep my phone on loud ring and vibrate in front of me at the Serenity Sisters' gathering. Waiting.

Me: Are you okay?!?

Ella: Yes. I'm just exhausted. Can you come get me?

She had a fabulous time. Blew her $20 on candy. Reconnected with old friends. Was a genuinely happy girl. Managed to get out of the house with her "good luck" jar of Nutella and spoon in her purse without me seeing it! Success story number #413.

October 26, 2013

I was not the only one struggling.

iArthur: I'm exhausted for no reason [Effexor®]. It's kicking my ass. I wish I lived in the 16th century and could have been either a Heretic or Genius.

I've grown tired of subverting the tendencies I've cultivated and analyzed for decades and are now out of vogue.

I want to be your partner, the companion to your children, and a father to our son.

I need to make stuff.

iMe: I miss Arthur, 3 dogs, Nigeria.

iArthur: I'm Arthur, 2 scared dogs, Suburbia.

Arthur, 3 dogs (one adopted by cohabitation), Nigeria, one transgender 13-year-old, one 11-year-old gem of a boy, one 5-month-old insomniac.

I like sleep, quiet moments, cleaning the house, and quiet, quiet, quiet.

Pls call me at xxx-xxx-xxxx

iMe: I am still cutting thru red tape with a machete.

iArthur: I know. I've never been more in love w/ you. I ❤ your machete.

October 27, 2013
  A day in my life.

06:20 Arthur and Jackson headed to hockey practice in Timbuktu. I
attempted to "sink in" with Jet . . . but he was restless and bored.
09:00 I stole "me" time to edit photos from a maternity session.
09:07 Boys returned from hockey smelling like rotten farts and rank
equipment. End of serenity.
11:00 Jackson tested his cooking skills out on a new pancake
recipe. Kitchen chaos begins.
11:30 A colleague, Deris, arrived for assistance with her resume.
We enjoyed some pancakes—a few fluffy and a few crepes from a
batch that was apparently missing the baking powder.
11:42 Deen, Ella's new 17-year-old trans acquaintance from the
Pride Center youth group, had stopped by with his mother to drop
off some old dresses he would never wear again. There were now 8
people and 3 dogs in the house.
The dresses were all Ella's retro style—I secretly questioned why a
trans man would have so many dresses?
12:00 Resume writing commenced. Baby bouncing resumed. Dogs
had momentarily stopped barking. Ella started her fashion show of
the new dresses. Arthur had vanished.
13:00 Lia, my life-long friend, arrived so Ella could assist her with
editing a video for a university course. Technology crisis after crisis
stressed out all the girls . . . missing power cords, 3 computers
with maxed-out memory banks, downloading into non-existent
accounts. We recalled how much easier life was with a pen and
paper. Arthur was texting from the bar to find out the name of the
crescent shaped white area on a fingernail bed.
14:35 Resume project for Deris was completed. Video editing hit an
all-time stressful high, and we resorted to headphones for Ella, still
parading in her new dresses and 3" heels, and calming tea for Lia. I
had no idea where Jackson was.
15:25 I heard pucks cracking against the fence outside, Jackson
testing out his new stick on the driveway—a forbidden event—but
I ignored it; at least he had been located.
16:45 Arthur arrived home with grocery list items: carbohydrates
for kid lunches and a cake.
17:00 SuperJen arrived to mind the children for Date Night.

Arthur wanted to go for a romantic donair. Ella and Jackson had a screaming match over the missing Nutella.

17:04 Monty was vomiting in the kitchen. Deris escaped to the calm of her child-free home.

17:38 We lit candles, sung "Happy SuperJen Day", ate cake, and gave SuperJen her custom superhero bobblehead. We loved our most fabulous kid-sitter and wanted to honour her.

18:15 Baby was fed and I changed out of puke-smelling fuzzy pants into jeans and a shirt I couldn't nurse in. I pulled up my unwashed hair, tweezed a few obviously unruly eyebrow hairs, and declared myself ready. Arthur and I ran out the door, not looking back. Lia, SuperJen, and the kids were home to finish their IT project.

18:30 Arthur and I pretended to enjoy an overcooked meal at a loud restaurant where we discussed our crappy financial situation and the poorly done chores.

Work sucked. Life was hard. But we were committed to making it better. I texted SuperJen to tell her I forgot to set out pumped milk for the baby.

20:00 Jet was not a complete wreck, but had voiced his negative opinions about the bottle situation. SuperJen exited the stage and we five attempted the bedtime routine. Lunches, gathering of shrapnel, resisting personal hygiene, the usual.

21:00 Would this day never end?!? Jet was down, I expected him to wake shortly to eat all night as usual. Jackson resisted bedtime, claiming his toothbrush had been stolen. There was a glitch in the final video project, and Ella and I worked feverishly to correct and upload the product.

22:41 I started one final load of dishes, because waking up to the pancake gunge would have been a crappy way to start a Monday morning, one more load of laundry started, dogs peed one last time . . . and I climbed into bed for a *relaxing* game of Candy Crush™ . . .

#everydayhero #perpetualexhaustion #everyfuckingday

October 30, 2013

The front door of the Gemstone does not face the street it sits on. The solid wooden door, set to face north over the river valley, faced a medium-density housing complex. It was built "correctly" in 1937, but in the 1960s a main artery was constructed to accommodate the growing subdivision, and the house was left looking askew. The Gemstone is sideways.

Guests were never sure which door to use, as either requires a walk around the side—truth be told it didn't even matter. At one side, visitors enter the proper but small foyer and catch a glimpse of the tin ceiling in the den, the heavy wooden trim and staircase, and the original French doors (missing one single pane of glass). At the opposite door, you trip over the pile of Ella's shoes and struggle to find a hook to hang a coat. Then the guests emerge into the large family kitchen with evidence of day-to-day stacks of bills and papers, books, dishes, and a large fridge in the middle of the room. Done up or exposed, both routes lead into the heart of the Gemstone.

It had been my experience, thus far, that the people we loved having in our lives had been supportive and politely curious about all that was happening in the Gemstone. Perhaps this was because some of the turmoil over the past decade had already produced the sifting effect of losing the bad-egg relationships. My motto had become "If you're not contributing positively to my life, you're not in it".

This attitude, of course, had resulted in some hard decisions about old friendships and how my energy was best spent. This arose as a topic at PFLAG. There is obvious heartache over family and friends who continue their ignorant paths of hurtful and mindless comments or actions regarding sexuality and gender.

Ella's closest friends had gracefully jumped gender ships right along with her. I'm not sure whether it is a sign of the times, or a sign of kind hearts, or some sense of voyeurism that they have an "alternative" friend. It may even be that they already knew, so it wasn't surprising. They posted kind comments on her beautiful photos, and continued to initiate social events: their friendships had prevailed.

Family members who had not been accepting of the change were a charged subject. I was so very grateful we didn't have many of those—some in the room at PFLAG had lost their entire families. It was simple to soothe them by saying they would find new friends, adopt new families, fill up those holes with allies—but the pain of those deep wounds was beyond what I could comprehend. The rejection rocked people to their core. My stance had been that others make their own decisions, just as we make ours, when it comes to logistical family events. I simply had no control over their attitudes and actions, but I could set healthy boundaries with the hopes that my children would learn to do the same.

November 5, 2013

Teachers: How is Ella doing?
Me: I really have no clue. She is a 13-year-old girl and tells me nothing about school!
I think she is exhausted getting herself up and out the door before 6:30 so she has time to decompress and mentally prepare for her school days. I saw more stop-motions and drawings produced last month than I have in the past few years . . . and she flits and dances around . . . so—good?

It was parent-teacher interviews. I had met a few of them, but I thought it important to show my face and be an involved parent when possible. I wrapped up Jet and headed into a gym swarming with proud and concerned parents. Iain and Arthur were working <insert resentment here>.

Math: Ella is completing her work in class, and her average is 74%.
I double check to see that we are talking about the right Ella. Ella, who painfully struggled for hours and weeks and months at the kitchen table last year.
She has a unit exam tomorrow. I am generally really pleased with her work.
Would have been good information before we agreed to let her attend the Givenchy Christmas Product Launch at The Bay this evening . . .
English: Wow, Ella really struggled with writing in the first person.
This is interesting because her entire life is a running monologue of nothing but what Ella is thinking.
Science: *The line is too long, and Jet is fussing. I skip out.*
Social Studies: *Teacher is absent. Perfect. One less line to wait in.*
Phys Ed: I am so glad you came. It's nice to have a face to go with a name.

We have already exchanged e-mails about Ella's need for a little leniency about undergarment "failures" and pain in her legs after her injections . . . and about Ella's ability to spin a tall tale and exaggerate physical discomfort . . .

We have worked through some issues, and she is doing well. She is changed on time, and with a little encouragement, she tries her best.

Great news for a girl who hates Phys Ed as much as I did. She enjoyed writing an essay on the history of bowling, punishment for forgetting her socks, better than bowling itself!

Media: She is LEADING her group. I don't know where they are going, but she dug right into making classic sound effects and writing and recording a radio script, old style.

Win. THIS is why we are at the Arts School . . .

Art: I think we have a friendship blooming. I LOVE her.

I am challenging her to move beyond the immature infatuations; no more simplistic drawings of shoes. We grow as artists as we grow as people. I can't WAIT to see where she is headed.

Win. Win. Win.

November 6, 2013

Facebook was plastered with a story involving the Mayor of Toronto having admitted to smoking crack cocaine and being publicly intoxicated. Arthur showed me quickly on his iPad plastered with every possible current event app and news website . . . news was another one of Arthur's addictions. The Mayor's drug use and unruly behaviours had caused public outrage.

Even in my worst drunken stupors, and there were many, never was I ever offered a crack pipe. What kind of circles do you need to be in to have that happen?

I knew too well . . .

All the uncommon girls in my group in Rehab had made bad decisions. They had gone to a dodgy party and been offered crack, becoming addicted on the first high. They had driven drunk one too many times and had lost their cars and jobs. They had gambled too long one night and finally emptied the nest-egg they swore they would never touch. They had passed out too early one night, or slept in too long the next day, someone had voiced concern about their children, and social services had intervened. Their gambling, alcohol abuse, or addiction was no worse than mine; they simply had made the wrong choice one too many times. It took me a long time to figure out that the THINKING that led to our collective behaviours was identical . . .

> *I am SO emotionally uncomfortable that I need something . . .*
> *Right now . . .*
> *To make me feel differently . . .*

I visited the Rehab Psychiatrist. I was wondering, after all my reading, if I had a newly diagnosable disorder. Borderline Personality Disorder? Double Depression? I needed some medical attention I could relate to. I was having some thoughts about jumping in front of city busses and thought I at least needed my medications adjusted. Alcohol chemically alters serotonin levels.

> *Rehab Psych:* How bad of an alcoholic do you think you are?
> *Me:* I'm doing okay in here.
> *Rehab Psych:* On a scale of 0 to 5, how bad is your alcoholism?
> *Me:* Maybe a 3 or a 4.
> Comparing consequences in my life to others. Minimizing.
> *Rehab Psych:* Carla, you are a 5. Treatment centers are for people who are a 5 out of 5. Rehab is the end of the line.

> *#FML #itsbad*

November 8, 2013

My kids will probably remember me as a mom who was on and off a diet wagon. The Master Cleanse Lemonade Diet. Weight Watchers® Points Plus. Cut the Carbs. I was just as addicted to food and binge-eating as I ever was to alcohol, but the effects of the former are not as socially reprehensible. My muffin top comes and goes, and Jackson occasionally brings it to my attention with innocent comments:

> 5-year-old Jackson: Mom, I saw your bum and I didn't even laugh.
> 8-year-old Jackson: What is that bumpy stuff on the back of your legs?
> 11-year-old Jackson: You're not as big as when you were pregnant, but still no *Sports Illustrated* ® model.

I jumped back on a wagon of sorts . . . trying to bring bad eating habits back into my consciousness.

iMe: Lent starts tomorrow!! I am giving up refined sugars, aspartame, and complaining . . .
Better for baby, better for me.
I suppose that makes tonight my Mardi Gras!
iGramma: Go for it! Only an hour left . . . xox

November 9, 2013
Pee Wee hockey tournament in the middle of nowhere—I was home at the other end of the province, making cookies but getting updates from Iain.

iIain: Game two. Warm-up in progress to Back in Black (at a wholly insufficient volume level in my opinion). Should be a better match-up than last night's 17-0 loss. The mood is pensive but good.
Inauspicious beginning, down by 2 just two minutes in.
OMFG the mother of all own goals.
Kid just ripped it into his own net . . . an incredible shot. Goalie was annoyed.
Jackson misses on an easy rebound from point-blank range as the first period comes to an end. The teams are not evenly matched, but it does not look like the fiasco of last night.
The teams are back on the ice. The puck is dropped and the second period is underway.
The Scorpions are missing chances left and right. The other team is not. 6-1 now.

The best part is the sound guy, who moves effortlessly from Tom Jones to Great Big Sea to Jethro Tull.

Goal! A beautifully executed 2 on 1 makes it 8-2.

12-4 final.

Jackson finishes game by flattening the high-scoring captain.

November 10, 2013

How do I stay love-based and not fear-based with these stories popping up on my newsfeed? This was terrifying; this was real.

Hate Crime Charge for California Boy Accused of Setting Transgender Teen on Fire

A 16-year-old California boy accused of setting fire to a transgender teen's skirt as the victim slept on a public bus in the city of Oakland earlier this week was charged as an adult on Thursday with committing a hate crime.

Richard Thomas was charged with aggravated mayhem, felony assault and a hate-crime "enhancement" after telling a police officer he committed Monday's attack "because he was homophobic", according to the criminal complaint.

The 18-year-old victim, Luke Fleischman, who was born male but identifies himself as gender neutral and goes by the name of Sasha, remained hospitalized in San Francisco with severe burns on Thursday and was listed in stable condition, a hospital spokeswoman said.

> The teen will require several surgeries to recover,
> according to a website posted by family members to raise
> money for the victim's medical treatment.[20]

November 11, 2013

We were conserving money by staying at Gramma and Papa's condo for our annual Cookie Day celebration. The extended family gathers at a community hall in a very small town to hand-knead 12 pounds of butter, flour, and sugar into delicious dough that is decorated, baked, and distributed to everyone's fattening butts. This was one of the few chances we have during the year to reconnect with extended family. It was the first time for most of them to meet Jet and Ella.

The day started with an agonizing fashion show of all the outfits Ella thought might be appropriate for the event. Gramma and I were the judges. While I knew her clothing choices are not a reflection of me as a parent, the unspoken rule was "You had better wear something that will make Gramma proud of her family and not embarrass Papa". I don't believe that we, as girls, should ever be *required* to dress a certain way, but I am not ignorant of the fact that sometimes fitting into a social norm is just easier.

Nope, too skimpy for the farmers.

Nope, too cold for winter.

Nope, too "out there" for my cousin the reverend.

Ella had run out of the foundation that looks good on her face and proceeded to use a clearly inferior product. The result was Snooki, from *Jersey Shore*. The face, along with her attempt at straightening already curly hair resulted in a pyramid configuration that was clearly not going to do. Would this ever end?

Me: Ella! I need you to go have a shower and wash off your face. Start over.

Ella: *resists*

---

20   Cohen, Ronnie. (2013). *Hate crime charge for California boy accused of setting transgender teen on fire.* Retrieved November 10, 2013 from http://www.reuters.com/article/2013/11/08/us-usa-california-hatecrime-idUSBRE9A702R20131108

We did arrive at the farm with a 13-year-old girl in respectable attire and baby Jet in an adorable Tommy Hilfiger outfit, gifted by one of my single friends (typically we sport second-hand cheapo clothes). I stood down. She forged her own way, with an occasional glare from me to let her know when she was acting *WAY* over the top. My family members were cautiously curious and asked me about her school, which washroom she used, and what the other parents thought about that. She was as she should be. Ella. Herself.

November 13, 2013

I was a walking "to do" list. I woke up thinking about what was left over to do today from yesterday. Laundry. Cleaning. Correspondence. I walked from room to room and saw things that triggered an "I need to do that", or a "Damn, I forgot about that". It was overwhelming.

In accountant's daughter style, I opted for Excel to help me quell my anxiety. I couldn't decide where to start, so I designed a weighting system to help me prioritize. Really, I just felt like hiding in bed with a few episodes of *Orange is the New Black*. I needed to pay attention to the balance of "have to" items vs. "soul food" items.

#listlover #unhealthyloveofexcel

November 17, 2013

iGramma: How are Pablum Boy and Hockey Boy and Math Girl? Oh yeah, and Tired Mommy?
iMe: Pablum Boy did not sleep, but he's cute.
Hockey Boy got a pass on hockey practice this morning because Iain is lazy.
Math Girl is now English Project girl and has overtaken the living room with bits of foam board and various construction shrapnel . . .
And Tired Mama? Sigh.

November 18, 2013

Sometimes when recovery programs get too programmy, I back off and simply use some handy slogans to get myself in a better headspace.

We did not cause it, we can neither control nor cure it, leaving only our own behaviours on which to focus.

- One day at a time.
- How important is it?

Dumbass! Why can't you get your shit together?

- First things first.

You fucking jerk, you are ruining my life!

- Just for today.

Grow up!

Some of these are obviously not conference approved . . .

November 20, 2013

The big kids were both back at Iain's for the first time in what felt like years. Our "week-on—week-off" arrangement had been the best one we had found, in terms of consistency for the kids, and ability to plan, schedule, and follow the ever-complicated lives of tweens. Ella had been with me for much of her transition though, approaching 6 months, the result of "women" being good teachers for "girls", and the resistance put up by her about being at her dad's house.

How I longed for some osmosis of common sense into her skull . . .

iElla: Ugh! Dad got mad at me for not wearing a sweater under my coat! First off, I don't have any sweaters there (hello, sweat marks!) And secondly, because I'm already wearing a tank top, bra, many a gaff underwear, and 2 pairs of tights plus a hairspray helmet! Can you please talk to him about it?
P.S.—He wants to get me another winter coat when this red one is already boiling.
iMe: Bras and tank tops and gaff do not count as warm clothing. It's winter, and you need to be safe and weather appropriate. Warm is more important than fashionable.
Believed no teenager. Ever.

November 23, 2013

What was my obligation to disclose that Ella is a biological male?

This question had haunted me for months. We had discussed the subject with therapists and other parents of transgender tweens and with Ella, but there seemed to be no easy answer.

Would you, as a parent of a teenage child, want to know if a visitor at your house identified as transgender? If Ella had a third nipple, we would not feel obligated to tell anyone about it. But, since she has a penis, the jury is out. What if she was "just" gay? Or "just" bisexual? Would you want to know then? Does your perceived right to know trump Ella's right to privacy?

> Me: Your dad and I have already discussed it and agreed that if you are sleeping over at a friend's house it is important their parents know.
> Ella: But Lucy doesn't know! What if her mom tells her? WHY do you have to tell her?
> Me: There is more potential for very bad fallout if they find out later and are angry that we didn't tell them than if we have a polite conversation beforehand.
> Ella: I'm not READY yet.
> *Weepy. Emotional. Ella wanted to be a common girl.*
> Me: You have a choice. I have a conversation with her mom before you go, or you can have your playdate without the "sleepover" part. *I was on my mother "high horse". I drew a line in the sand that I hated to enforce, but . . . my heart was breaking.*
> Ella: MAKE her PROMISE not to tell Lucy?
> Me: I can't promise, but I will ask her to keep it private.

I attempted to reach her mother a few times before we finally connected. I had 12 anxious texts from Ella asking about my progress.

> Mother: Hello?
> Me: Hi. I'm Ella's mom, Carla. I wanted to connect with you before you host Ella this evening. We are always torn as her parents about making this call, because it is kind of a touchy subject, but for everyone involved we like to be transparent.
> Mother: Okay –
> Me: Ella lives her life as a girl, but biologically she is a boy. She uses the girls' bathrooms and the girls' change room at school,

attends every activity as a girl. She identifies as transgender. So, activities like swimming, sleeping together, and such are awkward subjects . . .

Mother: Uh ha –

Me: Ella has chosen to not tell other students and her friends at school. I'm not sure if your daughter knows—but it is VERY important to Ella that we not tell her. Ella will confide in her when she is ready. It's not a secret, but it is private.

Mother: Okay—Lucy is usually progressive about these kinds of things. It's not an issue.

Me: That's wonderful, and I doubt the news will surprise her when Ella is ready. Please, if anything comes up, or if you have any questions, don't hesitate to contact us.

Mother: Sure.

Although the conversation had gone well, the lump in my throat choked me . . . not because I was embarrassed or upset about Ella being Ella, but maybe I was a hypocrite? If it's *her* privacy, why had I vetoed the decision and outed her? Safety. Distrust of society's reaction. An ounce of prevention being worth a pound of cure. If the situation was reversed, I would want to know to be better able to support the transgender visitor. Or at least that is what I told myself.

After this, I simplified the rules and adopted them for all children—trans or not:

1. Must have been to the home where they would be sleeping over at least once in the daytime.
2. If I can't speak with the other parents to confirm arrangements, it's not happening.
3. When you are horizontal, you are in separate rooms.

November 26, 2013

Jet was sitting and flopping over. He did not sleep without being attached to my boob. I didn't mind because he was happy and mostly easygoing when he was awake. I was madly in love with him—his little voice, his silly giggle, and his fearless blue eyes.

Some ladies were waiting beside me for a baby wellness-check, and chatting.

Me: His eyelashes are amazingly long!
Other mom: I know—it's not fair.
Me: I think somewhere along the way women have genetically altered their own eyelashes by breaking them with makeup and curlers. Some Darwinian thing.
Other mom: He looks like a really good boy.
Me: He is great—he has a friendly demeanor. They have their own personalities right from the get-go.
Other mom: So true. I get frustrated when mine is so fussy. I feel like I am doing a bad job . . .
Me: I remember a long time ago, waiting in a doctor's office with an insane 2 ½-year-old and a 6-month-old on my lap. I couldn't control the eldest—"he" didn't listen, "he" was strong-willed and very focussed—turns out "he" had autism. There was another mom sitting with a very well behaved 3-year-old. When the child jumped off his chair to grab a toy, mom hit him, and he sat back down. That was the day I learned that just because my child was behaving badly didn't mean I was a bad mom, and just because yours is behaving well doesn't mean you are a good one. I hold onto that.
Other mom: Thank you.

November 27, 2013

Ella and I fought over the bathroom mirror. She spent her customary hour primping and fluffing and I spent my typical 28 seconds pulling my hair back into an ugly pony. I'm too fat for my pants, have no time or interest in a haircut, and generally have let myself go. This is a "rainbow" day, starting at the Gender Clinic, progressing to Value Village to acquire more skirts, then to the Gender Psychologist, and finally to PFLAG.

I was exhausted from constantly choosing to cater to Ella's whims and desires. If I set healthy boundaries around needs vs. wants, perhaps I wouldn't be so resentful?

Other parents echoed this sentiment at PFLAG. They shared stories of going out of their way, beyond the call of typical parenting, to support their child. The fear was that they would "fall back into the dark place they were in before they were strong enough to come out or transition".

I was comforted by knowing I was not alone. Ella held us as emotional hostages, dangling the unfortunate fact that she had been unfairly treated by the universe by giving her the wrong biological anatomy. It was even more challenging for Arthur, who had not had 12 years to develop a thick "Ella-proof skin". Her egocentric, autistic, rigid, and self-entitled views of the world were such a hard pill to swallow. Guiding her was an overwhelmingly difficult task.

I was reminded though, that when I am tired of bloodying my forehead by hitting it on the same wall, I have the option of turning right or left. In that case, taking a new path to less conflict involves stepping back and setting new strategies in place. New household guidelines and consequences. Preparation and follow through. More work.

November 29, 2013

My Quirky Moms group arrived with appetizers in hand for an evening of wine and whine!

> Quirky moms: How is Ella?
> Me: OMFG
> Quirky moms: We all deal with such difficult challenges . . . but really . . . this is a new level of complicated.
> Me: I'm scared for her. I used to be fearful of bullies at school. Now I am fearful that someone will set her skirt on fire on the bus, or an ignorant mob will beat her up . . . the ASD makes it IMPOSSIBLY difficult to teach about danger and safety.
> Quirky moms: We are here to help with anything, any day, lovely lady.

November 30, 2013

My addiction of the week was cheese curds—the white ones that squeak when you eat them. I had been making excuses to drive the entire way across the city to buy them bags at a time, and ate them with reckless abandon. Jet's diapers smelled like poutine.

I was paying at the counter for our cheesy lunch. I had brought
Ella with me this time; an excuse to succumb to my cravings again.
I glanced over my shoulder and caught a glimpse of Ella spinning
around on her heels singing "I'm so pretty, oh so pretty," oblivious to
the construction men standing awkwardly around her. All she wanted
was to be a girl in her own little world . . .

December 1, 2013

Fuck. Relationships are complicated and difficult. I am not sure
whether working at making them better is more painful than trying
to get out of a bad one. Like I said to begin with, everything I let go
of has claw marks all over it.

The thought of putting in the effort and investment it takes
to have a "forever" partner, which is the flip-side of another soul-
crushing break, is a fine balance. I don't think I'm unique when I
contemplate my life alone—or in a different relationship—or other
rosier options. The grass is not greener on the other side; the grass is
greener where you water it.

> iMe: I am fried. Ella fried me ☹
> iArthur: Why the hostility today?
> Why don't you take a day off and I will take the baby?
> iMe: I am retreating to YOUR downstairs area full-time. YOU can
> have the rest of the house to do your complaining about "lack of
> space" . . . YOU and ALL the dogs and kids, doing ALL the daily,
> weekly, and monthly chores, food procurement and preparation,
> and ALL other logistical activities . . . this includes, but is not limited
> to, being sensitive to the emotional needs of ALL souls involved. I'd
> be happy to.
> iArthur: Wow. That's a lot to digest.
> Why don't I mull it over while I work my ass off at a new job that is
> underpaying me while I am the sole provider for my partner and
> family?
> Also, how to deal with an amazing debt load that I can't even begin
> to wrap my head around, an inheritance that I can't access, and a
> ruined credit rating.
> Let me mull your situation over while I deal with my emotional
> atomic crater and physical issues.

Let me have a few minutes to process.
Thx.

iMe: Let's have a complain-a-thon.
iArthur: No thx.
iMe: How about a thankful-a-thon?
I'm thankful for outstanding children.
iArthur: I've never been more loved.
iMe: I'm thankful for Turkish bread.
iArthur: I'm grateful for my extended family. I'm thankful for a caring and competent partner. Compassionate, kind, and thoughtful.
iMe: I'm thankful . . .

#wegotthis

Fierce

December 2, 2013
15:05

Ella phones: Merm!
Her latest nickname for me, coined from the most recent "ermahgerd"
obsession
My substitute teacher today PROJECTED the class list on
her computer screen for all 42 kids to read . . . ELIOT . . .
JOHN . . . GRANT.
Me: Oh, sweetie.
I swallowed my heart back down. It landed somewhere between fear
and rage.
Did anyone say anything?
Ella: I had some explaining to do, you know, the old "My full name
is Ella Margaret Eliot John Grant, after both my grandparents" thing
. . .
Me: Are you okay?
Ella: I just feel awful.
I heard betrayal, violation, and terror.
Me: Come home.
WTF!

I had worried endlessly about for her being bullied in the hallways,
harassed on the city bus, or beaten to a pulp on the street, but
the reality was that she had yet to experience anything so horrific.
What she had just been subjected to was being "outed" by the staff
at school—the people who have been charged with protecting her
private information.

Inconveniently, the principal was not available. I wrote a string of
e-mails to people I thought may have known the ins and outs of the
legal and ethical recourses.

When Ella arrived home sobbing, I sat down with her at the
kitchen table to try to assess, if even possible, what level of damage
had been done to the psyche of my little girl. We documented all
prior occasions when her birth name had been called out, displayed,
or otherwise shared without permission; all of which Ella had kept
quiet about until this point.

I was a furious mama bear. I had been catapulted into sympathetic nervous system overdrive: battle mode. Cortisol surging in my blood forced every possible scenario for making changes through my head. Common sense tried to counter these thoughts with the reality of the financial implications of waging a personal war, and the possibility of harm by further disclosing Ella's identity publicly. I tried my best to keep the intensity of my rage private—Ella needed me to be her mom and loving supporter, not the prosecutor for the rainbow world. Ella was the only one who could set the bar for how big a deal this was; I did not want her to gauge her feelings by my own.

December 3, 2013

> iMe: Why aren't you at school?
> iElla: I just couldn't☹
> iMe: Your sub teacher called to apologize profusely today. She feels awful and will NEVER do it again . . .
> iElla: Tell her it's ok—I don't want my teachers to be mad at me
> iMe: It's not okay. But it's nice she called to say she was sorry
> I made us a pan of almond crunch candy . . . with dark chocolate
> iElla: ☺

I was angry. I would have killed for a drink. I needed a break from my emotions—liquor did that for me. I spent some time reflecting on the *reality* of my life with alcohol . . .

Dear John(ny Walker) –
    I think we have been "on the rocks" for quite some time. I don't think I can ignore how dysfunctional we have become any longer.
    It all started out so wonderfully. That first night when I was 14, just you, me, and a deck of cards. You allowed me to be Me—I lost my inhibitions and could let go of my responsibilities. I called people I could not have called sober, saying things I could never have said before. And in the morning, you weren't angry I had blacked out couldn't remember most of our time together. I wasn't even terribly sick. Maybe my genes just know how to cope with the ethanol. I fell for you, and I fell hard.

You kept coming back, week after week. I could sneak into bars to be with you. You were the best dance partner—you didn't care if I lead or followed, didn't care if I stepped on a shoe or two. We went to house parties, camping trips, to the beach, and even golfing; what great times. I am glad my love of photography was also blossoming so I could look back and recover some of my blackouts, I don't really recall much. I was Crazy Carla, and you were my partner in crime.

What a fortunate girl I was when you moved to university with me! You eased my transition into a new environment where there was never a shortage of people ready to go out with us any hour of any day. My friends didn't even notice the intensity of my relationship with you because I made sure we spread our time around. You celebrated every exam, you softened every uncomfortable situation. You were the only one I knew that could lift the burden of responsibilities I had placed on my own shoulders.

Then this hero child tried to grow up. You took the edge off tumultuous lusty relationships as long as I was careful to be sure they were friends with you, too. You allowed me to freely explore sexuality and big-girl situations. I don't know when exactly I gave you power over my inhibitions, but I did.

I missed you terribly throughout my pregnancies . . . all those people in my face without you by my side. But, ever my loyal sidekick, you came back to me shortly after.

You walked me down the aisle.

You masked the pains of parenting.

You made lonely evenings pass.

It was in a detox ward I can only describe like *One Flew Over the Cuckoo's Nest* that someone told me you weren't really all I thought you were. A night-shift counsellor said you had stolen my soul, dug into my money, interfered with relationships that mattered, and damaged my ability to work. I thought then that I might leave you.

So, I did. Cold turkey. For two years, I lived without you. I was depressed, bored, and overwhelmed. My husband was gone. I was lonely and irrational. But when I just could not cope with my life any longer you came back without resentments—you had been patient and were willing to quickly resume our relationship of destruction.

You were NOT my friend.

You left me in dangerous places.

You erased my morals.

I have learned that blame doesn't change outcomes, and I know no one deserves 100% of the responsibility . . . but it feels unfair that you get off unscathed to take on more victims and I am left to clean up your trail of chaos.

I try to leave the past in the past now. I begin to deal with the shame I feel when I talk to my emotionally-abandoned children. I begin to fill the void that is left with spirituality and love. I rewrite my moral code and build my self-worth on a solid foundation. It is a leap of faith that anything or anyone will feel as intimate as you have felt to me for so long.

I'm saying goodbye. Goodbye to my best and worst friend. Goodbye to carefree wild nights and an easy out. Goodbye to the lies, dishonesty and isolation. Goodbye to numbness.

People on the outside have watched the highs and lows. I know they will help, when asked, to pick up the pieces and help me to begin to live my life . . . a vibrant, spiritual life of goodies. Without you, I can continue to dig myself out from under whatever is covering the better parts of me . . .

Carla

December 4, 2013

Principal: We try our best to make sure this kind of thing doesn't happen, and we feel just terrible.
I have spoken to the supply teacher, and she feels just sick about it.
We can't promise it won't happen again.
Do you *really* think the other kids don't know anyways? Maybe they do and just don't really care.
Blah. Blah. Blah. Bullshit. 💩

Everyone was apologizing, but no one was accountable.

I wrote a letter to the Minister of Education to try to hurry along the working group responsible for making the necessary changes to the provincial computer system to add a "Preferred Name" field, and the ability to "hide" a legal name. I sent it to my elected Member of the Legislative Assembly (MLA). I sent it to the chair of the school board. Ella had been failed on so many levels.

Dear MLA,

I am the mother of a brave girl in Grade 8 who is working her hardest to overcome some massive life challenges. Amid the normal pressures faced by a 13-year-old girl in a large classroom with a tight budget, she is also adapting to a new school we have moved her to this year because she identifies as transgender.

Transgender individuals are those that identify with a gender identity that differs from the one which corresponds to their sex at birth. Born biologically male, my daughter lives her life fully as a female. This information is not a secret, but it is private and confidential, and we only disclose it when we feel it necessary.

You would think the heartache and fear involved in concealing your biological identity would come from other junior high students in hallways, in change rooms, and on public transit, but this has not been the case—her identity has been publicly revealed by teachers and staff at school, in error, because we cannot change her name with Alberta Education until she has had a legal name change. There are no fields to enter, or display, her "preferred" names.

The process of changing her name was initiated months ago—with fingerprinting at the police station, completion of an Application for Legal Change of Name at a registry agent office and financial outlay, but the paperwork has not been processed yet. Even when this is completed, we will not be able to change her gender marker from male to female because it is not permitted under the Vital Statistics Act of Alberta without undergoing surgery. As a result, Alberta cannot completely protect her from embarrassment, accidental disclosure, and discrimination.

I am sure you can readily understand the gravity of a situation in which the full birth name of a transgender youth is projected from a computer screen for all to see, called out in error for any number of routine school purposes for all to hear, or questioned at the library for all to overhear. Usually, sharp-eyed individuals catch this beforehand, but just this week we had yet another incident where it was missed, creating a very alarming and stressful situation for a young woman with enough to worry about, and who ought to be able to trust the system not to complicate an already difficult journey.

For her, and others like her, this is an urgent problem that continues to cause emotional trauma and fear that someone, looking at a computer screen, will "out" her and violate her privacy by sharing that which she has chosen to keep private.

There are many challenges facing the school system, I know—but this is something with a relatively simple technical solution that seems only to require sufficient gravity be assigned to it from the top for the staff in the middle to enact a change.

With anticipation of a timely resolution and response –
Carla

December 5, 2013

I called lawyers who were all very interested, but started their conversations with a disheartening "Let's meet to talk about a retainer". I read decisions on court cases in other provinces. I read the Vital Statistics Act and the Freedom of Information and Privacy Act. I considered law school—it would have been cheaper to spend four years in law school than it would be to pay someone to file and win a constitutional rights suit!

My rage had dissipated into a motivating sense of injustice.

Me: Ella, my primary job is to love and support you. If you want me to drop all of this, I will. If you want me to defend your rights until we are homeless and broke, I will.
Ella: I hate this. It sucks. Roll call is the most stressful thing *EVER*. Every day. Every class.
Me: About the "legal name change" issue . . .
We could file a complaint with the Alberta Privacy Commissioner, but then your teachers may be "investigated" and I don't want them to not like us, or you. Maybe if the Minister of Education sees a Freedom of Information and Privacy Complaint go across his desk, he will start working on a solution with a bit more oomph? We could lawyer up to see if they would be liable for what you are going through. It is not professional for them to have acted like they did. If I did that at the pharmacy, I would be FIRED. And probably lose my license.

And then there is ANOTHER big issue—even with a name change, we can't change the M to an F on your birth certificate until you have had surgery—which you can't have until you are at least 18. We could file a complaint with the Alberta Human Rights Commissioner to try to change that—like they did in Ontario. It wouldn't change the LAW, but they could tell the Alberta government that what they were doing was discriminatory . . .
Ella: I get it.
Me: Remember the fingerprints and forms and stuff in August for your name change? The roll call issue should fade away for you within weeks, as soon as we get that. It is probably discriminatory to require someone to change their name to protect their gender identity, but this problem has a workable solution.
Ella: I'm not going to school until my name is changed.

I reflected on my thoughts of esteemed people who have charged forward and paved the way for political and social change. I had been naïve to think that we weren't going to be called on to be *that* family.

Ella: I'll buy a blonde wig.
Me: Seriously, Ella. You could be outed in a very big way if we pursue this publicly.
Every Google search for Ella Grant or "Eliot" Grant could bring up a news story about being trans . . . forever. We can't get that back once it's out there.
Visions of coming home to crosses burning on our front lawn.
Ella: I'm outed either way, Mom. Either I must tell the security person at the airport that I am trans, or the lady at the pharmacy, or the teachers at school . . . or I can be known as a trans person who tried to do something about it.

She was torn. She was not sleeping. She was plagued with anxiety and nausea.

December 6, 2013
I used to love going to bed. Snuggling up, resting my busy mind. Now, not so much.
I sank into the squeaky mattress where a snoring man lay. I fought off three dogs to get to my spot in the fur covered blankets that

smelled like breast milk, because I had not had the energy to wash them for a few days. I played my maddening five games of Candy Crush™ and was timed out, defeated for yet another day. The light bulbs buzzed, and I counted the minutes until the baby started to cry.

Jet was usually in bed with us, too. The soother no longer soothed him. I counted 18 legs—two large adults, one small baby, and three dogs (one of each size) in the bed.

I had eaten almost the entire pan of candy I had made for Ella myself and laid there uncomfortably full. I stared at the small triangle of angry red paint that still existed next to the ceiling fan in our room—another unfinished home reno project.

December 7, 2013

The Carla Grant Sleep Training Strategy
1. Wait until the baby has developed object permanence
2. Kick the snoring man out of the bed
   a. To eliminate it as the cause of the baby's awakenings
   b. So the man can function at work the next day
   c. So the tired mom can sleep when baby finally does drift off
   d. To ease the guilt caused by someone else witnessing me not consoling my child
3. Create a better bedtime routine—be home every day at bedtime
   a. No 21:00 hockey practices
   b. No recovery meetings that run to 21:00
   c. No 18:00 naps (for mom or baby) that keep everyone up late
4. Put baby in his crib to sleep . . . drowsy but still awake
5. When baby protests at 22:00, 23:00, 00:00, 01:00, 02:00 . . .
   a. Go into baby's room
   b. Turn on his mobile
   c. Give him his soother
   d. Tell him how much you love him
   e. Leave
6. Wait 4 minutes and repeat step 4
7. Repeat until either:

    a.   Baby sleeps
    b.   Baby communicates he is HUNGRY
    c.   Mom collapses out of exhaustion and climbs into the crib
        with baby . . .

Report from Day #1 of *Mom Sleep Training*
- There was hope
- Sleeping diagonally in a king bed alone ROCKED, and reinforced the importance of a baby who sleeps independently
- Baby only fed at 02:00 and 07:00, the rest were out of habit
- 7 minutes of fussing baby for a future of sanity was worth it

December 8, 2013

> iArthur: What does my queen want for Xmas?
> Please make it under $30
> iMe: I already have everything I need . . .
> xox

December 10, 2013

We had just finished eating our unbalanced dinner of perogies and bacon bits when my friend Julie arrived at the house to cut our hair. It was a great trade for the photo shoots I had done for her military husband's departure, and again for his safe return from Afghanistan.

I didn't like my hair blonde, so Julie gooped me up for a new dark winter do. I fed a fussy Jet, who had just popped another tooth. Julie attempted to decipher Ella's teen girl secret code for what she wanted done with her hair. Ella was weepy and barely keeping it together—her anxiety about going to school was at an all-time high. She was having frightening thoughts of harm.

Arthur arrived at the door swearing and throwing things around because no one had come out to the truck to help him unload his shopping trip. I was not sure if I was embarrassed *for* him, or that I was *with* him. He and his foul mood left almost immediately, likely to escape the madness that was our home.

Angie, the lab, was hiding directly under the hair-cutting chair because she had decided Julie was her new best friend. I had purchased red cans of compressed air that make hissing sounds to deter the dogs from barking. They work brilliantly, but Angie was guilt-ridden and eternally upset by the red cans, that seemed to accuse all of them of wrong doing. She wanted to go home with Julie. It took some effort to get her into her kennel, away from the falling curls in the kitchen. Benny was hiding upstairs, barking occasionally, and licking his dicky.

Jackson was imploding upstairs, fluctuating between sobbing and door slamming because his new Lego® set was missing pieces. While I'd gone upstairs to attempt to console him, black goop still burning my hair follicles, Monty jumped onto the table and ate what remained of my bowl of stale microwave popcorn left from earlier.

I typically enjoyed the snipping close to my ears, and the thoughts of how it would feel to brush out newly cut ends, but on this day, I could hardly hear it over the disappointed 11-year-old, the wailing 6-month-old, the eccentric 13-year-old, and the barking dogs. My ears were congested with the cold I had developed secondary to never sleeping and being ultimately run down—and I couldn't even self-medicate because I was still nursing.

This hour-long blip in my life at one point would have been embarrassing for me. At one point in my life, it would have been a great reason to beg for sympathy, or at least act like a martyr. Now it was just my reality.

iMe: I will NEVER have time to do any writing. My life is a gong show.
iGramma: If your life wasn't a gong show, you wouldn't have anything to write about.

December 11, 2013

I sneak in some time for pictures of baby's first Christmas.

December 12, 2013

If Ella's distress wasn't motivation enough, this was. The world, unlike our home, wasn't always as accepting.

Two Transgender Women Killed—So Why Can't This City Call Them Hate Crimes?

Despite major gains in 2013, the LGBTQ community is reeling from two murders in the past week.

It looks like Cleveland has a deadly hate crime problem.

On Dec. 5, Betty Skinner, a 52-year-old disabled transgender woman, was found dead in her Cleveland assisted living facility. She had been beaten severely and died of blunt force trauma to the head.

Nearby, less than a day later, a 22-year-old transgender woman named Brittany Nicole Kidd Stergis was found shot to death in her car.

The murders were the second and third killings of transgender women in Cleveland in 2013. In April, Cemia "CeCe" Dove, 20, was found tied to a concrete block at the bottom of a Cuyahoga County pond.[21]

---

21   Fleisher, M. (2013). Two transgender women killed—so why can't this city call them hate crimes? Retrieved December 12, 2013 from http://www.takepart.com/article/2013/12/12/state-transgender-rights-movement

December 13, 2013

> iMe: Does 50 feel old?
> iIain: Nope.
> Me: *Then why does 37?*

December 15, 2013

> iArthur: Ella was cute today; she asked me if I was painting like "artists do".
> I mentioned that all artists have their own visual vocabulary, like musicians have a musical style, or authors in their writing, or actors with their voice and mannerisms.
> It was lost on her.

I was just glad Arthur was creating. He fashioned a 4'x4' painting for my parents for Christmas. It was the first hint of ambition, motivation, or genuine communication I had seen in what felt like years. That was the spark I loved. It reminded me of how it feels to do what makes you alive inside.

December 16, 2013

> iElla: It happened again!!!!!
> iMe: Tell me more?
> iElla: Merm?!?
> iMe: What class? Teacher?
> iElla: Attendance was on the screen when I walked in later than usual. There was a health class in there the block before and some of the kids just stayed for media, so they'd had plenty of time to observe. She closed it when I asked and did call out the right name. But THEN she invited a student, who was misbehaving, to her desk and she spent a lengthy time staring at her screen . . .
> Oh gawd, I feel AWFUL!!!!!
> Can u PLEASE pick me up?
> MERM!
> iMe: I have to feed Jet first! Can you wait until the final bell? I'll come get you then . . .
> iElla: Ya ☹

December 17, 2013

Message on the phone . . .

"Hi, Carla. This is the principal returning your call. I will start with an apology and then I would like a little bit more information.

"I have started my own follow-up and made a couple of changes, but I am still very concerned and upset that this has happened. Again. I'm very concerned about how she is. So, if you wouldn't mind getting back to me, that would be great. Thanks so much."

iArthur: How is Ella today?
iMe: Oscillating between weepy upset and angry vindictive.
iArthur: No school for her this week then?
iMe: I don't know.
I'm upset and can hardly even think.
I don't even want to call the principal back . . . I'm tired of being the polite accommodating mom. I think I'll just file the Freedom of Information and Privacy Complaint and let them contact her.
iArthur: Don't call her back. File the complaint.
Fuck them and fuck their ineffective administration.

December 17, 2013

Me: Jackson, can you please take the pile of stuff on your way downstairs?
Jackson: I have to go to the bathroom . . . so later.
Me: Just take it on your way!
Jackson: I have to go upstairs . . .
Me: What's the big deal? Just help me tidy up, and get it out of here!
Jackson: The wifi in the basement bathroom sucks.

#firstworldproblem

December 17, 2013

iGramma: Happy £¥%&ing Full Moon! How is Ella doing?
iMe: She is home from school today . . .

Mom diagnosis: fearful anxiety
iGramma: Not surprised. Is she going to Iain's?
iMe: Arthur is imploding. Iain's car is broken and has quashed the
kids' birthday plan with him tonight. Jackson whined and cried
until I got him tickets to the hockey Christmas celebration at the
Metropolis hockey game. Ella wants to stay here.
Jet bit his finger while eating a cookie today . . . he cried.

December 18, 2013

Report from Day #10 of *Mom Sleep Training*

- There was no hope
- Jet was once again in the king bed along with the rest of
  us, he resisted the change to his sleep routine after days of
  consistency on my end
- I would now employ a new strategy of **waiting it out**, instead
  of crying it out . . .
  1. I would wait until he was old enough to understand
  2. I would wait until he was able to tell me what was going
     on—was he cold? Thirsty? Lonely?
  3. I would wait until I was ready to bring an end to our
     lovely breastfeeding bond
  4. I would wait—and I would soak up the immense amount
     of joy that he evoked, through my sleepy eyes, as long as I
     needed to

December 19, 2013

iGramma: It's a new day. Do you have new energy? xox
iMe: Well . . . I started writing the complaint to the Privacy
Commissioner, so I guess that's more energy than yesterday when I
just wandered around contemplating it . . .
iGramma: I now call procrastinating "pondering". It's much less self-
critical. I'm trying to be kinder to myself but not with sugar!

December 20, 2013

I finally connected with Fabulous Lawyer, a man I had been
playing phone tag with for a few weeks. He seemed keen and
knowledgeable on the phone, sympathetic to the struggles faced by
gender and sexual minorities, and although he was busy, he offered to
review a human rights complaint for me before I filed it.

He started our conversation by telling me that I had opened his
eyes to an important cause. He had reviewed the landmark case
about the changing of gender markers in Ontario from the summer
of 2012 and was confident the same could be done in Alberta. I was
vaguely aware that similar cases had probably already been filed in the
province, but the more the better in terms of pressure.

He was willing to work on the case pro bono! He had colleagues
who would likely be willing to assist us, and he was keen to get
started in the New Year.

Facebook: Pro Bono Lawyer—BEST CHRISTMAS GIFT EVER!

I was elated. I made giddy phone calls to everyone I could think of
to share the news. Maybe we could enact positive change.

And then, to top an already fabulous day, Ella's new birth
certificates had been printed and arrived.

My days hadn't felt very inspired for a while; there hadn't been
enough laughter or light. And if you can't laugh—it just feels too
hard.

December 21, 2013

iArthur: I never had to be asked/told to do my chores
Carpet Diem
Carp Diem
Carpe Dien
I give up
Auto correct is my Noss
Boss

December 22, 2013

Arthur, Jackson, and Angie headed out on a road trip in a truck packed to the rafters with the 16-square foot painting and baby paraphernalia, just shy of midnight. We were ready for a long-anticipated Christmas at Gramma and Papa's ocean house! I was looking forward to being with my mom—not needing to utter the words "Can you get the baby?" because she already knew.

Ella, Jet, and I headed out on an expedition to tidy up a few loose ends. Makeup refills for Ella to replace her foundation so she "doesn't have to wear the one that oxidizes and makes me jaundiced."

We made a quick stop to try on a houndstooth peplum top she spotted in a window. Peplum is a prime trans clothing candidate—a fashionable way to hide anatomy.

> Ella: I'll just pop into the change room for a minute . . .
> *Jet fusses in the stroller.*
> Sales Lady: Oh . . . you can't see your mom! Don't worry, she'll be right back! Aren't you precious?
> Me: I'm the Mom! See the bags under my eyes?!? She's the 13-year-old sister!
> Sales Lady: You're NOT serious!
> Me: Oh yeah. For real.
> *Hearty laugh.*

December 23, 2013

Ella, Jet, and I wait in line at the WestJet counter at the airport with strollers and luggage and everything we had forgotten to send in the truck when it had left a few days earlier.

> Attendant: Carla?
> Me: Yes . . .
> Attendant: Jet?

Me: The baby.
Attendant: "Eliot"?
Me: *Head nod in Ella's direction, attendant looks Ella up and down but does not say anything . . .*

And we repeated this routine at each of seven required pit stops en route to the doors of the aircraft. Each time, Ella cowered behind me like a guilty teen about to be busted for lying. I presented the tickets and ID and stood confidently in front of her—as if in some way my physical presence could shield her from a verbal assault. This wasn't Russia, why did we feel like we were doing something wrong? For me, airports were on the list of places where you don't even bend the rules. Ever.

When we stepped on the plane, I brushed my hackles back down and was more resolved than ever in my decision to pursue legal change. No one deserves to be shamed for simply being who they are.

December 24, 2013

The Baby Doctor, who had cared so astutely for me and delivered my Jet safely, had tragically died.

Influential Doctor Remembered

When Michael began to read the long list of online memorial tributes to honour his wife [the Baby Doctor], he noticed that almost everyone mentioned how she had been there for her patients in times of joy and sorrow.

"She was a family physician in [Suburbia] for more than 30 years. She delivered more than 2,000 babies," he said, adding that in some cases, both the mothers and the new generation of babies were delivered by [the Baby Doctor].

Sometime early in her practice, she treated a young patient who had been the victim of a sexual assault. In the 1980s there was no official protocol for how to examine or treat such patients. The protocol that was later adopted by the Alberta Medical Association, as a standard procedure for dealing with children who have been victims of physical and sexual abuse, was largely developed by [the Baby Doctor].

"At the time, she was the only physician in the [Metropolis] area who would do medical exams on kids. No other physician would see them, because it was such a taboo. She would see them right away," said the executive director of the [Metropolis] Sexual Assault Centre. "The area has a number of very special services for victims of sexual assault that are unlike those found anywhere else in Canada."

Yet all through those years of working with victims of sexual assault and working with other physicians to establish procedures and protocols, [the Baby Doctor] also studied and developed practices to allow for natural childbirth within the safe environs of a hospital.[22]

For me, she defined legacy. I didn't know what to do with that kind of sadness.

December 26, 2013

Branches of my extended family were preparing to leave the ocean house. It had been a few short days with 12 people and two dogs celebrating the holidays together. We ate the 10-pound chocolate Santa, the kids adventured on beaches and cliffs (Ella scaling them in style, in heels), and I enjoyed all the helping cousin hands with Jet.

We were eight; my grandparents, Uncle David, Auntie Laurelie, Gramma, Papa, Jeff, and I. Jeff and I were mostly oblivious to the adult nuances and silent conversations which polluted the air. For us, it meant trips to the mall to go bowling, and to Zellers to spend the coveted Club Z points. We were the only grandchildren: Grandma and Grandad were generous with their gifts, their money, and their compliments.

22   Jones, S. (2014). *Influential doctor remembered*. Retrieved January 11, 2014 from http://www.stalbertgazette.com/Influential-doctor-remembered-20140111

My Auntie Laurelie rarely brought her female partners with her, even after 15 or more years in a committed relationship. Grandma sometimes asked her what that "thing was doing these days", but it was obviously not a safe place for Laurelie to be herself. Laurelie was still hiding in a closet in the home my Grandma grew up in from the 1920s. I suspect this double life of secrecy and disapproval played some mammoth role in Laurelie's struggle with mental health issues.

My Uncle David rarely brought his male partners either. His forever love, Lyle, was stuck pretending to be a "roommate" living in David's basement for decades. He was always working at the casino over the holidays. Even when David's lovers had joined us in his earlier youthful days, I was quickly shut down as a child for innocently asking where David's "fun friend" went?

Stories of hidden lives and being cast or ostracized by family are shared at almost every PFLAG meeting. Not everyone is in a place where they can be accepted for who they are, where they are.

December 27, 2013

Christmas celebrations, for me, had been overshadowed with more sad news. I received word that another recovery friend had ended her own life. I wondered what message the universe was trying to send me . . .

Alcoholism was no joke. It was life or death. The news rocked me. We were a lot alike, my friend and me. Although I knew the statistics surrounding alcoholism, it was hard to accept that her demons finally got the best of her. It was also a shocking reminder that no one, regardless of race, education, money, prestige, or support is safe from the clutches of addiction. It arises from pain, and ends in pain.

Rehab for me had been a commitment to spending the first six months of 2009 being locked up with 48 women in withdrawal.

Our days consisted of roll-call at each of three well-rounded meals (designed to nourish bodies suffering from neglect), assigned chores, three hours of group sessions in the mornings and afternoons, evening meetings in the community, and structured weekend programming. Walks were allowed each evening from 20:00 to 20:30, only with a partner, bag checks, and occasionally drug tests were carried out when we returned.

I had quit smoking the day we were committed, so not being allowed outside much was a blessing in disguise. If I was to live a life of honesty, I knew I couldn't continue lying to the kids about any of my nasty habits.

The building itself was a dormitory with small common areas, shared bedrooms, and communal bathrooms. It was nicely appointed and well maintained, but locked and secured, make no mistake. Think starter show home meets prison.

I now have a much different impression of the "clients" than I did when I arrived. I thought the girls were harsh. Opinionated. Troubled. Dishonest. Sick. Not like me. Over the course of my stay, they transformed in my eyes into broken children and wounded soldiers who, for a variety of reasons and choices, had succumbed to addictions. They came from Corrections Canada, Family and Social Services, Indigenous and Northern Affairs Canada, and from "functioning society", like me.

This group shrunk over the course of treatment. Women left for breaches of curfews, positive drug tests, and threats of violence. The graduates included:

Shelby: Soft-hearted country girl. She had been wounded by the fanatical and ostracizing religious beliefs of her parents. Her boys were grown, and she was an exemplary corporate employee on the surface. Her years of pain had led to theft at work to fund a life of drinking and gambling.

Nellie: Overweight, alone, and sad. Her pension money had been whittled away, one pack of smokes at a time, at a crappy casino.

Stirling: An armor of arrogance and beauty over an immature soul. She lost a sister at a young age, and was left to cope on her own at the hands of a bulimic, narcissistic mother. Her family culture of children being removed from the home by Social Services had not skipped her generation.

Emily: Daughter of two small-town school teachers who, at one point, had everything going for her. She shared her genes with her severely disabled twin sister. She partied too hard a few summers and acquired a nice addiction to crack cocaine. She had lost her man and her little girls.

Sandra: A horrifically abused child. Her mother watched, likely unable to escape the abuse herself. She carried on the tradition with an abusive husband and a soap opera life for her own children. She was homeless and on the streets, not equipped to deal with her darkest demons.

Lindsey: Her mother had died when she was young and she was raised by a father who ignored her and an uncle who abused her. Her children had been taken away. She was too drunk to be able to care.

Donna-Lynn: Small-framed, 60-ish free spirit, who smoked pot daily and who had been drinking from sunrise to sunset for 40 years. While in treatment, her husband told her he was leaving her for her best friend, and Donna-Lynn had now lost the only thing she ever had.

Grace: A beautiful spirit in a body that caused her anguish— childhood alopecia had caused her to lose all her hair at 12-years-old, and the emotional torment of cruel teenagers, coupled with abuse from a grandfather, wounded her irreparably.

Me: A pharmacist who hadn't lost her job . . . yet. A mother who hadn't lost her children . . . yet. A proud DIY-er who hadn't lost her home . . . yet. A truck owner who hadn't lost her wheels . . . yet. A girl who held the world on her shoulders and whose default escape was drinking.

For a while, I wondered how I could possibly "belong" in the group. I minimized my own traumas. I didn't deserve to be in a room with women who had been raped by their fathers, or hung by their hair in outhouses, given my comparatively posh lifestyle.

Shit happens. Events are processed by little minds, little hearts, and little souls in whatever way they can be at the time. We simply can't measure the profound impacts that trauma, in all its forms, has on people; it changes everything. The causes of trauma can't be compared. Hard is hard. There is no harder.

I deserved to be in the room just like everyone else. Once I accepted that, and learned to listen, and about how to pay attention to when my own buttons were pushed so I could learn to unplug them, I began to grow and heal.

#uncommongirls

December 28, 2013

Ella got a text, out of the blue, from a friend she hadn't seen since grade 5.

iAlice: Hey, "Eliot"! It's Alice.
What's new?
iElla: Well, I'm a girl named Ella now.
iAlice: Cool.
Do you want to hang out at the mall next week?

January 3, 2014

> ilain: In your opinion, did E behave well enough over Christmas to merit another trip?
> I have not told her about the trip to Costa Rica in April yet.
> iMe: She enjoyed this trip. She was interested in the scenery and the interesting buildings.
> Only a few afternoons of revoked privileges: one for being a self-entitled brat to Arthur, and one for taking photos of Jackson in the bathroom (her retaliation for Jackson calling her a stupid trannie . . . brothers always know how to stab deep.) Yikes.

I was reminded that most of the challenges I faced when parenting Ella were not gender-related at all. They were typical 13-year-old problems, typical girl problems, typical autism problems, typical headstrong child problems, and broken home family dynamics problems, yaddah yaddah. Putting them all together resulted in a perfect storm of sorts.

Difficult to parent is the child whose neurons do not connect actions to outcomes.

January 5, 2014

I never wanted to be a hockey mom, not because I actually *knew* any of them, but because I had heard stories of behind-the-scenes political maneuvering and of intense parents-turned-demons in the stands. My brother Jeff was not a hockey player, so I did not grow up in rinks; Papa and I enjoyed watching *Hockey Night in Canada* together in the winter months, and that was the extent of it.

As fate had it, or perhaps by divine geographical intervention because we lived where ice forms, I had a sporty child who *wanted* to play our country's national pastime . . . minor hockey. I avoided team "parent positions" like I avoided the Parent-Teacher Association at schools. The less involved I was, the less likely I was to get caught up in any turmoil. I didn't need any more fucking complications in my life.

There came a point in Jackson's third or fourth season (when I finally understood icing and offside calls) that I shifted, and began enjoying being part of it. Games became a place where I could yell!

Not obnoxiously, and not in the calibre of the mothers wielding cowbells, but I could be loudly supportive, and the other parent-benchwarmers didn't care.

#anonymouslyvocal

As time progressed, so did my love of standing on the bench, or along the boards, with a big camera lens shooting Jackson and his teammates looking like NHL superstars. They loved my pictures, and in a way, it became my unofficial "parent position" as team photographer. Connected, yet on the sidelines, was a comfortable place for me to be. Even on the receiving end of play-by-play texts felt satisfying . . .

> ilain: A tense affair here at the Sports Centre.
> The Scorpions get their game faces on.
> 0-0 halfway through the second.
> Jackson making a better effort than usual.
> But inexplicably penalized for something no one saw.
> He sits in the box like a wrongfully convicted criminal.
> A tight defensive battle it remains. 2 mins left in 2nd.
> Disaster! With 1:07 left a shot goes off Gavin's melon, into the air, and falls behind him for a goal.
> The period ends in a furious scramble around the enemy net but no equalizer is forthcoming.
> Gavin is playing a blinder. Could be 5-0.
> GOAL! Nicholas picks a corner from 30 feet.
> Nice passing leads to a 2nd enemy goal. They seem to have more zip.
> Scorpions come close. The tide could be turning . . .
> 4 mins left but the Scorpions go to power play.
> 1:06 left. Still down one.
> Face off deep in the enemy zone.
> Over. No win. Great game.
> iMe: Thanks for the play-by-play.

January 10, 2014

Fighting with Ella to squeeze her size 10 feet into "appropriate" footwear had been an ongoing challenge since the transition. She wanted stilettos, platforms, kitten heels, and Louboutins. We wanted flats, winter boots, sensible walking shoes, and Sketchers.

The compromise for the winter was a pair of warm boots with a 3-inch heel. These would withstand the -30°C wait at the bus stop. Except she lost one. We then owned ONE size 10 black winter boot with heel.

She followed this up with a serious case of frostbite from wearing open-toed shoes in the snow one weekend with her father.

Has she learned? Nope. Never will. Is this an autism obsession? Is this gender-specific pleasure denied for too many years? Is this just Ella's quirky sense of style? Is this just 13?

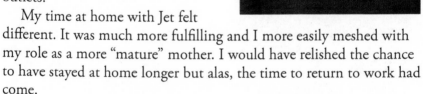

January 13, 2014

I had always been a better part-time at-home mom than a full-time at-home mom. When Ella and Jackson were 5 or 6-months old I started itching for some adult conversation and some motivating professional outlets.

My time at home with Jet felt different. It was much more fulfilling and I more easily meshed with my role as a more "mature" mother. I would have relished the chance to have stayed at home longer but alas, the time to return to work had come.

#billstopay #returntotheratrace

January 16, 2014

Ella: I don't mean to be rude, but did you drink when you were pregnant with me?
Me: Never, sweetie. There were other complications with the pregnancy. You struggled inside.

Apologetic.
Ella: I don't understand how it's fair that I have autism *and* a penis.

I vehemently believed on a root level there was nothing *wrong* with my children, or any person for that matter. I felt whipped when I witnessed my children hurting. I felt helpless knowing that I couldn't change the world so that the innate perfection I saw in them held true for them as well. It wasn't their "failures" that weighed on me, nor my broken expectations; it was the things that, by higher design, they were destined for before they started making their own decisions. Those were what sucked. My biggest burden as a mother was knowing they are suffering through things that I had no power to control.

January 17, 2014
I took lattes and Jet to connect with my friend Marie. She told me how her son's quirks had intensified, and they hung a diagnosis of ASD on him. That is how you access supports. That is how you know what books to start reading.

> Marie: The occupational therapist said I could claim things like his iPad as medical expenses.
> Me: I'm not sure, but I'll check with Papa, my in-house accountant.
> We watched her beautiful Parker rock and flick his fingers repetitively in front of his eyes, watching the same show obsessively—over and over and over. We talked about her concerns for the younger sibling, as he hit his head on the wall repetitively. She questioned whether he was mimicking, or showing early signs. She knew the odds of another diagnosis were high.
> I text her the list when Papa sends it to me. I read it over.
> "Prosthetic Breasts*"
> *Right on!*
> *For mastectomies only
> *Damn.*

January 24, 2014

Arthur had gone to pick up the car from the shop. The annoying repairs, now completed, were due to being hit by someone reversing at a red light. Who does that?[23]

A NHL hockey game was on the agenda as well. His time with unruly drunk old bar friends, I imagined.

> iArthur: I'm getting barraged by afterhours work calls . . .
> iMe: As soon as you leave the game they'll stop calling.
> iArthur: There is another problem: the people here are making transvestite jokes . . . I'm sure it's a coincidence but I'm leaving.
> iMe: Hard to change the world.
> iArthur: If it was my staff you would be engaged to a mass murderer.
> It hurts me a lot.
> iMe: Lots of intolerance and ignorance out there.
> Either speak your piece or let it go . . . don't fester.
> iArthur: Done.

I have refused to listen to the punch line of racist jokes. I have never enjoyed others trying to fake accents at another's expense. I will never understand how humans could be so downright cruel. It is only our ego that benefits from cutting another down to elevate yourself. I don't share insulting memes on Facebook—actually, I unfriend those who do. I don't have room in my sphere of energy to battle the negativity disguised as humour.

I have lost sleep over the potential backlash to having written these pages. The haters, the trolls, the excessively opinionated. Why can't everyone just leave everyone else the hell alone?

February 2, 2014

I watched a squirrel frolicking around in the large pine tree in front of our house. This little one was likely the offspring of my nemesis, Pervis the Squirrel. Things were getting way too serious in my life. How I imagined the spiritual realm of the squirrel to remind me to stop and play, to not hoard my nuts, and to get my work done. This was not the first time the squirrels had given me some reality checks.

---

23   Jackasses, say my editors. .

Squirrel Encounter #1

They first invaded my life when we were living on the East Coast. We moved across the country in a Corolla with a spirited 2-year-old and a 6-week-old baby. The house we had rented had a stunning view of an unspoilt bay 25 minutes outside of the city. I could spit from the upper deck and hit the ocean. It would have been a fabulous summer ocean cottage, but failed miserably at being a year-round home.

The power went out every time the wind would blow, and the dial-up internet was barely fast enough to support simple e-mail contact with any friends or family. Iain was at school most days, leaving me in isolation with no car, no adult contacts, to hang laundry to dry and chop firewood. I was a pioneer.

I met Pervis, the squirrel, while I was handwashing endless baby utensils, breast pump parts, and sippy cups. He would scale the kitchen window screen. We didn't realize he was living IN the house until later that winter, when one night he flew across the pantry at an unwitting Iain, who I thought might have a heart attack.

Luckily, it was a rental property and it wasn't our responsibility to try to evict Pervis or his family. We moved out before Pervis did.

Squirrel Encounter #2

One stormy night, the ceiling above our bed was making drip-drip-dripping sounds. Iain climbed a ladder to confirm that there, in fact, was a leak, and as a temporary fix for the night, placed a red bucket up to catch the water.

It was the next storm when we realized we had never done anything about that leak and he, again, went up in the middle of the night to ensure the bucket was catching the rain that poured through the old shingles.

Iain was teetering, balanced on two joists in the ceiling space, with a flashlight clenched between his teeth when he discovered, to his horror, a squirrel had drowned in the bucket. Somehow, he managed to get the dead squirrel out of the attic and down the ladder, hovering over me resting in our bed without me asking what was going on—I surely would have been horrified by the sequence of events.

The following weeks revolved around setting live traps, feeding squirrels, and eventually catching one or two in what was a humbling lesson of man vs. nature.

Squirrel Encounters #3 and #4

*Years later, at the Gemstone, the squirrels had once again invaded.
I was a brave girl, but not brave enough to climb up into the dodgy
attic space filled with ancient wood chip insulation to uncover whatever
horrors had been living there for the 75-ish years the house had been
standing.*

*I could hear them scratch-scratch-scratching on the backside of the lath
and plaster walls. I watched them taunting me, chirping loudly at me
outside, as if to say "Thanks for the free warm place for the winter! Just
loading in more nuts now so my whole family can join me!!"*

*One morning, Jackson came into my room, excitedly trying to
convince me in his 5-year-old way that a "Squirrel was in da' hall, right
by ma' room!" I ignored the claim until I saw the trail of water down the
hall where the squirrel, having had a bath in the toilet, indeed had been
running around inside the house.*

*I called pest control people, who told me they rented traps. I already
owned traps. I needed someone to come and FIX this problem.*

*On another particularly tragic day, I sat at the kitchen table drinking
too much wine while the children were decorating gingerbread houses in
preparation for Christmas. Earlier in the day, I had discovered that not
only had the freezer stopped working, but the washer also would not turn
on. I emptied the freezer into a box on the back porch; the one good thing
about Alberta in the winter is it is cold enough to salvage frozen foods
while thawing a freezer.*

*I had spent part of the afternoon at a funeral for the mother-in-law
of Cathy, my first kindred-spirited friend in Suburbia. I discovered that
"Eliot" had been troubled by diarrhea at school when he arrived home
in borrowed jogging pants with a note from his aide, saying that "Eliot"
claimed it was "a little slippery" down there. It was around the end of
the first bottle of wine when I discovered that "Eliot" had run out of
underwear.*

*Cathy called to check on my appliance "situation"."I cried. She met
me outside the backdoor a while later, and I had a "secret" cigarette. That
was when we spotted the squirrels—hanging by their little grappling hook
hands onto the siding of my house: fucking. As if the realization that the
squirrels were now multiplying in my attic wasn't enough, they had also
chewed into the frozen meat and pizza that lay outside in the sun.*

*My only consolations were the flowers Cathy had brought me from
the funeral and the package of new underwear for "Eliot". That is a good*

friend. Even "Eliot" agreed that she was truly wonderful when I later washed the red underwear in the newly-repaired machine and turned all his shirts pink.

February 3, 2014

It snowed, again. Arthur had been better this year about keeping the driveway clear. It's not hard to miss a snowfall or two and suddenly have the inches of snow accumulate into unmanageable mounds of snow and ice many feet deep. I figured being pregnant and then having a new baby should be excuse enough to get out of that job.

Winter months are sometimes very hard for Canadians. It's dark when we wake, still dark while we get ready for the day and dark again by mid afternoon. It's cold. Really cold. Like -36 ° C cold. Even seasonal affective disorder lights aren't enough to keep the winter blues away for most people. Vitamin D comes in pills or drops, and socialization is limited to people's homes and indoor public places.

Thailand was my retirement plan. I considered (okay, not really) possibly even emptying out the narcotic safe on my way out of work on my last day to fund my future life of leisure. It was an accepting country for Ella, too, although the sex trade and lady-boy lifestyle was a bit of a concern. Jackson would love the elephants and cheap, amazing food. I would like the warmth of the sun and of the gentle people. I would especially like the maid and the personal driver.

It's the years between here and there that are the big questions marks.

February 4, 2014

Ella has relocated her eight million bags of miscellaneous shit to Iain's house in preparation for a respite week I had planned away with Jackson and Jet.

> ilain: Ella is having visions of hurting other people—running over people in a car, drowning the baby, often she is the one doing the harm and it is scaring her. Could visual hallucinations (as opposed to random dark thoughts) be caused or accentuated by her antidepressants or hormone shot?

iMe: She is not on antidepressants. But she probably should be . . . to help quell anxiety and pervasively negative thoughts, as well as "stuck" thoughts. That's why I booked the appt with the Youth Psychiatrist last December.

ilain: She told my new girlfriend that this has been going on for years.

iMe: It has been. It's just been more intense lately . . . as her anxiety has been increasing

ilain: Horror movies and *Bones* episodes don't help.

It is worrisome. I'd have expected to hear about this from you if you knew about it. Meeting of the four adults when you return.

iMe: I did tell you about it. I also took Ella to see the Family Psychologist the day I first discussed it with her . . . and the school counsellor.

I have been concerned about her general anxiety for months . . . but nothing happens quickly

ilain: Alright. I know you've discussed the anxiety. But I don't recall hearing about seeing images of bloody violence and harm. She knows it's not real but that they're more than just thoughts.

iMe: After the Family Psychologist's assessment and my conversations with Ella, I don't believe she is in urgent danger . . . If she needs to see someone sooner, you can take her to Emerg and wait for a psych consult

Iain secured an urgent mental health appointment. Synopsis: She was not worried. The disjuncture between visions and who she appears to be was wide enough not to worry and there were no accompanying psychotic signals. That was the end of Iain's heightened concern; he was assured that there was no immediate danger.

Later, I explored the issue further with Dr. Gender. The phenomenon is known as horrific imagery, and is in rooted in anxiety. The thoughts are particularly worrisome for the person having them, though, because they *always* depict actions which are *contrary* to the nature of the person. He described it to Ella like this . . .

Dr. Gender: When someone holds a new baby, there is always a thought that runs through their minds saying, "You might drop the baby," to cue your body to be extra careful with the precious child you are holding. For most people, they don't even recognize the original thought, and just naturally hold the baby more securely.

Your brain pays extra attention to that thought, and gets stuck on it. And your anxiety blows it up in your head into something scary—which can even prevent you from doing something you enjoy, like holding the baby.

Same as when you are arriving home to an empty house. There is a thought that flies though most minds completely undetected that says "Be careful, there could be something awful inside," and it makes them more cautious when entering. Your brain says "NOOO! MY FAMILY IS ALL DEAD INSIDE!" and it gets stuck there. And you feel bad for thinking about your dead family . . . but that wasn't the intent of the protective thought to start with.

If we can control your anxiety, these thoughts will diminish. They won't paralyze you.

And that made her feel better. The images continued, but the guilt of being a bad person for having them went away.

February 5, 2014

I have always loved my kids one at a time. They didn't have to compete. They could just be the centre of their world and I could enjoy the uniqueness that is them without compromise. It's not half the parenting work, it is roughly $1/1,000^{th}$ the work.

Jackson, Jet, and I caught the plane to Vancouver Island. We fulfilled Jackson's grocery wish list of goldfish crackers, beef jerky, tortellini, and root beer. He created an elaborate overview of all the Olympic hockey teams and the tournament format.

His big request while we were at the ocean was to surf. Gramma hooked him up with a surf teacher, and off they went in search of  waves. I stayed huddled on the beach with a toque, mitts, parka, and camera. Jackson froze his little body into a popsicle covered in a wet suit while the snowflakes were flying.

People looked at him in awe, not because of his superhero bravery for surfing at such extreme temperatures (truth be told, there were many other insane people in the water), but because of his CRAZY pink hair. He was raising money for the St. Valentine's Day Hair "Massacure"—a charity for sick children. He sported the glowing coloured hair for a few weeks—long enough to stain my sheets and tub a luminescent pink—then shaved it all off.

I was so proud of my brave, compassionate child.

February 17, 2014

It made me SAD[24] that my kids knew how to pack little suitcases to go to "Dad's house" when they were just 4 and 6. It made me SAD that I was the cause of a logistically complicated childhood. Divorce sucks.

> iMe: Need Jackson's hockey stuff, and Ella's school rolly bag, pencil case (green, maybe in the rolly bag?), flat iron, and some clothes, please.
> ilain: No idea on clothes. Might necessitate visit. Will bring rest.
> iMe: Orange dress, both grey dresses, black/metal heels, purple flats, green skirt, black skirt with ruffle on it, and black turtleneck dress.
> ilain: Gawd. Ok.

I failed.

I failed.

I failed.

I failed by creating a family on unstable footing.

I failed by not instilling in them, by example, the importance of commitment. They were not privy to all the adult details, and I dreaded a day when they may perceive relationships as being disposable.

I failed by being the crazy lady, unable to cope in healthy ways with the onslaught of traumatic events that unfolded around me.

The flip side to my ever-changing relationship status was that I was an example of someone who decided that "settling" was never enough. I hope they saw that I had enough respect for myself to not continue in relationships that were no longer serving my highest good. I never really *believed* in forever marriage. I wasn't a girl

---

24   SAD—a big feeling word goes here, but I can't name it. It's not on my feelings list.

who played out fantasy weddings; I didn't have every detail of the "big day" conjured up in my head. I saw tremendous value in the commitment, and many of the honorable values attached to the traditional notion of marriage, but not in the event itself.

I know you're out there . . . the statistical 25% of adults who want a "do-over". A different partner, more kids, fewer kids, a different career path. I do not regret anything in my life; I trust that I have experienced everything for a reason. That said—yes, some of them were very poor decisions.

February 18, 2014

> Ella: 87% in science
> 100% in media
> 53% in gym
> Me: Oooohhhh. What are we going to do about that?
> Ella: I can't run or jump. It outs me. I can't stretch with kids sitting in a circle across from me.

I stuffed down my hatred of shopping at malls and soothed myself upon arrival with poutine, extra cheese curds. We had tried the skort from Winners—too obvious. We had tried long shirts—can't conceal anything when in motion. We had tried loose jogging pants—obvious bulge.

Compression shorts two sizes too small worn underneath baggy running shorts two sizes too big finally worked. $120, but I equated it to a child with cerebral palsy needing a brace.

February 26, 2014

After playing phone tag with a contact at the Freedom of Information and Privacy Commission for weeks, I finally received and opened a letter from them stating, in legalese, that without publicly identifying Ella they would be unable to investigate whether there had been a breach of her privacy.

It was ironic that the body responsible for making sure that information people had a right to keep private could only do so if they didn't hold that information private. I certainly understood to be fair, transparent, and ensure a fair process was upheld, certain steps had to be taken, but really?!?

This response was almost as pathetic as the one I had received from the Minister of Education, stating that maybe I should contact the school principal about the issue. They were clueless.

Ella had moved along her continuum of needing EVERYTHING to be private and having NO ONE know about her biological gender to becoming more comfortable expressing who she was, and wanting to do some good for the community that was supporting her. I tried not to push for this movement to take place—it certainly was a very personal choice for her.

Together, we wrote them back and gave a green light to investigate using her real name, but to not publish it in any findings that may arise from the proceedings. We felt this issue needed to cross the Minister of Education's desk again—from a public body that had some teeth to make changes.

March 2, 2014

Fabulous Lawyer had become the central coordinator of our Alberta Human Rights Commission complaint. He was an articulate, motivated, young lawyer known to the LGBTQ community. We had only met a few times, but already I was eternally grateful for his support. He had been made aware of a few other complaints that had been filed with the commission and was eager to have ours heard in a timely manner.

I was the primary contact for our medical and support professionals—trying to convince them of our worthy cause. Nobody wants to be contacted by a lawyer.

I wrote an affidavit to support our case:

In the matter of a Complaint to the Alberta Human Rights Commission by Carla Grant on behalf of my minor daughter.

1. I am the mother of E, the individual for whom I am bringing a human rights complaint.

2. E is the eldest of my three biologically male children. I share custody and guardianship of E with her father. The past few years have been ones of enormous transition for E, and for our family.

3. As a young child, E was effeminate and fixated on the female gender role: sparkly shoes, princess dresses, tea sets, and crystal-cut chandeliers. We sought the professional opinion and advice of a psychiatrist regarding these feminine characteristics when E was just 5 years old, and were encouraged to keep E's feminine inclinations private. These interests persisted through the elementary school years, where E generally had female friends and came to detest most stereotypically male sports and activities.

4. In October of 2012, then 12 years old, E approached me with questions about gender reassignment surgery. Unsurprised, but ill-equipped to field these questions on our own, her father and I consulted with our Family Psychologist, which led to a referral to Dr. Gender. An eventual diagnosis of Gender Dysphoria was made in March of 2013. From there, we were referred to the Endocrinologist and to a Gender Psychologist. We have continued to see this team of professionals on an ongoing basis to support E and the rest of the family. E transitioned to living full-time in her identified gender role, female, in June of 2013.

5. She applied, and was accepted, to the Arts School outside our district so she could enter grade 8 as a female with relative privacy. Administrative staff and her teachers were made aware of her transgender status so they could keep watchful eyes for any trouble that may arise. Our family is acutely aware of the discrimination and violence that is focused on this gender minority segment of our population.

6. In September 2013, I initiated the process for a legal name change in Alberta. This took months to complete and we didn't receive the Legal Name Change Certificate and new Birth Certificate until the end of December 2013. I learned that it is possible to get a legal identification card from Alberta Registries that has a female gender marker, but the Birth Certificate is the foundation document required for gender changes in many instances. Our inability to change the gender marker on the Birth Certificate has led to a series of associated problems.

7. Without a Birth Certificate that designates her as female, we are unable to change the gender marker with Alberta Education.

On at least seven separate occasions at her new school between September 2013 and December 2013, her legal name, not her female preferred name, was called out or displayed for all students to see by both regular and substitute teachers. If her stereotypically male legal name wasn't enough to give away the fact that she is transgender, the "M" certainly does. Since then, her name has been legally changed, but the "M" remains.

8. These public disclosures of private information cause E an enormous amount of stress and anxiety. After most of these incidents, I received texts and phone calls from her begging me to come and get her from school. She felt sick and was frightened she would be a target of the sorts of hate crimes she has seen on the news. She did not want to return to school and, on a few occasions, stayed home for days until we were able to get her to return, though I am unsure of the benefit she derived from this, given her level of anxiety and its profound effect on her ability to concentrate in class.

9. Without a Birth Certificate that designates her as female, we are unable to change the gender marker with Alberta Health & Wellness. E and I went to pick up her prescription for her hormone-suppressing medication and were told that there was a problem with the prescription. This has happened on more than one occasion and is the result of two scenarios. When E presents at the pharmacy counter as a female, well-intending pharmacy staff often change her gender marker to "F". The result is that I am required to disclose she is transgender to front-line technical staff in an uncomfortably public environment.

10. Without a Birth Certificate that designates her as female, we are unable to change the gender marker with Passport Canada. In December 2013, she flew with me and her infant brother from the Metropolis to Vancouver Island, to visit her grandparents. At the time, her ticket had been purchased under her legal name and "M" status. E was terrified about being "called out" at the airport and even considered not taking our Christmas vacation. At the airport, seven airport and airline staff people looked at the "M" boarding pass for this obviously "F" young lady in heels and a dress. Only

two of them asked me to clarify, and even though they were polite about it, E hid behind me like a scared little girl.

11. I understand that in Alberta we cannot change the gender on the Birth Certificate from "M" to "F" until she has had her *anatomical sex structure changed to that of the opposite sex,* but the referral for surgery, among many other requirements, demands she be 18 years old. At this point in time, E is thinking she will probably have gender reassignment surgery when she is able. E's body is still changing, and she has years of physical and emotional development before we would consider such permanent options. We are also aware that there are many transgender people who never have any surgeries and continue to live productively in their identified gender. This leaves E as a young teenager with a future of unnecessary public disclosure and years of anxiety, stress, and the real possibility of harm.

12. It is not a secret that E is transgender, but it is a private matter, and we choose to disclose it only when we feel it necessary. All E wants is to live as the girl she feels she has always been inside. As the situation currently sits, she is continually experiencing pronounced and unnecessary psychological stress of a particularly intense sort, and daily fear at a crucial time in a young lady's life. We need to procure documentation that is consistent with how she presents on a day-to-day basis to try to keep her safe and able to lead the normal life of a teenage girl without limitations, discrimination, and constant trepidation.

13. E has given me her permission to file a human rights complaint on her behalf because she and I believe that the requirement to have anatomical sex reassignment surgery before being able to have the gender marker changed on a birth certificate is unfair and discriminatory.

14. I make this affidavit in support of an order that the Alberta Government be directed to change the gender marker on E's birth certificate immediately.

Dr. Gender, our saviour at the Gender Clinic, wrote a passionate and articulate letter from a riverboat on the Mekong River to support Ella while attending the World Professional Association for Transgender Health (WPATH) conference in Thailand. Our wise and wonderful Gender Psychologist wrote her letter of support. The Endocrinologist provided written support, too.

And that was it. Fabulous Lawyer filed it, and I waited for word that changes were happening, like they were in other provinces.

March 5, 2014

My one-on-one trip with Ella and the baby to Gramma's ocean house was, as expected, different than my trip with Jackson. Ella was primarily interested in her wardrobe. It was a challenge to get her into flats on the beach—and in the end, the compromise was a pair of wedge flip-flops.

Ella had been planning the detour to an abandoned ski hill for months. We followed the Google satellite map up a foggy, windy, gravel road until we hit the remains of a ski chalet at the base of a mountain. There was obvious ski runs cut out, which were now barren and starting to grow over.

With the baby sleeping in the truck, Ella and I explored as far as we could possibly walk in three feet of slippery slush. We never spotted the ruins of the actual chair lifts, only the spooky sensation that we were 20 years late to witness a mountain that once crawled with life. Ella clawed her way to a graffiti-ridden wall so I could shoot a portrait. Her corset had been pinching her since the security screen at the airport, and she attempted to take it off. In a smooth move, she lost her balance and dropped her silicone breast form into the snow.

Ella: Merm!!
Me: No way. Your crisis! It's too slippery for me.
Ella: Help me!! I've lost my **BOOB** and I *NEED* you to get it . . .
Me: Not a chance.

She crawls along the concrete wall trying to gather her femininity to recompose.

The trip did give us a chance to hash out a few things and compose a long e-mail to Iain . . .

eMe: Iain—
We have had a chance to talk over a bunch of things this week and here are some of the highlights . . .

Costa Rica
   Ella is scared about flying through Texas (and a bit fearful about flying in general). She has the best documentation we can get for her—but some reassurance and empathy towards her situation will go a long way. I tend to advocate for her like she is a young child, so she doesn't face any discrimination head-on by herself.
   The thought of being forced into jeans for the whole trip is traumatizing her. This is a psychological aversion for her, as I have shared with you before (from Dr. Gender), and if her clothes are appropriate and not provocative that she should not be forced to wear pants. That said . . . we have discussed extensively the need for "appropriate" clothes in a tropical country.
   Bathing suit? Ella hasn't swum for over a year now. I am available to take her shopping Thursday after school to get a few things, if that helps.

General life stuff
   I know you are not comfortable with Ella's flashy sense of style and persona. However, we do not get to dictate what "kind of girl" she is going to be. I completely agree with you that the life skills are lacking (respectful behaviours, getting along in groups, minding other people's feelings, being "helpful" in general) but the things she likes to wear to make herself feel beautiful are beyond us—if they fall within guidelines. For me . . . no boobs, no butt, no belly, and no back is appropriate. Being "dressed for prom" or "overly formal" is okay with me. It's who she is. It is not a reflection of us. It reflects her.

Shoes—we need to limit the time she is spending in heels to ensure her Achilles tendons are not shortened. A couple days a week at school is plenty. We will need to make sure she has appropriate flats for the rest of the time.

Ella has the appetite of a 13-year-old biological male. It is critical that she have healthy food choices available. I know her choices are not always appropriate—and are often gluttonous but we can help guide this with simple guidelines (only one serving of any packaged lunch snack, one portion of food cooked at home, etc.)

At the end of it all, Ella is a smart girl who you think would "get it," but she just doesn't. Going back to rule lists, drawing things out, being clear about expectations and very precise in explanations about when things go wrong will make life easier for all of us.

c

March 8, 2014

A budding successful trans actress from the USA had been coming in and out of my news feed for a few months. Laverne Cox had a fabulous role on *Orange is the New Black,* and she had been featured on a few talk shows that were shared on Facebook.

She was in the Metropolis doing some speaking engagements, and Ella wanted to attend the private workshop she was hosting, "Ain't I a Woman", exclusively for trans women. I excitedly signed Ella up—even though I had trepidations of her being exposed to the more frightening side of the gender minority world; the true tales of violence, discrimination, and damning stereotypes. I knew it was important that she become comfortable seeking community with her peers. I imagined being trans could be lonely in redneck Alberta.

What I loved the most about Laverne was her acting as a "possibility model" instead of a role model. She never misses an opportunity to point out in her gracious and charming way how inappropriate it is to grill transgender people about their genitals and surgeries, and flawlessly moves the conversation into a discussion about the real issues that trans people, especially trans women of colour, face. Kudos to you, Laverne.

March 10, 2014

> Ella: If I die on the operating table when I have my gender reassignment surgery, you have to promise you will make them finish it.
> Me: It's a big surgery, we would be sent to the best professionals in the country. They have really great techniques for male-to-female transitions.
> Ella: Oh, I know all about the surgeries. I'm just worried that if I don't make it that I'd be buried a guy, or even a *half* girl.
> PROMISE ME you will make them finish it, even if I'm already dead.
> Me: I promise, Ella, I will ensure they finish.
> Ella: Pinky swear?
> Me: Pinky swear.

Ella welled up with tears. The depth of her conviction about her gender truth was so apparent. She was not concerned about dying . . . only that she might die with a biologically male physique.

March 12, 2014

Through the months of January and February, my diabetic Uncle David had landed in ICU and then in an extended hospital stay for a serious diabetic ketoacidosis. We were lucky not to have lost him. This event, though, highlighted the severity of his ongoing dementia at 68 years old—a nasty combination of insulin dependence and forgetting if you've eaten or taken insulin.

My aunties worked very hard to clean out, list, and sell his place for his move into an assisted living facility. Uncle David was fortunate to have means to move to a decent building with prepared meals and homecare available. There was a woman in the dining area celebrating her 107th birthday the day we moved David's new bed in. Our society is severely lacking in options for the not-healthy-enough-to-be-alone-but-not-old-enough-to-be-here-yet folk.

David was mangy, three months overdue for a haircut, and I happily offered to chauffeur him—any busy work is favorable to just sitting around trying to think about new things to talk about.

> Uncle David: Well, we must go find Jim.
> Me: Who is Jim?
> Uncle David: Jim has been cutting my hair for 30 years. Stick with what ya know, ya know?
> Me: Where do we find Jim? Do we need an appointment?
> Uncle David: I've never had one before. I will recognize the place.

So off we go in search of Jim. Turned out, it was not too complicated, and the two-chair barber shop at the base of a dated apartment building was empty and waiting for us.

> Jim: David! I've been so worried. Where have you been?
> *Glint of delight in his eye—they hug.*
> Uncle David: Well, I got into trouble with my diabetes and was in the hospital for 3 weeks.
> Me: 3 months.
> Jim: Come. Sit down. Let me clean you up. Tell me about it.
> David, we've shared so much together! Movies, wine . . .
> *Quick glance in my direction and fleeting eyes toward his old friend.*
> Uncle David: She is safe.
> Jim: Oh. Carla. I was MADLY in love with your Uncle David and he just threw me away . . .
> Turned a blind eye to me and carried on with that other guy . . . the piano player!

This launched them into a long and animated hour of talks of unrequited love, hidden lives, and tragic losses. I shared Ella's story with them—they suggested supports and commended me on allowing her to stay true to her spirit. I felt honoured to have felt a sliver of David's *real* life. Not the one I knew from Christmas dinners or from disgruntled tales of Uncle David being too cheap. This was the honest core of a man I hardly knew.

I was saddened when I dropped him back at the doors of his new old-folks home. These were not his peers. These were predominantly heterosexual cisgender old-school seniors in the last phase of living. I hope that by the time Ella is 68, there is a more appropriate place for her to be.

March 15, 2014

This was the month I acknowledged, and accepted, my own looming mid-life crisis. I was nearly 38 and about to head back to work, leaving my sweet baby Jet in the hands of strangers employed at a daycare, surrounded by diaper genies and snotty germs.

I knew the grind of working and juggling a family. It was late nights of meal planning, crisis intervention, and homework review. It was early mornings of dragging kids out of bed and stuffing food they don't feel like eating down their throats to get to somewhere else on time. It was working thousands of hours to pay for the daycare spot where kids get sick, and then can't go because they are sick, for the honour of being able to work at all. This is how North American families raise children.

I resented the continuing education credits I had to complete and the money I had to outlay to reinstate my licence and return to the pharmacy. I enjoyed the work environment and my friends and coworkers at the store—but FUCK. I was relishing motherhood this time. And I was enjoying not being in the front-line firing squad of bitchy housewives out of refills of their Prozac® and fashionistas enraged about the price increases of Botox®. I was tired of working hard to make oodles of money for someone else.

I wanted to be making photographs of the empowering moments of women, and attempting to capture the uniqueness of oddities of society in breathtaking stills. When was it time for *me* to spend my time doing what I loved?

My final decision was to give up self-doubt and just start living. I built a website to showcase my photography and designed a few flyers. I started searching out clients and models. I began shooting children with autism spectrum disorders for an exhibition I had always wanted to create—a fundraiser to highlight the glimmer of light in the eyes of these children when they are engaged, with their passions, the special way they clench their hands with delight, and the way they stretch to the tips of their toes to more deeply feel the sensations around them.

Facebook: I have given up self-doubt for Lent.

No likes.
No comments.
I immediately questioned my decision. Was I too philosophical for my friends? Was I becoming airy-fairy and too "programmy"? Maybe I had the wrong friends!?!
Nope. It was just a prime example of my self-doubt—waiting for Facebook likes to validate my life goals. So, I gave myself a Gold Star ★, and I carried on being brave.

March 16, 2014

iGramma: Dear All or Nothing Daughter,
Re: Many Projects
I know all about that.
Love,
Your All or Nothing Mother

I love Gramma (I imagine by now, you probably do, too). She was a constant infusion of love and grounding insights that undoubtedly made me a better mom, friend, and partner.

Gramma demonstrated, by example, a wonderful way of being. I occasionally sense the vastness of the hole that will be left inside me the day she is no longer walking this journey beside me. It's not possible for her to teach me how to live without her. It will bring me to my knees.

In my younger years, she allowed me to take uncooked packages of ramen noodles and homemade sugar-free chocolate milk (designed for Jeff) for lunch, not because it was healthy, but because she knew I needed comfort food at lunch during the awful time that was junior high.

I easily recall many magical days, such as the blizzardy "snow day" in grade 2, when the whole town lost power and Gramma and I sat in front of a cozy fire with our fluffy Bichon, Muffy. It felt warm despite the snow rapidly accumulating outside the windows and the smell of warm, cozy dog comforted me. Gramma, like a magician, pulled a simple craft kit out from wherever she had it neatly tucked away and we passed the hours easily, together.

My Mother was a woman who did what she had to. She worked years on the road to fill the bank while Papa established a clientele. She had been a frightened young mother who learned to be a nurse and advocate for Jeff with his juvenile diabetes, just a few years after I was born. I took on the role of the "hero-child", not because she demanded it, but because my *little Carla brain* thought mom didn't need any added stressors. Even when frightened with nightmares, I often resisted going to her for comfort, not wanting to add my fear onto her load.

I don't recall many tumultuous patches with my mom. There were a few incidents, many of which involved underage drinking, that I knew disappointed her. When I was about 13, she declared herself on "strike" and refused to do any household tasks until the rest of us stepped up and owned our responsibilities; a clear example of the consequences of crossing her boundaries.

I know now that I will not have the same relationship with my children that my mother and I share. We are different people, in different times and in different places. I am fortunate to have a tangible example of how awesome it can be.

March 17, 2014

Jet was spending most of his days sitting on the floor spinning himself around in circles, playing with Tupperware and the few remaining toys that the dogs had not eaten. He was not eager to crawl, and I delighted in that. The new moms I knew from the baby class were down on all fours doing crawling demonstrations to encourage their babies. I was doing nothing to stimulate any sort of development in that regard. I knew what hell would break loose when he started to move.

Jet had developed a fear of Rosie the Roomba®. The result of this unfortunate course of events was that the amount of dog hair stuck to everything had increased exponentially.

March 28, 2014

Ella was not yet ready for her trip to Costa Rica just days prior to departure. She had her "Ella Margaret Grant", "M" passport to take with her and a few summery dresses, but was missing a few wardrobe essentials for a tropical holiday. She was disheartened that she hadn't been swimming in over a year.

The anxiety of shopping typically kept me garbed in ratty shirts from university days and worn-through shoes with threads barely holding them all together. Ella was my polar opposite—she delighted in the chaos and gluttonous expenditures.

Five grueling hours in a mall with Ella and Jet and over $500 later, she was ready.

> • 1 bathing suit with slits for cups in the bra and a skirt that started at an empire waist line
> *This was a diamond found in the rough . . . The Bay.*
> • 1 new summer dress that did not require dry cleaning, ironing, or special undergarments
> • 4 pairs of compression shorts so she could comfortably wear pants or skirts with flat fronts
> • 1 pair of FLAT flats. No wedges. No heels. No patent leather . . .
> • 1 pair of flip flops

Jackson already had his 2 pairs of shorts, 2 t-shirts, swim trunks, snorkel and fins, and a pair of shoes packed up and ready. Simple.

March 31, 2014

I turned 38. I celebrated my birthday with poutine and a nap. The only thing better would have been a new jar of my Auntie Danelle's dill pickles, home grown on the farm.

April 7, 2014

With the big kids gallivanting in Costa Rica, Arthur and I were free to run away.

I tended to my excruciatingly itchy prickly heat rash covering 63% of my body, Arthur nursed the blisters on the soles of his feet and his crispy red lobster sunburn, and Jet burned up with fever and exploded with traveller's diarrhea. It was our third day in Mexican paradise.

We had planted ourselves beside a tropical pool overlooking the Mayan's turquoise waters. The couple next to us introduced themselves and their only child, Gracie. Mom had an enormous My Little Pony tattoo on her back, and I thought she was exceptionally funky. They had travelled from England, away from the "type of people" who vacation in Majorca.

> Cool girl: I must say, you look fabulous for having had 3 kids.
> Me: I feel about 50 years too old and 20 pounds too large—but I do appreciate the compliment.
> *The stunning cool girl thought I was a hotty mama! Unlike Ella, who continually described me as having looked "like I had been run over by life".*
> Me: It's certainly not from putting much effort into eating well or taking particularly good care of myself.
> *Though I was secretly proud of myself for having dropped 25 pounds in preparation for this trip.*
> Cool girl: Everything in moderation?
> Me: Not even a little bit!
> *Belly laugh.*
> Cool girl: Gracie will be our only child. I'm loving just having one.
> Me: I thought we would have one more because of the split between my older kids and this "only child". But in all honesty, I'm so in love with being able to dote over just him . . . I'm not so sure anymore.

She had mistaken us for American because we were not displaying the maple leaf proudly on our bodies and luggage. This lead to comparing tales of the drunken Canadians that had invaded the serene pool space the afternoon before. A sunburnt child being tossed around from one drunk adult to another. Cigarettes, which would surely prevent the delivery of their 100th birthday card from the Queen, according to Gracie, were dropped carelessly in the pool. Beer spilled in rivers running across the reflective concrete.

I had been those drunken fools in years past . . . crazy Carla. At each meal when the waiter brought us free cocktails and Arthur and I sent them back in exchange for virgin mojitos, I felt a bit sorry for myself. I was addicted to the craziness.

But each morning when I woke and could recall the night before in its entirety and having made no particularly bad decisions, I was grateful for sobriety.

April 13, 2014

> ilain: I am at Payless Shoes . . . with you know who.
> iMe: For what? Does she need more?!?
> ilain: Ach, I don't know.
> Sale.
> Bigger problem is the 17 yr old hitting on her.
> iMe: Chase? That guy is creepy jeepy. Ella knows that.
> ilain: I don't think she's getting the message.

I didn't know if Chase was female or male, straight or gay, or anything in between. From all Facebook and gossipy tales though, Chase was anything but asexual. Ella liked the attention. I didn't like the risk. Typical teenage problem with an atypical twist.

April 14, 2014

I wasn't sure if it was the lunar eclipse of the full moon that was making me so irritable and high strung, or if something else was up energetically speaking. I had fought with Arthur about finances, scolded Jackson about being a grumpy self-entitled brat, and picked at Ella about her attire. Jet was spared the wrath of my mood; who can get angry at someone who is content to amuse himself with a sock for an hour?

I listened to a few TED talks.[25] One talked about the high bar we have set for ourselves as parents by naming "happiness" as the goal for our children.[26] Happiness is impossible to define, and even harder to maintain or explain. I agreed with the speaker that maybe the Hippocratic Oath was a more reasonable parenting style (a verb only since the 1970s). My goal . . . just don't do too much harm!

The talk had sent me immediately back into a small scene with the chip sample lady at Costco who, just the day before, had scolded me for allowing Jet to chew on the flyer they handed me at the door.

Chip lady: Don't let him eat that! It has **ARSENIC** in it. I used to work in the paper industry.
I yank the paper away from Jet, secretly hoping he SCREAMS about it, and she will feel badly about commenting on my parenting.
How dare she judge me? She has NO clue about the challenges I have faced.
I was livid and my face was numb.
Me: Your chip dip is AWFUL.

My reaction to her comment had been totally disproportionate. This was not the first time this had happened . . . just the week before, a woman at our table in Mexico had mentioned to me that the baby I was ignoring was eating bits of paper chewed off a pamphlet he was examining.

Me: I would rather he ate paper than scream all meal.
Judgemental interfering woman: I would rather he scream than choke.
I RAGED inside.

---

25   TED is a nonprofit organization devoted to spreading ideas, usually in the form of short, powerful talks. www.ted.com
26   Senior, J. (2014, March). For parents, happiness is a very high bar [Video file]. Retrieved from https://www.ted.com/talks/jennifer_senior_for_parents_happiness_is_a_very_high_bar?language=en

On another occasion at work, when a childless co-worker commented that a mother should "take the screaming child home", I erupted in defense for the attacked mother (who, of course, hadn't even heard the comment over the tantrum-throwing toddler).

> Me: Maaaaaybe that child had autism and she *can't* settle him. Maaaaaybe she is a single mother who has no choice but to pick up his medications right now.
> Maaaaaybe you should shut your mouth about things you have NO clue about . . .

The button inside me that got pushed when parents are judged for how or what they are doing with their children was a large, hot one. It probably served some purpose earlier in my life—to protect myself from comments about inadequate child-rearing while I was drunk, and possibly to hide behind my own inadequacies of raising challenging spirits.

I think the way I began to unplug that button was by validating my own value and strength as a mother. The more confident I was in my parenting decisions, the less I needed others to validate them. Raising children is a difficult, underpaid, never-ending, and often thankless endeavor. It's the best job in the world, and the hardest by far.

April 15, 2014

Maybe in my fragile, full-moon state I shouldn't have subjected myself to any more "educational" material—but since I couldn't sleep anyways with my jittery legs I indulged myself in another TED talk. I should have opted for an episode of *Criminal Minds* instead.

Decker Moss[27] gave 18 minutes of poignant, educated facts and personal accounts of being transgender. He talked of his coming out, his emotional and physical transitions and about continued obstacles with misgendering, documentation, life, and legalities. He eloquently explained how gender occurs between the ears, not between the legs. He imagined a world where people are free to choose the gender and pronouns that are true for them. I was foolishly sucked into reading some of the comments left by listeners. I think I need to stick to the cardinal rule of never reading comments on a post, EVER.

27   Moss, D. (2013, December). Hey doc, some boys are born girls [Video file]. Retrieved from http://tedxtalks.ted.com/video/Hey-Doc-some-boys-are-born-girl

Ugh . . . just because you "feel" like a man, doesn't mean you are one. If a Dog felt like a Cat and acted like a Cat, would that mean the Dog is a Cat? NO. It's STILL and WILL ALWAYS be a Dog.

Sorry cupcake. Gender isnt [sic] assigned by a doctor. Your [sic] a boy or a girl and that's all there is too [sic] it. Cant [sic] change genetics. Blame your mom for drinking while you where in the womb.

What an absolute fucking freak of nature. The nerve of this creature to demand a world where when we meet someone we ask them "what pronouns do you prefer"? Get the fuck out of here!

April 24, 2014

I went to the registry.

> Me: I need the form to change the gender on a birth certificate.
> Lady: Was there an *accident?*
> *I'd love to have known what kind of accident she could have possibly been referring to . . .*
> Me: A what?!?
> Lady: Like an error, a mistake?
> Me: Yes.
> Lady: I don't think there is a form for that.
> Me: Then how do I request the change?
> Lady: Maybe Vital Statistics does that?
> Me: That is profoundly unhelpful.
> Lady: Sorry, you can have a legal name change form.
> Me: I have already changed her name. Now I want to change her gender.
> Lady: Yeah. I don't know anything about that. Maybe a surgeon can help?

Ugh. I eventually found a form online and sent it to Fabulous Lawyer . . . I kept pushing . . .

And Ella was bummed out. She had been very strong for a very long time, and I think she was crashing a bit. Her last Lupron® shot just about did her in—tears and uncertainty.

And Jet was now proficiently scooching from room to room. I needed to install baby gates.

And Jackson was mourning the loss of the ice that had melted away from the outdoor rink down the street—it had been his easy winter hideaway.

And Arthur had vanished. Escaping.

And I was supposed to be doing my pharmacy homework for an injection certification course at the insistence of someone I no longer felt compelled to work hard for . . . and a few hundred hours of photo editing I could barely stay awake for.

It wasn't our shining moment.

May 2, 2014

It was now four months past the date of the big "outing" at school. I had been naïve to think things could happen quickly in the bureaucracy that is the Government of Alberta.

I checked in with the Office of the Privacy Commissioner, who admitted to having just sent a *first* contact letter to the Education Minister and the Metropolis Public School Board.

Nothing was happening quickly with the human rights complaints. It sat in a pile of other complaints.

And children continued to be at risk in classrooms across the province.

May 3, 2014

My adventure into photography land had started to result in paid work—motivation for me so I was able to buy the lenses I longed for. There were some maternity shoots, some family sessions, and a few birth stories—which were by far my favorite and the most difficult to work into my life.

The downside to this was that I had to *deliver*, and couldn't fake this one—a big family wedding. I found a second shooter for moral and technical support and dove into my first wedding. Egad. Luckily for me, I am very able to stay distanced from the emotional craziness that is a wedding—I'm not a girl who had been dreaming of being wrapped up like a white parcel and "given" to her husband. Perhaps this was also the reason Arthur and I were perpetually engaged.

iMe: I'm freaked right out.
iGramma: They'll never see the blurry ones.
iMe: What if they are ALL bad?!?
iGramma: Capture the emotion. That's what they want and that's what you always do so well. Once you get started tomorrow, you'll be fine. Try some shots at rehearsal tonight!
iMe: Is there one?!? F@%# I didn't know that!!!

Like an unstoppable force, the wedding happened. It all happened. The hair crisis, the sleet and rain, the poorly-lit, tacky hotel room. And I was there, taking photos, like a smooth imposter photographer.

They loved them. I saw room for potential and improvement. Did I want to be a wedding photographer? No. I did, however, believe dabbling in an array of photography genres would make me better to shooting the subject matter I longed for; after all, how different is the pressure of catching "the kiss" than catching the moment a mom holds her newborn for the first time? I had never felt braver than when I was being vulnerable.

May 11, 2014

iGramma: Happy Mother's Day to the BEST mom ever . . . I hope today doesn't wear you out, like other mother's days!

A traditional Mother's Day meal out was a nightmare for me. One that usually consisted of misbehaved children, underwhelming cuisine, and an inflated tab. I had released my expectations for the day to be anything but like any other day—when moms worked hard and shit happens. 💩

We had developed our own little tradition, though. Off we went to A&W for a "Mama Burger" and a trip to a greenhouse to inspire things to come when the cold chill finally left the early morning air. It was uncomplicated. It was our thing and I liked it.

I attempted to take a photo of all my children.

May 23, 2014

iMe: This is the outfit for "Queer Prom". I realize it is "older" than her and elegant for 13. It's an "over the top event"—more like a safe costume party than a junior high dance. She will be with her peeps. Could you pick her up at 11 p.m.?
ilain: Nope. Not at 11 p.m. She's 13, and she's getting picked up early.

She's still young, regardless of the event. The intensity of her anxiety often fogs up my parenting goggles.

May 24, 2014

Jet was 1! He dove face first into the cake. The rest of us enjoyed eating the bits of smashed up cake for breakfast. Gramma and Papa joined us for the weekend, so a trip to Toys R Us was in order. Arthur selected an abstract, hard plastic, red, animal-like thing that all children walking into the store claimed was cool. Papa chose a Fisher Price Zoo for our monkey. We enjoyed a meal out, where Jet showed off his spitting skills to the wait staff.

I had simplified my expectations of birthdays. Ella and Jackson had lavish parties when they were young—friends, piñatas, and cakes I had paid others to intricately decorate.

May 26, 2014

> iMe: I have an appt with Jean-Paul, the principal of Suburbia Junior High, to discuss the possibility of Ella returning for grade 9 on Thursday at 15:30, if you want to join.
> ilain: Would love to, but swamped here.

I needed my chart to evaluate this one . . . not even just a pro/con list. My left-brained "Ella Returning to Suburbia Junior High Decision Rubric".

Pros to Suburbia Junior High	Pros to the Arts School
• Ella wants to • Academics are superior, teacher is outstanding • Transition back into peer group before hitting high school • No more city bus rides • She has made a hash out of the urban environment, and the faster she is out the better	• The arts program at the Arts School is well known and produces outstanding students who do well in the industry—one where Ella may go • Hold steadfast to be able to push the breach of privacy issue further • My adult brain tells me that she is/will be more accepted in the liberal arts environment than in a conservative stuck-up small suburban high school

Cons to Suburbia Junior High	Cons to the Arts School
• Sending Ella for grade 9 back to the school where she attended as "Eliot" for grade 7 is INSANE • Reinforces that when things are not perfect she can leave instead of working to fix it • She hasn't hit the best parts of the Arts School programming (the higher-level courses) • It was HARD WORK to get her into the school, and we likely won't have another chance	• Ella remains where she is—moderately successful in a few subjects but highly anxious and exhausted • I want to minimize the sentiment of places she can't go because she is trans

Ella's decision-making process: I want to. So, everyone should want me to.

May 28, 2014

Boobs. Now, I had been a teen obsessed with my non-breasts for a long time. I pestered my mom long enough for her to buy me a training bra for the raisins on my bread board. It was normalizing to have a bra strap to snap and something tangible to obsess about in a mirror. Ella was me to the power of 10 million.

iElla: *Ella spams me with links to breast forms*
I'm a size 5
Nvm, I'm a size 6
So that would make me a 32C
More links to fake-perky-nipple-boobs and mastectomy prosthetics
Merm?
Got some fake nails and elbow length black gloves
iMe: I'm tired.

May 29, 2014

Sitting in the principal's office at the school where Ella attended grade 7 were myself, the long-haired, French-Canadian principal Jean-Paul, and Ella's most awesome teacher, Ellen.

Jean-Paul: Some 'udder district principals and I met las' year and **ALL** agree that we would **NOT** have a Gay-Straight-Alliance in da' school. We support diversity, but we choose to not single out **sex**. Kids dese days are overly sexualized as is.
"If we teach them about sex, then they will have sex" rings in my ears.
He doesn't even know the difference between sex and gender!!
Ellen: What will she be wearing? I simply don't know if the kids here are ready for her.
Me: She will likely be dressed like you or I would for church, every day. At least for a few months until she likes something new . . .
Jean-Paul: **IF** she coming here for the academics, she are welcome. If she coming here to be "champion of sexuality", it will be a problem.
Me: Ella doesn't want a GSA. She just wants to live as the girl she is. It will be me on the front step with a rainbow flag, if there are any problems.

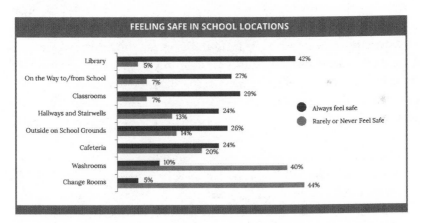

Published findings from the Canadian Trans Youth Health Survey, entitled *Being Safe, Being Me,* shows how clearly unsafe these kids feel in school.[28] I envisioned Ella hiding in a library for the entirety of her 9th grade and never peeing, ever.

28   Veale J, Saewyc E, Frohard-Dourlent H, Dobson S, Clark B & the Canadian Trans Youth Health Survey Research Group. (2015). *Being Safe, Being Me: Results of the Canadian Trans Youth Health Survey*. Vancouver, BC: Stigma and Resilience Among Vulnerable Youth Centre, School of Nursing, University of British Columbia. Retrieved from https://saravyc.sites.olt.ubc.ca/files/2015/05/SARAVYC_Trans-Youth-Health-Report_EN_ Final_Web2.pdf

May 30, 2014

> iMe: On another note . . . there is a family doctor in the
> Metropolis who is taking referrals for transgender patients to
> better coordinate their care. Do you think it would be worth Ella
> switching family doctors? Family Doctor knows NOTHING about
> her . . . he hardly even looked her in the eye last time we were
> there. Might be worth having someone more invested in her well-
> being over the next few years.
> ilain: *No response*

The medical community, in general, has done a very poor job of embracing this segment of the population. They were not educated about gender variance, and many, until recently, probably never even knew they had any in their care. The norm is for the physician to become visibly uncomfortable and refer, denying any potential help that they could possibly offer.

The Endocrinologist was needed in our case because of Ella's age, and the complexities of navigating puberty. It's the horror stories of mature, sound-minded adults who simply desire a prescription for estrogen or some spironolactone that any medical doctor is competent and able to deliver—but WON'T. They are left to wait and wait, bearing their incredible burden every day, and we already know the well-documented dire consequences.

Get educated, doctors. Get as comfortable with a patient you thought of as male needing estrogen as you are sticking a speculum in a biological female. Educate your staff so they stop humiliating patients at your desk. There is no need to loudly question someone about a gender marker they may not be able to afford to change. Keep uneducated opinions to yourself. Speaking with staff about the "weird" or "odd" patient is at least unethical, and at most a violation of your oath to do no harm, when someone overhears that bullshit.

#endrant

June 1, 2014

> iMe: Good news. The building where RONA used to be is going to
> be a Value Village!!
> iElla: Oh.
> My.
> God.
> Can you order some new boobs for me?

June 2, 2014

> iIain: Ella drama. Becoming very tiresome, and I would like
> an extended summit meeting with all parents at the earliest
> opportunity.
> 4 a.m. texts she sent from the basement about vomiting "4 times"
> in the night. Something is going on at school that we don't know
> about.
> We are approaching a very hard line on the suffering Hollywood
> starlet routine, and a crackdown is coming re: accountability. We
> will need to be on same page. The diva has to go. She's had her fun,
> time now to get real.

June 3, 2014

Five months now since the outing. I connected with Fabulous
Lawyer. We decided to press the Human Rights complaint harder,
knowing other similar cases were being heard. We couldn't wait for
the "anticipated regulations", in case they never came to fruition, or
didn't include minors, or a million other outcomes I played through
in my busy mind.

More e-mails sent. More closed-door meetings happened. More
red tape. Where was that machete?

June 6, 2014

Papa is a brilliantly quiet, and quietly brilliant, man. Throughout
my childhood, his life was organized into lists and spreadsheets and
drawers and cubbies. I understood very easily where he was coming

from and where he was going. His creative niche was woodworking, and the smell of sawdust still takes me right back to playing in his woodshop when I was young.

He invited Jackson to join him on an out-of-town weekend course—the product was to be a hand-crafted longboard. We delivered the young skate fanatic to Papa, and they went on their way. A weekend all to themselves. Eating out every meal. Sawdust and tools. They both loved it.

They were both very proud of their gorgeous project. It had given Jackson another little break from the unusual occurrences at the Gemstone, and Papa a chance to reconnect with the "middle" grandchild who was too often quashed between Eccentric Ella and Baby Blue Eyes.

June 7, 2014

iElla: In a dramatic turn of events, my Jehovah's Witness friend asked me if I could go to Pride parade with her.

June 10, 2014

iMe: You coming to the meeting at Suburbia Junior High?
ilain: Fuck, no. Sorry. Seriously. I know it's important.

After Ella gave the principal a socially inappropriate, and autistically common "too tight for too long" hug, we sat across from Jean-Paul at his intimidating desk. I was expecting a fight. Ella was clueless about the behind-the-scenes maneuvering that had occurred on her behalf. I had a bitter taste lingering from the tone of our last meeting and was not optimistic about this one either.

Jean-Paul: So. Ella. You need to know we support you 100%. I want you to benefit from academics with the rest of da school. Come, let us have a tour of da washrooms.

And off we went, with the obviously newly-educated principal on a tour of all the washrooms. Ella was asked if she was comfortable with using each of them. He had already had a key cut for the private changeroom if she chose to use that for any reason.

> Jean-Paul: We have no GSA, but we encourage diversity. I also asked someone from the Institute of Sexual Minority Studies at da L'University to speak with da staff at da September meeting to make sure we can support Ella da best way.
> I think, though, Ella, it might be easier to no do physical education this year. I do not believe the teacher is an accommodating person and I know da changing is 'ard for you.

Ella cheered. Excusing her from a mandatory class was a blessing for Ella—the girl who hated sweating and being out of breath and who had obvious physical limitations when trying to be discreet with her body. I imagined the conversations that must have occurred between Jean-Paul and the higher-ups ending with "Let's just not deal with the fallout from the other parents by excusing her from being required to change anywhere." Regardless, I was pleased that Jean-Paul had done his homework and had changed his tone. Ella was thrilled, and the decision was made. She would return to Suburbia Junior High for her grade 9 year—the same school she had left as "Eliot" just a year earlier.

June 11, 2014
This was NEWS!

> Mr. Fabulous Lawyer,
> This is a follow-up to the correspondence that my client, the Registrar of Vital Statistics, received from your office dated June 3, 2014, in which you requested a timelier response to a request to amend your client's birth record rather than awaiting the development and proclamation of regulations to deal with circumstances like your client's.
> I am pleased on behalf of my client to inform you that upon **sincere reconsideration, the Registrar will process the application for an amendment to the birth record** [my emphasis] of your minor client.
> The Registrar is eager to assist and guide your client directly through the amendment process. I would recommend that your

clients contact Ms. Very Helpful, and she will be able to assist in a speedy turn around on this application.

To amend the child's legal birth record, Vital Statistics will require the following documents:

- **A Statutory Declaration**
- **Written consent from the child**
- **A letter from a physician or psychologist**
- **A $20.00 amendment fee**

I trust this will be to your client's and your liking and that you will not hesitate to contact me at your earliest convenience should you or your client require any clarification.

Government Lawyer

June 14, 2014

iElla: Can you take in my purple dress and ask if it can be done for Thursday? There's a tailor in the mall. Remember, hole at base of zipper and 2 inches off each strap.

iMe: I think you have enough other dresses to choose from . . . pick one that won't cost me any money?!? Why don't you wear the fancy silver dress?

iElla: Not enough boobage.

Speaking of boobage, have you ordered the new ones yet?

June 15, 2014

I had never been so sick of boobs in my life.

iElla: What cup size are the new bewbies?

iMe: Whatever you asked me to order . . . 6, I think?

iElla: I meant are they 30C or 32C or wat.

Did you order the cleavage creator?

iMe: No. Please leave me alone.

I don't wanna taco 'bout it.

Why don't you wanna' TACO 'bout it!

'Cause I'm NACHO friend anymore.

June 16, 2014

iElla: I'm a teary mess.
iMe: Why?!?
iElla: Well somewhere between the stress of school and the birth
certificate change and how sick I feel I don't really know . . . and

Alberta Gives New Birth Certificate to 12-year-old Boy who was Born a Girl

A 12-year-old transgender Alberta boy has been granted a new birth certificate that recognizes him as male.

A child was presented with the new document on Sunday in the Metropolis during a Pride festival brunch hosted by the city's mayor.

A spokesperson for the minister says the new certificate simply has an "M" instead of an "F".[29]

iElla: ALL THAT HARD WORK AND WE GET TO GO TO THE BACK OF
THE LINE ☹
iMe: The reason we worked hard was because it was important.
And we helped make an important change. We got what we
wanted . . . an "F" birth certificate and for the schools to fix their
computer to protect trans kids.
I'm proud of us, regardless of who was "first".
iElla: I know I know.
We do all this work for a good cause and nobody even gives a
damn.
iMe: I'm delighted for the boy and his family. They are not unlike us
☹
It takes an army of people on all sorts of different fronts to make
changes . . .
I was saddened I didn't know more of them. Where are they? How do
we connect with each other? Why are we all typing mad complaints
and duplicating research alone on parallel paths?

29   The Canadian Press. (2014). *Alberta gives new birth certificate to 12-year-old boy who was born a girl*. Retrieved June 15, 2014 from http://globalnews.ca/news/1395508/ alberta-gives-new-birth-certificate-to-12-year-old-boy-who-was-born-a-girl/

Like mother like daughter, Ella and I both pouted a bit, mostly over Blizzards. Other trans people and parents had been fighting this battle and had hit this milestone first. As petty and ridiculous as it sounds, silver was hard. It wasn't the big Human Rights Tribunal I had envisioned, but I know our efforts put pressure on the issue, created more awareness, and were certainly a catalyst for change.

We stuck with "Ella was the first *male-to-female* trans minor to have her birth certificate gender amended in Alberta!"

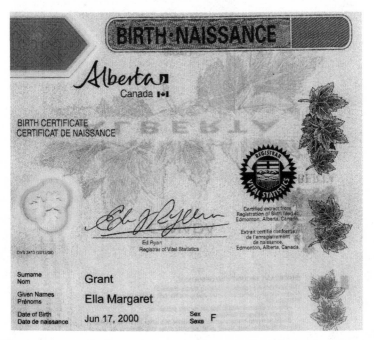

We systematically began changing her name and gender everywhere we could—the bank, the school, the doctor, the pharmacy, the summer camps, her SIN, her education funds . . . it's everywhere.

> Ella: Does this mean I wouldn't have to tell my boss that I'm trans?
> Me: That is exactly what this means.

June 17, 2014
Ella had a new ride for her 14th birthday. She was excited she could fix her lipstick in the little mirrors. Something to lighten her mood.

June 22, 2014

I had a very sick baby. It takes time and exposure to develop immunity to all the things that live in snot. Jet was spiking fevers of 104, had an infection in both eyes, one ear, and his chest.

And off to work I went, leaving poor Arthur to deal with a sweet little one who only wanted to be consoled by nursing. It tore me up inside. This was quite unlike the sentiments I had going back to work with the older two—then I was ready for adult connections and not concerned more with "mommy-and-me" this and that, surrounded by all the physical stuff representing the new age of parenting. With Jet, the bond was much more fulfilling and organic. I was just nurturing his little soul.

June 23, 2014

Ella did not finish grade 8 at the Arts School on the high note that I thought she would. She sulked home on the last day of classes, impressed with nothing but the leftover pop and candy she got to bring for the end-of-year celebrations. She did not make plans to see anyone over the summer, she didn't want her copy of the yearbook, she was totally done with the school we thought would be a good fit for her, but in the end, wasn't.

On top of the end of a momentous year of change, however, was an underlying anxiety and mood I recognized all too well. I saw her struggling, and I was frustrated with my "co-parenting" staff who only saw the negative consequences of those struggles.

iMe: The men are all against medications. I would like to tell them to shove their opinions up their asses until they show up and help her out on their own . . .
I would like to tell them (and I might) "Why don't you take this opportunity to do your own research and meet with experts to collect their opinions, reflect on all the people in our family who benefit from appropriate treatment of mental health issues, and analyze the results of all your "strategies" to date. Then, and only then, will I meet to discuss this as a group. Until that happens, I want veto power on this one."
iGramma: And why don't you do just that?
iMe: I might . . .

Her anxiety was crippling. I couldn't see the eccentric, flamboyant spirit I knew her to have. She was awfulizing everything, dealing with her horrific imagery, binge eating, and struggling with concentration.

I did not engage with the men in what I knew would be a disagreement about treatment waiting to happen. I started her on the medication and just waited the necessary 4 weeks for her chemistry to respond.

iIain: Ella was lovely this week. Why the change?
iMe: Prozac®

June 26, 2014

The boobs arrived in a discreet brown paper covered box, carefully labelled, with no obvious sender.

iElla: Euhhhh Merm can I get off the bus at your house, pick up my package, then can you drive me to Dad's?
iMe: No. I will deliver the package when it is convenient for me.
iElla: Uhhhh can u please try to drop off the package before 4? Sorta a personal package that I'd rather not get in front of Dad. Merm? Hello?
iMe: Out front.
Nothing. Radio silence. No feedback yet . . . Wait for it . . .

iElla: MYYYYY MILKSHAKE BRINGS ALL THE BOYS TO THE YARD

The bra is thin and the nipples on the breast forms show through
iMe: That can be easily fixed with a thicker bra
iElla: Also, what's a full bra and what are nipple covers?
They look enormous from the side but not so much from the front
Oh, and new breast forms plus old breast forms equals one very happy Ella
With both I'm about a 34C
iMe: Both is excessive . . . don't be greedy
iElla: Keep in mind I'm short and fat, so they aren't disproportionately large
Just the new ones are heavy and kinda sag . . . might just be the bra though . . .
iMe: Boobs ARE heavy and they DO sag!!

June 30, 2014

> iElla: Hey Merm. I came up with an idea for a movie and I was
> wondering if you'd be able to do the filming with all my friends at
> your house this weekend?
> iMe: Working. Again.
> iElla: Till when?
> iMe: Midnight
> iElla: Oh. Are u on a break?
> iMe: No. No supper breaks. No pee breaks.
> iElla: Oh ☹ **sends virtual hug**

I was selling a bit of my soul to fulfill my mat-leave commitment.
I loathed it. Even though I had only been back a few months, I was
trying hard to resist collapse.

July 1, 2014

> iMe: Happy Birthday, Jackson!!! 🍁🍁🍁🍁🍁🍁🍁🍁
> 🎂🎉🎂🎉🎂🎉🎂🎉
> ❤ mom xox

Jackson was having a wildly wonderful summer largely due to
the freedom afforded by having a mother who was too burnt-out to
engage and a sister and brother who both demanded the remaining
morsel of her energy. He biked and boarded. He went dampolining
and swimming. His easy-going nature and positivity were such a
blessing amongst our chaos and change.

July 2, 2014

I was contacted by a former pharmacist intern of mine who thought of me when she was asked to recommend someone for a teaching position in a Bridging Program for internationally trained pharmacists. My plate was already full, but I interviewed regardless and was offered the part-time teaching contract.

I needed *ANOTHER* job like I needed a fork in my eye.

The job meant a change in my free time to work ratio, which now approached 1:99 and encroached on the hours I should really have been sleeping.

It meant early mornings and late nights of curriculum development and digging deep into therapeutic textbooks I hadn't read since graduation. It meant working until midnight in my retail location, arriving home to nurse the baby at 00:30, 03:30, and 05:30, then getting him up and out the door to day care when it was still dark to be ready to teach twice a week. Oh, and teenagers?

It also meant a break from the punishment of retail and working with motivated, engaged learners driven to licence and work in Canada. It meant being able to share my years of pharmacy with people who would benefit in a life-changing way. It was a job that reignited my interest in pharmacy and I dove in, knowing it would either be the end of me, or a new beginning.

July 3, 2014

The list of things to **NOT** say to the parents of a transgender child, or to me anyways.

1. God doesn't make mistakes.[30]
2. Are you sure this isn't a phase?
3. They'll feel differently when they get older.
4. I hope you are in some good therapy.
5. How does that work? Are *they* even allowed to use my bathroom?
6. How could you force her into this?
7. Is she having *the surgery*?
8. I don't believe in "transgender".
9. He'll always be a boy to me.

---

30   "Yes he did. Have you seen me?" ~ Ella, 2014

10. You can do what you want in your home, but don't expect anyone outside to act any differently.

11. She's going to have such a difficult life now.

12. It must be the hormones in that cheap meat you fed them.

13. Those clothes attract too much attention—can't she just be more discreet?

14. Why can't you just let her be gay?

15. She is too young to know.

16. How could you let your child choose to do this?

17. Hate the sin, not the sinner.

18. My kid wanted to be a dog—

19. Don't come crying when she gets bullied.

20. You're doing this because you've always wanted a girl.

July 5, 2014

Ella was already making big plans for fYrefly. This was her first year attending as a young adult who could stay for the duration of the camp. I was understandably anxious after seeing the hooker that came home after the previous year's event, but I was also moderately hopeful she had learned *something* over the past year. I also implicitly trusted the competence and finely-honed facilitation skills of the leaders and counsellors.

There had been some communication about an all-gender swim during the event. Many in the group had not been swimming in many years—understandable in this population, some of whom have bodies in all stages of transition that wouldn't necessarily be accepted by everyone at a small town "family swim" on a Sunday evening at the local pool.

> iElla: Do they provide shirts for swimming or what?
> Also, can my bforms get wet?
> iMe: Wear your old ones—the chlorine could eat up the new ones.
> iElla: What if they were in Ziploc bags or something?
> iMe: No swimming in a pool with boobs worth more than my first car.
> iElla: Wait . . . you can get a car for 280 bucks?
> iMe: No.
> 280 each. And I bought that Sentra 20 years ago!

And in Ella fashion, the product returned from fYrefly was as outrageous as ever, but happy. She had connected with her true peeps and bonded with kindred spirits. There was no way Suburbia was ready for this.

"Remind your daughter that the best thing she can do with her body is to use it to mobilize her beautiful soul".[31]

~ Sarah Koppelkam

July 7, 2014
Ella was back at Film Camp.

I was thrilled to see this small change on the consent form following last year's discussions . . . this is how changes start to happen.

Registrant Information (Please print clearly)

Last Name: _____

First Name: _____ Middle Name: _____

Preferred First Name (if different from legal): _____

---

31   Koppelkam, S. (2013). How to talk to your daughter about her body. [Web log comment] Retrieved July 3, 2013 from http://www.huffingtonpost.com/sarah-koppelkam/body-image_b_3678534.html

iElla: I'm the leading lady in a horror movie! Grey suit and all—like my favorite Hitchcock blonde, Madeline Elster!
iMe: I love it when you find your groove.

July 14, 2014

iElla: List for Suburbia Junior High—Tell me if you approve
High-waisted shorts (I tried some on for a costume and they were flattering)
Oversized/print/long tops
Leggings
Wedge sneakers
Graphic tees (they look pretty cool with pleated skirts)
And hair bows—LOTS of hair bows
Also, high top (Converse®) sneakers or Osiris®
Add ballet wrap tops. Like the ones that fold over and wrap and tie in the back
And hoodies and beanies. Those look good on everyone. Speaking of hoodies, there're some really nice ones at the store . . .
iMe: Then you better start earning some money! I'll start a list of extra chores you can do for money.
iElla: Oh.

July 17, 2014

Over the years, Iain and I had tried various separation arrangements with the kids; week-on week-off was the best we could arrange to minimize emergency pick-up-forgotten-shrapnel trips, to make plans for a full week cycle and follow them through, and to not have them missing either of us for extended periods. At times, I resented the 50-50 concept because I often felt that I bore the lion's share of the coordination, which tipped me far beyond 50%. To be fair, I could never have given that up; I am a true control freak.

Perfectionist Me: If I don't do it, it won't get done *right*.
Conceited Me: My way is the *best* way.
Resentful Me: If your dad had done this, then *I wouldn't have to* . . .

As the years have passed, I gained much more trust in the benefits of co-parenting. My arrogance and control has waned into humility and respect. With Iain, they had Monday evening "welcome-back" dinners at Tim Horton's, special bath nights (which needed only a candle and scented bubble bath), family walks, and a solid commitment to international exploration. With me they had the comfort that comes from being grounded in a home like the Gemstone, the freedom to make more messes (but more chores to clean it all up), the predictability of schedules and plans, and the unconditional love of canine companions!

I love it when they are with me; I love it when they are not. That is not just lip service. I don't pine for them . . . I *like* leaving the bathroom door open, and I *like it* when my leftovers from the night before are still in the fridge the next day. I don't know if this was a decision I'd made soon after my separation or if it was just a coping mechanism, but I didn't need any more SAD[32].

July 19, 2014

Now having firmly accepted the realization that I would never be mother-of-a-daughter-giving-birth, I allowed myself to become engulfed in birth photography; to live vicariously through my camera. Don't think medical textbook, or those awful videos you may have been forced to watch in prenatal class. It was capturing loving connections between mom, dad, and baby. It was strength and elation. For a girl who is not great at noticing subtle emotions, there is nothing more charged than a birth.

iSalome: 03:21 I think baby is on the way.

I was a fly on the wall. I captured little moments passing by while she was in her birthing trance, supported by her husband in their bedroom. Big brother passed the time with a cherished friend watching shows and eating birth day treats downstairs. The expert hands of the midwives guided her through contraction after contraction and Salome brought childbirth back to its simple, organic beginnings. It was hypnotic.

---

32   Another hard feeling word I can't pinpoint.

While birth photography was an impractical full-time pursuit for a working mom of three requiring childcare and a certain amount of stability, it was a newfound passion and my gift to the moms-to-be in my life.

July 25, 2014

Jackson thinks it would be funny and somehow changes a setting in my iPhone to autocorrect "Jet" to "Acid". I didn't know how to change it back. Nor did I have the energy to even bother Googling it.

July 26, 2014

> iElla: Merm! Can I sleep over at my friend Jewel's house tomorrow night? She invited me.
> iMe: Is Jewel from fYrefly?
> Gender? How old?
> iElla: Yep
> Girl. I don't know.
> She does drag makeup and I do video . . . she wanted me to help edit a drag makeup tutorial for YouTube
> iMe: I have no problem with you hanging out ☺
> I do have a problem with a drag video online and negative/ dangerous publicity ☹
> iElla: She's doing the makeup on herself.
> iMe: Ok. No names?

Once you put it out there, you can never get it back. The digital memory of the internet can be so damaging. I have often thought about how grateful I am there were no cell phones in my youth. There were very few places a video or photo would even be taken, let alone spread in a viral fashion in a short period of time. I don't know how I would have handled the social repercussions or the emotional fallout of *everyone* seeing me doing stupid things at varying degrees of intoxication or sobriety.

August 2, 2014

Ella begged me to drive her into City Hall to meet a group of kids from fYrefly—a reunion of sorts. I ran through my typical list of excuses, and then I agreed. I put my curriculum work away and went to just hang out with my kids and a camera.

Jet and I sat by the fountain and just puttered. Ella flitted around with her friends, showing up every hour or so, eventually leeching every dollar I had out of my pocket. She mostly enjoyed the company of her new friend Jewel.

When Jet voiced his frustration, and demanded to go home for a nap, we arrived back to the car with the same enormous pile of baby debris we had left with piled into the stroller. But not the keys. I could clearly see them sitting on the front seat of the car, locked inside. With my wallet. And the phone charger for my now-dead phone.

I was stuck downtown with a hungry, tired baby and a flat broke teenager. I was angry but managed to pull together a plan involving Arthur, AMA, and a kind man who let me borrow his phone.

"Mama said there would be days like these . . ."

August 4, 2014

After a weekend of napping in the afternoons to prepare for midnight shifts at the pharmacy, chauffeuring teenagers to and from hockey, and seemingly necessary shopping excursions with an 18-month-old under my arm and the dogs barking from their kennels behind me, I was ready to collapse. Jet woke at an unruly 04:41 and refused to sleep again, my body had only been resting since 00:49 when I arrived home from my shift to nurse him back to sleep. This was the unfortunate pattern of my life.

In my sleep-deprived fog, I rummaged through his clothes, trying to find some that were clean enough to send him to daycare in. We hit the McDonalds drive-thru for a muffin to round out his nutritiously empty lunch of cupboard scraps. I didn't even take it out of the McBag—I don't have the gumption to attempt fooling his day-moms into thinking I had it together.

I met an Al-Anon program friend at the best greasy spoon in town for bacon and eggs. Sleep was the one single thing that would make the largest difference for Arthur or me, but as much as we had tried to instil some healthy sleep habits, the baby simply wasn't a good sleeper. The inconsistency of my late evening shifts did not help.

I told her the story of the crappy muffin in the McBag as evidence of how close to the line of personally unacceptable I was. I couldn't give up my shifts at the pharmacy at the risk of losing benefits and having to pay back a five-figure sum for my maternity leave. I had made a commitment to teaching—and that part I was enjoying.

Friend: How can I help you?
Me: I need a wife.
Friend: I can do that. I'll be your Step-Wife.

And that was that. She made a weekly meal plan, did the shopping, prepared the food and left me with a simple list of how to make what, when. She did our laundry, folded the clothes, cleaned the house, and attempted to control the uncontrollable dog hair. She ensured there were healthy snacks for hungry teens, she changed over the beds, she introduced baby Jet to new foods. She was an angel of sorts.

This week's menu:
- Stuffed Dijon glazed pork tenderloin with garden greens and roasted asparagus
- Spaghetti and meatballs in Bolognese sauce with warmed French bread
- Barbequed homemade feta hamburgers with all the fixins' and Greek pasta salad
- Grilled garlic shrimp on saffron rice with sautéed mushrooms, tomatoes and shallots

#priceless #lovemywife

August 6, 2014

> Ella: I'd like to hang out with Jewel this weekend.
> Me: We can try to make that happen. It's an inconvenient drive to
> pick her up . . . Can't her parents drive?
> Ella: Her mom only takes the bus, and her dad's truck is a company
> vehicle. But I REALLY want to spend some time with her.
> Me: Is she your girlfriend?
> Ella: Yes . . .
> *Blush. And that first-love kind of smile.*

Jewel and Ella had attended school together at the Arts School, but they hadn't really connected until Camp fYrefly—the blessing and curse of a camp that teaches kids they can be exactly who they are with confidence. Until I had to strap Ella back into the confines of reality of the culture we live in, that is. They connected.

They spent the weekend together, sitting next to each other, occasionally holding hands, and feeling less alone. They did each other's makeup and discussed their future in our safe home environment.

They slept in different rooms—just as I would have required for any couple their age. House rule—if you are horizontal, you are not behind closed doors. I was secretly glad Ella was on Lupron®, which kills testosterone levels, rendering erections and sperm production unlikely so their fertility as a couple was not a concern. The last thing I needed was another chapter for this book entitled "My Daughter and Her Girlfriend's Natural Biological Child", all rights reserved. We did have a few conversations about the risks of STDs being real and serious . . . resulting in the anticipated eye-rolling responses.

It matters not to me who Ella loves. It matters not what body type she finds attractive. I was simply pleased Ella felt loved.

August 7, 2014

The big kids and I headed to the dreaded mall to start some back to school shopping. Jackson was predictable—mostly the same as the previous year in a size or two bigger and slightly more edgy. Ella, on the other hand, had completely changed her entire persona about five times in the past few years and demanded a new and more suitable wardrobe. She slayed me.

She was stopped walking down the mall corridor not once, but TWICE, by complete strangers simply to compliment her on her amazing outfit. I have never had that happen in my entire life. Ever. She was a show stopper— regardless of the outfit, location, or disposition.

August 15, 2014

This was us, 104° F. It made me very sad, and stressed out about childcare— kids that look like this are not welcome at daycare. Luckily, I now had a Step-Wife who could parachute in when my distant family couldn't. He wasn't miserable. Just hot and needy.

And spotty. I think maybe a Dalmatian reincarnated? Snazzy!

August 24, 2014

Ella and I travelled the entirety of the city to meet her new family physician. Dr. Awesome was a kind woman who delivered a lot of babies, judging by the number of enormous belly bumps in the waiting room. Although not accepting new patients, she had made it known that she would travel the transgender path with Ella, and others, aiming to educate herself and provide support in a professionally appropriate capacity.

The appointment was mostly a "meet-and-greet". We discussed medications, lack of exercise, deep breathing exercises, and future planning.

Ella: How could you have left me alone in that hallway?
Me: Why? It was only for a minute.
Ella: That sample cupboard on the wall was FULL of estrogen! Patches, creams. They were calling me like "I'm right heeeeerrrrrreeeee, Ella, but you can't haaaaaavvvvvvveeeee me . . ."
Me: I have *never* heard of anyone, ever, considering estrogen to be a high-risk theft item before!

August 25, 2014

Me: I am having crazy anxiety about you going back to Suburbia Junior High.
I was worried about Jonah the bus bully.
And all the other Jonahs of the world.
Ella: Mom, it can't be any worse than being an effeminate, gender-confused, autistic boy in grade seven wearing plastic glasses with no lenses, giving out hallways hugs, and rocking pink shoes . . .
Me: I suppose, when you put it that way, you're correct.

I'm Trans, I Get Bullied, I'm Fighting Back

I'm no stranger to harsh words from ignorant people. I was bullied as a kid like many of us were. I may not have had a singular face to my bully but the consistent verbal attacks from people who felt that my gender presentation, even as a child, was some kind of attack on their own, have left the collective imprint of emotional bruising caused by one. I was born a girl and dressed like a boy. I begged to keep my hair short and cried every time my mother tried to put a dress on me so she just gave up trying and let me dress how I wanted to most of the time, unless it was some public outing in which she did not want my own presentation being a reflection of her identity which I think was a subconscious act to be protective.

I was repetitively asked "Are you a boy or a girl?" throughout childhood and adolescence and usually followed by "Fucking dyke!" It wasn't just kids either. When I was 12, a Portuguese female customs officer loudly asked the question in front of other travellers. When I answered, she said, "Next time you come through here, try looking like one."

This consistent public humiliation left me scarred for life. This hurt is triggered every time someone violates a part of my identity now.

Words can be violent. Especially in the context of someone who is transgender and language used around our bodies.

We spend most of our lives confused or hating ourselves so when people crawl into our psyches and compound that self-loathing, it becomes dangerous. We feel alone and unwanted and freakish.[33]

August 31, 2014

We gathered at a funky downtown diner to celebrate the decision to drop the formal Human Rights Complaint now that Ella had her "F" Birth Certificate. Iain, Ella, Fabulous lawyer, and I. Fabulous Lawyer had never met Ella in person and it was important for me that he had an opportunity to lay eyes on a young lady whose life had been so dramatically altered by his kindness, legal knowhow, and persistence.

Ella complied with my requests to dress in respectful, somewhat professional clothes and acted in a manner I was proud of. These concerns have nothing to do with gender, but are rather common ground with parents of a teenager.

We talked of challenges yet to come—the Freedom of Information and Privacy Complaint not yet resolved and the ongoing social struggles of gender variant youth. Fabulous Lawyer was sympathetic and connected, giving us new ideas and options for ongoing advocacy. I would continue to do my part just like he had done for us. It remained my job to pay it forward.

---

33   Silveira, L. (2013). I'm trans, I get bullied, I'm fighting back. Retrieved August 25, 2014 from http://www.huffingtonpost.ca/lucas-silveira/adult-bullying_b_3287841. html

Live

September 2, 2014

iMe: Have a great first day of school with Ellen!!! I LOVE YOU ☺
I waited for it.

iElla: Merm! I have squat for a lunch today (2 apples and a bag of almonds). Can you please transfer me 5 bucks so I can go to Wendy's or something and get some lunch food?

First day of school back at Suburbia Junior High. No "incidents". I almost didn't know what to do with myself.
Second day. Nothing.
First week. Still nothing.

Me: Has anything *happened* at school?
Ella: No.
Some kids stare and then I do this:

The time and energy invested in worrying about the future, or fantasy as it would be more accurately known was, once again, wasted. The paralyzing fear of my baby girl in harm's way faded to a more comfortable level of angst, and the days continued to pass uneventfully.

I was reminded though, at PFLAG, nasty things do still occur—regularly. Officers in uniform being beaten by their colleagues at work, without recourse, and the harassment rarely being reported for fear of retaliation and retribution, fear of losing their livelihood over their identity. Of sexual harassment within the medical field by some of those entrusted to uphold dignity and morals—to do no harm. Make no mistake, people continue to die over this—suicides, murders, and missing persons.

September 9, 2014

> ilain: Can you attend the parents' hockey meeting tomorrow a.m.?
> iMe: Yep. Tell Jackson to pick a number as per the e-mail.
> ilain: 14 is good
> iMe: 17 is available
> Done . . . he is 17
> ilain: Wendel Clark!

September 24, 2014

> eJean-Paul: Hi Carla!
> I see Ella almost every day and things seem to unfold very well.
> Ellen told me that Ella is interested in attending the school trip to
> Washington! When you have a moment, I would also like to talk to
> you about this. I just have a few questions related to passport and
> accommodations.

It honestly hadn't even crossed my mind there would be any complications when I told Ella that we would absolutely consider the upcoming school trip. She wasn't permitted to go to Boston a few years earlier because her then-abhorrent behaviour in general did not warrant special rewards. This trip was a different story, a pleasant reward for having endured an incredible amount of shit in just a few short years.

Passport. Border crossings. Roommates.

The school was accommodating, in a strange "issue avoidance" kind of way. Just as they had opted to pull her from physical education to avoid the change room issue, they now offered her a single room to avoid the entire roommate and disclosure issues. Ella, of course, was thrilled with the outcome, so I did not pursue the issue. Instead, I got very busy doing what I needed to do to get a new passport for my girl—a task made possible by the Alberta Human Rights Complaint pressure and Birth Certificate amendment made just a few months earlier.

September 27, 2014

iMe: Peekers, Gramma!

September 29, 2014
I was adept at preparing for circumstances I could anticipate. It's the oddballs that really got me.

Ella: MOM! The nurse came into the class today to talk about the HPV vaccine. They gave it to all the girls in grade 7 and now they know it's beneficial for boys too, so they are coming to the school to vaccinate all the boys! You CAN'T let that happen!
Mortified.
Mom: I'll make some calls . . .
What are the chances that the ONE gender specific vaccine would be offered to girls in the ONE year she was living as a boy, then change indication and be placed on the routine schedule in the ONE year she presented as female?!?
School nurse: Yes, that's right. We will be sending a note home for permission and then vaccinating the boys in a 3 shot series.
Me: Here's the situation. Ella is a biological male, but lives fully as a female. Transgender. What name do you have in your system?

School nurse: "Eliot" John Grant.
Me: How do we get that changed, so even the permission letter being sent home is addressed correctly?
School nurse: I have no idea.
Me: Could you please investigate and let me know if there are any problems?
I will withhold consent and make an appointment at the Health Centre to have it done privately.

The vaccine is to reduce the risk of contracting certain strains of Human Papilloma Virus—the sexually transmitted virus that causes genital warts and causes cervical cancer in women. They figured since only women have cervixes, only women needed the vaccine. But more research has obviously shown that if they also reduce infection rates in the men who transmit it to the women, everyone is better off.

And I wonder . . . since Ella will never have a cervix, and may not continue to have a penis . . . does she even need it? My vote is yes, just to be safe and keep all her partners safe in the future. Can't hurt, might help?

October 1, 2014

Some astute parents had identified a very definite hole in the support system for LGBTQ youth in Suburbia and the surrounding area. I'll remind you that this is an affluent town populated largely by dual 6-figure-income Caucasian families. The unofficial entrance survey screens out minorities, those without social status, and those with gender and sexuality variances.

Until this point, the options for Ella to have been connected socially with anyone in the community were very limited—a few summer camps, a youth group at the Pride Centre, which required parents to be available for transportation into the Metropolis, or a one-off chance acquaintance.

Outloud, a group for all LGBTQ youth and allies, was formed, and Ella was thrilled. A few times a month she could count on free pizza, supportive guidance from in-tune parents, and a safe space to be herself. Some weeks they planned activities and had guest speakers in to talk about various youth-related issues, other times they just chilled and basked in a place where they had finally found their people. Regardless of the topic, Ella always came home with a smile and newfound energy.

October 9, 2014

Arthur was not coping well with the mess and stress of our family. As hard as it was to stand and witness someone's implosion, I knew better than to try harder than he was to make it better for him.

> iMe: He is a traumatized child with the arrogance of an adult, and the coping mechanisms of a baby.
> I've pushed him this week into doing some honest financial planning, and he is not handling it well.
> I am in desperate need of an AA meeting and can't even make that happen.
> iGramma: I take it something significant has happened.
> iMe: Just reflecting on reality ☹

October 13, 2014

> iElla: Merm! Halp! Do you have any panty liners?
> iMe: Why? Did you get your period?
> iElla: Pfft I wish.
> No, I need to hide pit stains.
> Merm HALP!

October 20, 2015

By this point in time, I
had become schooled in the
underground world of the
transgender community. We had
shopped online on sites that,
along with Jackson's pellet gun
shipments across the Canadian
border, probably have me on
some federal watch list.

We have tried a variety of gaff underwear, cleavage creators, tapes,
and makeup. We have ordered cups and mastectomy bras from cancer
websites in a variety of sizes, materials, and shapes.

Ella once showed me a full-body silicone suit with a fake vagina. A
prosthetic. I really had no idea such a thing existed. When I Googled
them myself in private later, I discovered all sorts of such things—
little silicone vaginas in underwear, strap-on vagina apparatuses,
vaginas galore!

Ella seemed to mostly have found her groove with her Under
Armour™ and eccentric clothing, though to my chagrin, she still
bordered on inappropriate at times. My discomfort was partially that
the "in" styles for the summer of 2014 for 14-year-olds make me
feel like a 1945 prude. I prefer a few things left to the imagination!
I justify the dress code in the name of safety. But the deeper I dig,
the more I wonder if I am just as much a discriminator as the next
person—only *biological and beautiful females* should show that much
skin. The societal messaging is disgustingly ingrained.

> ilain: Umm, what's with the gargantuan Ella boobs?
> iMe: They are C cups . . .
> ilain: They are gargantuan.
> And a girlfriend!
> *The cat is out of the bag.*
> iMe: We can get smaller ones when they need replacing
> It's partly how she dresses them up (I do not condone push-up
> bras with them)
> Jewel is sweet. I am thrilled that Ella feels lovable ☺
> She is so dysphoric with male anatomy, I am not surprised that she
> would feel better with a girl.
> ilain: Not sure to feel joy or horror.

October 25, 2014

What do teenage girls do on their 3-month anniversary? Ella and Jewel arranged rides and begged for money. I gave them each $20 and told them to be the politest citizens they could.

They asked to be dropped off at Earl's, a business casual restaurant Jewel had never been to, and where Ella demanded to dine often, loving the chicken vindaloo. I didn't hear another word until they were out of money, and smelling even better than when I dropped them off.

> Me: How was your evening?
> Ella: Awesome. We split a pizza and the waitress told us how, like, awesome we were and drew a big smiley face on our bill! And then we split ice cream at Marble Slab, it's so delicious. And then we, like, checked out the lingerie store—I LOVE their corsets. Can you buy me one? And then we checked out the makeup at Rexall. L'Oréal is making a new lip-liner . . . And OMG I really need some of that . . .
> Jewel: Uh-huh.

They were both grinning sweet smiles that made it obvious how smitten they were with each other. They were both simple enough to really enjoy common interests in their strange parallel ways—makeup, food, and girly accoutrements. Once again, I was struck by how esteeming it is to be cherished by someone. They were holding each other up through some hard days.

November 1, 2014

> Facebook post: Does anyone have a Halloween costume I can borrow for Jet? Just to take some photos in?

"Staller-mother" move. I picked up a monkey suit, complete with banana, early in November but never did take the picture. I hated Halloween anyways.

November 4, 2014

Arthur called me out for disclosing Ella's story without her explicit permission. He questioned after all the work we had done to help her live safely and discretely as her true gender, why I would ever choose to out her? Of course, I tried to always use a high level of discretion, but I was frequently asked by new people in my life the standard "get-to-know-you" questionnaire.

How many children do you have? Three.

How old? 1 ½, 12, and 14

Boys or girls? Well . . .

At this point, I could have simply said the oldest is a girl, and the others are boys. But I rarely did. I launched into a simplified version of the story.

I did it in the name of public awareness, but what was my underlying root cause? I'd love for my motivations to be pure . . . "The more people I make my acceptance of trans people known to, the more people will know it's okay to accept trans people," "Planting a seed that makes people less ignorant," "Maybe the person I am speaking to has a personal LGBTQ connection that they are wanting to be able to speak about." Maybe I simply needed people know of the chaos I continue to deal with at home? Maybe for some twisted shock-and-awe factor to have a better story than the next person?

When is "Ella" simply a girl, not "Ella, who used to be "Eliot"?"

November 11, 2014

iMe: I need to come get you when Acid is down . . . we need to go do your Lupron®.
*Jet
My boss is in tonight. You have a choice of me or him ☹
iElla: Frick frack.
iMe: Or chest hair and a beard . . .
I know all options suck . . .
iElla: You. And a ginger ale.

It was also Gramma's birthday—Remembrance Day—which I almost always forgot!

November 15, 2014

Jet was now the same age that Ella was at our first-ever Cookie Day nine years ago. Ella was playing her quirky game of peek-a-boo by covering her ears. A very early example of a typical cross-sensory autistic trait, not yet recognized.

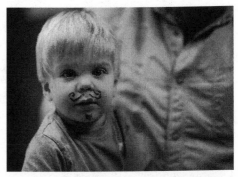

Jet was slow to talk. I had never been too concerned with milestones, but he did not have the token "50 words by 2 years and making 2-word phrases." Arthur was more concerned than I was, and for different reasons. He was searching the internet for typical behaviours; I had my eyes out for atypical warning signs. There is always a seed of "will this happen again" with any lifelong disorder or condition. I dipped the kids' urine for glucose when they were young and sick, just to rule out my brother's diabetes.

I made some calls—I was a strong believer in early intervention.

November 16, 2014

The Christmas lists had begun.

> iElla: Merm!
> the lipstick set is all samples (1/4 of the full size)
> *Sends link to lipstick that will give Iain a heart attack*
> everything is full size!
> also this!
> *Sends link*

IT'S INSTANT
IT'S RETRO
IT'S PERFECT

November 20, 2014

This was the first time I solemnly acknowledged Transgender Day of Remembrance (TDOR). It was a validating reminder of the importance of my continued part in advocacy work, and a painful reminder of the realness of the fears of those who identify as transgender.

Since 1999, the TDOR, on which those trans people who have been victims of homicide and suicide are remembered, has taken place on this day in November. The TDOR raises public awareness of hate crimes against trans people, provides a space for public mourning, and honours the lives of those trans people who might otherwise be forgotten.

Transgender Europe's Trans Murder Monitoring project revealed 226 documented killings of trans people during the last 12-month period, October 2013 to September 2014[34].

This was a time to reflect on the cruelty, hatred, dehumanization, and discrimination of trans people. It isn't being transgender that is killing people—that alarming statistic is captured by the suicide rates. It is society's reaction to gender-variance that is the primary issue. A palpable sense of disgust, voyeuristic curiosity, and arrogance emanates from those too ignorant to be giving voice on the matter. Society demands we be "honest" and "true to ourselves", and then beats and murders those who live authentically.[35] Ella is correct when she says, "I'm not more likely to be abducted than any other girl on the street, but when the assailant discovers I'm trans I'm more likely to die."

December 7, 2014

iMe: Gramma—I'm sick.
My head hurts.
I'm cranky and needy. ☹
iGramma: Poor babies ☹

34   Transgender Europe (TGEU). (2014). Transgender Europe's Trans Murder Monitoring project reveals 226 killings of trans people in the last 12 months [Press release]. Retrieved from http://www.transrespect-transphobia.org/uploads/downloads/2014/TDOR2014/TvT-TDOR2014PR-en.pdf
35   Tannehill, B. (2014). Transgender day of remembrance: A call to action for trans people and our allies alike. [Web log comment] Retrieved November 20, 2014 from http://www.huffingtonpost.com/brynn-tannehill/transgender-day-of-remembrance-a-call-to-action_b_6184766.html

I tottered on the fence between the ethical thing to do (calling in sick so I could comfort my baby and save other babies from his germy snot) and the necessary thing to do (show up to work and fulfil my corporate obligation). Then, like every working mom has done, I loaded the child up with weight-based doses of Advil® and Tylenol® and prayed they would control the fever, at least until after nap-time, when I could more easily arrange help.

December 14, 2014

I was noticing more and more how Arthur and I were walking parallel paths; each of us not wanting to reach out and connect with the other for fear of falling off our own rail on a diverging set of tracks. We were very different people and our priorities were also.

I spent time in my head supporting those I love, waging humanistic battles, excelling at work and doing what I could to keep myself emotionally well. It was probably a good thing that Arthur spent time doing other things, like feeding into his cleaning addiction.

> iMe: Back by 3 so I can bathe before work?
> iArthur: I'm in line at the car wash.
> Only 6 cars in front of me. ❤
> Orange is a wee bit filthy inside. Someone spilled peanuts (?) all over the passenger seat and down bedside it.
> iMe: They are cheesy owls. It was Acid.
> iArthur: There also seems to be a hundred McDonald's monopoly stickers and candy wrappers in the driver's door. ☺ Was he in the front seat?
> iMe: Leave me alone. I don't mess with your space. Don't criticize mine.

Jet had already started following me around the house, closing doors I hadn't bothered to open and vacuuming up little things with the mini Dyson®. He was doomed to be a Mini-Arthur, pointing out "muss"es and cupboard doors that needed "cosin" everywhere.

December 25, 2014

We are a white privileged family; by birth, by design, and by societal creation. We have been blessed with more gifts under the tree than anybody would ever need, more food to eat than some people eat in a lifetime, and more family love and acceptance than some ever bear witness to. There are days that I am bogged down in the woes of superficial problems, but I will never take any of these wonders in my life for granted . . .

December 28, 2014

My Christmas guests had left, and Jet's health had once again tanked. Fever, cough, miserable. For being a pharmacist, I often wait just a little too long before taking my children in to the doctor, erring on the side of "It's likely viral, and antibiotics won't help anyways."

Walk-in-doctor: This is a very sick little boy.
Me: He's punky, for sure.
Doctor: I'll write you a note to try to avoid triage, but you need to take him in to the hospital.
Me: Really?
Flip to logistic mode because feelings[36] surrounding sick children are SAD.
We travel into the city to go to the Children's Hospital, and I notified Arthur and my boss.
iMe: Acid has pneumonia and a collapsed lung, we are at the hospital. Can you cover my shift?
*Jet
iBoss: No. I can't.

WTF!!! This was a slap-in-the-face example of how clearly out of line my current employment situation was with my values. So, what do I do? Like a good employee, I left my baby at the hospital! With Arthur, of course, but *I needed* to be with him. I wanted *that* to be *my* job, not the bullshit at the pharmacy . . . angry customers mad at me for their petty insurance plans problems and their poor planning. I was skilled at keeping an attitude of service for the customers most times, but I was no longer willing to sacrifice myself. I didn't know what was next, but I knew what had to end.

December 31, 2014

There was no way I was going to make it to midnight. I barely made it to 8 p.m.

> iGramma: You are probably crazy busy . . .but do you remember the kind of yummy Ben and Jerry's or Haagen-Dazs ice cream you forced down my throat with all the big yummy stuff in it?? Feeling sorry for ourselves 'cause our evening plans are cancelled . . . ☹

> iMe: I am so your daughter.

What do we do to ring in the New Year? We painted Ella's room white—a long postponed decorating project to move past the visual reminders of all things "Eliot". A blank slate. A fresh start. A new year.

We did this, in short bursts between Jet's Tylenol, Advil, Amoxil, and Ventolin doses, in the windows of time he felt well enough to not be attached to my boob. Also in between Jackson's hockey games, my stupid midnight shifts, and consequential afternoon naps. It took a while to whiteout history.

In Arthur fashion, she now owned a
bed that was too big to fit in her room, an
infuriating maneuver to me because the lack
of space and storage was the precipitating
factor for the renos to begin with.

> iGramma: Why didn't you have him
> exchange it?
> iMe: Because the bed is now built and
> glued together. Impossible to get it out of
> there!
> iGramma: Crap. Close the door. You've created a new "Ella"
> environment for a fresh start; that's your job. She will make of it
> what she wants; that's her job. As I recall, I closed your door for
> years . . . and look how beautifully you turned out!
> iMe: LOL. With a pile of unfolded laundry in the basement!!!
> iGramma: Well I had a basket of ironing in the deep freeze the
> whole time you were growing up . . . especially if either mother-in-
> law was expected! I wish I had known then that it probably didn't
> matter to them at all . . . xoxo

January 1, 2015
  6 years sober.
  I feel a need to speak to the concept of addictive thinking, and a
bit about what I have learned about alcoholism. There is still much
debate about whether distorted thinking causes an addiction or vice-
versa, whether its origins are rooted in nature or nurture, or exactly
what it is that flips the switch, tipping people over into destructive
behaviours. Regardless of the cause, I am the result. I can absolutely
attest to the fact that even when a substance is removed from my
system, the obsessive and crazy thinking continues in full force. They
never taught us at Rehab how to "quit"; they helped us dig out some
deeply rooted toxic belief systems and encouraged us to live well
without our favorite coping mechanism.
  "Alcoholic" is a shaming word. Mostly I felt fear though, not
embarrassment. I was apprehensive of the professional ramifications
that a leaked AA secret, or proof of admission to Rehab, would have
had on my future—I researched the possible downsides of treatment

on the sly before I sent out application forms. Not being a practicing pharmacist has huge ramifications.

I was confident that reactions to my treatment plan from friends and family would be loving; it usually came with an understated "It's about fucking time". People on the outside could have easily weighed the possible outcomes: continued misery and serious consequences versus the potential benefits of turning my life around. On the inside, though, my thought processes were pathologically diverted to sanction and preserve my drinking . . . all the motivation I could muster was focused on *getting my next drink*. Intelligence does not trump addictive thinking, it made my planning and reasoning about alcohol even more intense. I alternated liquor stores, I planned my entire week around the moment I could turn my brain off with ethanol, I never put myself in a situation where I would be forced to control my intake. #dontjudgeme

Trying to resist the urge to drink produced so much restlessness, irritability, discomfort, and anxiety that determination alone could never overcome it. It was rarely about wanting to be drunk, but about a need to feel *different*. Most alcoholics have very low self-esteem despite having confidence in their capability. I often feel quite insignificant—even when my resume would suggest otherwise. The negative feelings about my deepest self are not based in fact—they are belief systems I developed as coping mechanisms in my little-girl brain that, until I took a painstaking look at, I didn't even know were there. They made me vulnerable to escapism, and alcohol did that. The feeling of liquor burning down my throat was the doorway to relief of the weight on my shoulders. My connection to that escape was stronger than my connection to everything that mattered—my partner, my kids, my friends, my existence.

I write in present tense here to illustrate the point that, regardless of when these ramblings are read, they will likely hold true. Addiction is deeply engrained in the fibre of my being. I become more willing to share my sordid backstory the further I get into sobriety. I am an alcoholic with a few years under my belt, and that doesn't have the same superficial instability as when I was newly into recovery. I know that I will always be one drink away from being back "there" again; brutal truth be told, sometimes I *want* to be back in detox. I often long to collapse in a place where people are *trying* to help me, where strangers already know I am probably *not okay*, even when I say I am. My brain conjures up theories that letting myself fall apart is a reprieve from holding me all together—a great example of a very distorted thought pattern.

And now what? I continue, one day at a time. I continue to attend meetings and read literature to keep my recovery active—my distorted thinking pops up daily, in all areas of my life. AA often speaks of alcoholism as being "cunning, baffling, and powerful" and I can vouch for all three. I am much better at recognizing it, but call on sponsors and friends often to help me sort out life situations before I mess them up all by myself. SMART recovery, writing, going for evening walks, immersing myself in photography, coffee with friends—it's all part of my recovery plan. A plan to move closer to my best, and farther from my worst.

January 3, 2015

For Arthur, life at the Gemstone oscillated between "Everything I ever wanted" and "Why the fuck did I ever want any of this?"

> iArthur: Ella has been difficult (making faces when she thinks I'm not looking and making snide remarks), but I have not taken the bait.
> Pls bring home a small bag of love . . . it's been a night.
> ♥

January 5, 2015

> iGramma: I hear our baby has a fat lip ☹. Boo boo??
> iMe:

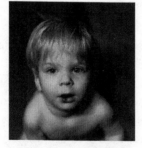

> iGramma: Bad news: Full Moon
> Good news: It was yesterday

January 7, 2015

My days off were chock-full of kid appointments. Big kid, middle kid, tiny kid. So much for attacking *The Carla List*.

Self talk: Kids are *ON* the Carla list.

Kids *ARE* the Carla list!

> I hope they will gracefully remember that I was tired.
>
> I had intentions of being great; some days all I could be was okay.
>
> ~ unknown [37]

January 13, 2015

I had been coughing for weeks. My mental health was suffering. I was drowning in the dark of winter, the stress of my home, and the outrageous work schedule I had created for myself.

As a pharmacist, I certainly knew how to self-medicate. I purchased a bottle of cough syrup and glugged some—straight from the bottle, as all pharmacists know is best. An hour later, my cough had not settled, so I drank some more. When I arrived home in the middle of the -34°C night, I drank some more—it warmed me up inside where I hadn't felt anything in a while. I spent most of the night hallucinating; it was a mixture of pure exhaustion, too much dextromethorphan, and a touch of alcohol in the syrup.

I was maxed out on my antidepressant dose, not wanting to add anything new because I was still nursing. I could not find a crack in my self-inflicted timetable to get myself to a meeting or to see my own mental health support network.

I hijacked Ella's appointment with her new amazing physician to steal five minutes alone. I was honest about how close to collapsing I was, and she responded by prescribing a few weeks off work to get back into my program. If I didn't want to slip, I couldn't stay in slippery places.

---

37   Unknown. Likely a wise and honest mother.

iArthur: Are you ok, sweetie?
iMe: No.
I need to get my head on straight.
iArthur: Rest.
iMe: I need a mulligan.

January 16, 2015

I chose to not air all my dirty laundry, out of respect for a man I love, the father of my baby Jet.

But know this—Arthur is a deeply troubled man who grew from a profoundly wounded child. The repercussions of this are far-reaching—finances, intimacy, connectedness, parenting, logistics. We were not well, and I worked long and hard to not be pulled down into the vortex of nastiness.

I hung onto the days not so long ago when I trusted him. Days that were better, where there was more joy—making plans, being curious, living well. And I hung onto my program and my sponsor for the wisdom and guidance to stay well within something unwell.

January 19, 2015

iGramma: Statistically, this is the most depressing day of the year, 3rd Monday in Jan. Failed resolutions, Xmas bills in, gloomy weather, etc.
Good news is that it's half over already! I'm having a decent day; hope you are, too. xoxox

January 27, 2015

It would have been hard to argue against the fact that we needed a new fridge. The piece of cardboard duct-taped in place to hit the trigger button to ensure the light went off inside was worn out and ugly. The icemaker was leaking water out of the back of the freezer unit and would have undoubtedly ruined the hardwood underneath eventually. We had saved the money, thanks to some sound financial decisions made months earlier—all in conjunction with holiday sale prices.

Arthur was the head of our 2-person fridge committee. My only caveat was that the fridge has the freezer on the bottom, and a water/ice maker. I thought it would have been a given that the fridge should fit in its hole.

iMe: If you had a fridge that didn't fit, would you:
A) Cut the newish granite counter, notch the wall and move the light switch so it will fit into an awkward looking hole in a load-bearing wall
B) Sell the fridge and buy a smaller one (now not on sale, but possible) even though it would be significantly smaller and at a loss because the large fridge was dented trying to force it into the hole
C) Resent the man who bought the fridge
iGramma: C. For a very long time.

The fridge sits unceremoniously in the middle of the kitchen. Ella asks every few weeks about what the plan for the Fridge of Resentment is, and I politely remind her that it is a sore spot for me and the she should *shut the hell up* about it.

February 3, 2015

I loved my Step-Wife. She was the only one out of all of us who was enjoying the new Fridge of Resentment still in the middle of the kitchen.

This week's menu:
- Golden beet stew
- Slow cooker Moroccan beef stroganoff
- Roasted chicken with carrot-infused wheat berries and green beans
- Italian ground turkey stuffed zucchini

February 15, 2015

I have heard and read countless stories of the emotional anguish gender non-conforming people endure, especially before coming out. Too often, it is a suicide attempt at the end of years of pain and unrest that brings the core issue to the surface. This is excruciating for parents and loved ones to witness—a person in extreme distress over who they really are. These are the parents that rightly say, "The decision between a happy <gender> and a dead <gender> is so blatantly obvious".

We were fortunate that our path of gender discovery did not have this tragic twist woven in. We did not, however, escape without some self-harming behaviours and emotional turmoil. She was smoking away social distress, sneaking off to "blaze" at lunch with her peeps. Some of this, of course, was teenage curiosity. Some was an all-encompassing desire to be accepted and one of the "cool crowd"—the age-old desire of every teen.

> ilain: Ella cut her arms to bits.
> This is trendy grandstanding and it must be stopped. Ella must not let the idea take root that this is cool. It isn't—it's fucking stupid.

From what I have learned about cutting—and other self-injurious behaviors like carving and burning—it is a psychologically-motivated, impulsive action to make oneself feel better. Although there aren't any theories as to its origins, the exact roles of biology (serotonin deficiency or overly active endorphins), personality, and environment are still in question. I didn't need to analyze it to death, but I did learn enough to know that it isn't uncommon, and that it arises from an overwhelming need to feel "better"; to get a rush, to end numbness, to punish oneself, or to communicate with others.

The natural response to self-harm is tied to the polarity of our human innate sense of self-protection. Iain fell into the "recoil and anger" part, and I fell more into the "outpouring of empathy" at the other end of the spectrum. Neither good cop nor bad cop were helpful. What eventually did help was advice from the Gender Psychologist to validate Ella's emotions as best I could, and try to help her identify healthier strategies to deal with whatever it was that weighed so heavily on her shoulders.

I had naïvely hoped she would stand by her announcement that she was "too pretty for that", referring to the nasty physical consequences of drugs and smoking. I didn't believe she felt pretty anymore—she was now much more aware of the petite curvy girls around her and so genuinely dysphoric about her own body. As much as we try to hammer into our children how beautiful and unique they are, at times it's a bit like trying to shoot a nail through a colander helmet made of steel.

The most useful parenting advice I ever received about how to help guide this socially awkward child through the evil that was junior high came from Temple Grandin, a woman with autism well known for her insightful descriptions of sensory issues and visual learning, and for her intuitive designs of cattle feed lots.

She answered my posed question from a small corner of a large stage at an autism conference, hiding off to the side out of the glare of the lights, out of the intense sensory stimulation. She was wearing a tacky cowboy shirt, but likely had no clue that her attire was in any way odd to most.

"I'm pretty sure dealing with teenage girls is not a life skill I will ever need again. Just get her through it, engulf her in groups with common interests, and move on."
~ Temple Grandin

March 2, 2015
Monday: I entered the Gemstone kitchen to find Jackson, laughing uncontrollably, chasing a condom filled with water—now about the size of a watermelon—around the kitchen floor. He had asked me if he could have one from the samples I had purchased to teach contraception to internationally trained pharmacists. They needed help—"No, you don't roll it out and put it on like a sock" I said to my male students from Egypt who had never seen one in their lives.

I screamed like a crazed tyrant for him to pick it up and take it outside.

The more he squeezed, the further it shot away from him. I, of course, had bought slippery condoms lubricated with spermicide.

Jet started wailing. He feared the overfilled prophylactic.

Monty attempted to get out of the way of the balloon shooting across the room, but succeeded only in jumping over it and nicking it with his claw.

LITRES of water exploded in spectacular fashion. I was understandably annoyed.

Tuesday: I arrived home from work to find a weepy Ella. She was tangibly anxious in that "I want to tell you, but I don't want to tell you" kind of way.

I promised not to tell her father.

She melted into a puddle of tears. She was buying and smoking pot and cigarettes and simply could not suppress the guilt. Jackson was implicated as well.

We talked it through. I witnessed her flush the remaining stash of weed.

I forbade the behaviour, but I knew it was a rule I could not possibly enforce.

Wednesday: I arrived home from work to discover a white powder in the upstairs bathroom.

It was not cocaine.

It was the remains of a discharged fire extinguisher. Jackson and his uninvited and disallowed friends were my prime suspects.

Shortly after, my phone rang and it was Jackson's grade 7 teacher calling to report a 20% drop in his social studies grade . . .

Thursday: I quit my job.

March 4, 2015

iArthur: Can we get a Labrador puppy? An acquaintance's parents are breeders and the litter came last night. 10 bundles of love. Pure bred, guaranteed, and $900.
Ready in 8 weeks.
iMe: No
iArthur: Ok. Thanks. I've picked a black girl from the pictures.
The kids will be SOOOOO EXCITED!!!
You are the BEST!!😲😲😲😲😲😲
iMe: No
iArthur: We will call her Mary. I think it's a great name for a dog. ☺
Mary, Ben, Angie, and Monty. 🐶🐶🐶🐶
iMe: No
Do. Not. Get. A. Dog.
iArthur: Can I get 2? ☺
iMe: Sure, if you want to move out ☺

March 5, 2015

I was worried about my kids.

Without labelling them or willing universal events . . . I knew they would experiment with illicit drugs. My take on the 2010s is that the world of substances has been normalized, and it would be ignorant to believe my kids would avoid it; my fear was that they would like it. My goal was to steer them towards making *less harmful* decisions (let's face it, pot is not in the same league of danger as crack . . . although too often one leads to the other), and trusted me enough to seek help and guidance if, or when, they need it.

The people who were most successful at Rehab were the ones who *wanted* to be there. Those who did not fare as well had been coerced by forceful families meaning well, by the justice system, as bait to regain custody of their children, among others. Family support is essential, but "doing it for my family" never supports sobriety. I landed there when I was ready. I wasn't mature enough in my first stint in Detox to have dug as deeply into core issues as I needed to maintain sobriety. I'm one of the lucky ones who reached a turning point before I hit the endpoints of addiction—jobless, homeless, alone, or dead.

March 6, 2015

Having some newfound mental space gave me time and motivation to reach out to old friends. I had become isolated and distanced from them, and I missed the girlfriend connection.

iMe: I quit my job. Sick of midnights and weekends and unappreciative bosses . . .
iLisa: Ooh la la! How exciting!!! Full time photography?
iMe: Not quite yet! Probably still pharmacy, just not retail . . .
When is ball hockey? That's another reason I'm glad I quit . . . to be able to go to games and hang with other slightly neurotic moms!
iLisa: Thanks for putting the slightly part. I appreciate you not completely indulging my self- destructive behaviours ;)

March 8, 2015

There were few things in life that I will set an alarm for before 6 a.m. International flights, lunar eclipses, and a skiing trip with my kids that had been repeatedly postponed for much too long was the current shortlist. We picked a date, watched the forecast, and dug out the winter gear. Ella hadn't been on skis for a few years, and I opted for her to wear my snow pants and ski jacket—it was also a perfect excuse for me to sit in the lodge and just attempt to get caught up on my writing. Having a block of time unattached to Jet, work or chauffeuring services was a treat.

We drove for hours to find sunshine and fresh powder. The kids became kids for a while and left the stresses of junior high, household chores, and reality behind. I enjoyed watching them stick their heads out the sunroof on the highway . . . experiencing life as a dog?

I set up shop for the day, next to an outlet and beside a window. The sun beamed in, warming my feet and my soul. The table next to me was inhabited by a younger European couple and their parents . . . and a 13-day-old baby. Mom and Dad took turns holding, burping, changing, nursing (of course, mom took most of those turns ☺), and doing a few runs. I was almost two years' post-partum and still wasn't sure my uterus wouldn't fall out when I crashed down a black run; this mom was astonishingly brave.

The kids reported back every few hours demanding food and recanting their escapades. Jackson was slightly frustrated with Ella's ultra-cautious and exaggeratedly terrified demeanor on the slopes, but mostly he was amused.

March 10, 2015

> iArthur: Mama, I am having a pretty tough morning.
> Angie ate all my crackers and then I dumped out the whole dog water dish. 😩
> Then the Dyson® vacuum stopped working because I drained the battery.
> Daddy charged it up and filled up the water dish.
> But then I used up the freshly recharged Dyson® to vacuum it all up and now it is really broken . . .

March 18, 2015

My short stint of official unemployment had given me time to brush up my resume, which on paper I'll admit makes me look accomplished (at least until someone reads this book ☺).

A technician at work, Sarah, told me about an instructing position open at a college. Turns out . . . her former instructor was a pharmacy classmate of mine . . . who knew Sarah from the pharmacy technician program . . . and had stayed in touch with her because her sister had hooked Sarah up with a roommate . . . who ended up being her girlfriend! Small world. And then there was a Facebook message . . . and the rest is history. That's how these things happen.

I bought a new dress for the interview, cut my hair short, and had an extra-long nap so I looked better than my typical near-death exhaustion. I nailed the interview and was offered an amazing job—working with an eager multi-cultural adult learner population in a positive environment with flexibility, room for work-life balance, and Christmas and summers off!

April 8, 2015

> iElla: IT'S MONTY
> ON THE PIANO
> CUTENESS OVERLOAD
> iMe: He looks terrified.
> iElla: HE JUMPED ONTO THE BENCH
> AND INTO MY HEART

April 11, 2015

Ella had an invitation from a friend at school to attend a birthday party at the Metropolis Waterpark. I thought it was lovely that she had been invited.

She was off on a mission to procure a gift. She purchased a large bottle of French Vanilla coffee creamer, because it was his favorite, with the change she scrounged up from the bottom of her oversized purse. With the rest of her ~~pennies~~ nickels, she bought the skimpiest string bikini I had ever seen at Value Village.

> Me: Ummm . . . NO.
> Ella: Whhhhyyyy not? It fits me perfectly.

I felt more comfortable with her in the one-piece full-coverage suit with the empire waist and strategic skirt overlay we had wangled. I felt better when she was at the Suburbia pool in swim lessons with old ladies who were more likely to gossip with each other, but less likely to be rude or threatening towards Ella.

What kind of mom would let a curvy transgender teenager with poor social judgement wear something that could only draw negative attention? Or any other teenager? Not me. I pulled out my veto and quashed the "bold is beautiful" and "curvy is the new sexy" social messaging, and possibly her esteem along with it, in the name of safety. Authoritarian power parenting move or not, safety is non-negotiable.

April 23, 2015

Ella was off to Washington. "F" passport in hand—a task easily accomplished once she had her "F" birth certificate. She had a jam-packed itinerary and a single adjoining room to Ellen, one of the chaperoning staff. I again swallowed down the bad taste of the "single room offer", knowing it was an easy solution to not have to deal with other parents and other contentious gender issues—but it worked for Ella.

Amazingly, she squeezed herself into one suitcase. No stilettos, no glam, no outrageous—I asked myself where my Ella had gone?!? Too tired? Growing up?!? Just a pair of red Toms, some well-worn Sketchers, leggings, denim shorts, and a few t-shirts.

No airport incidents! A rare occurrence for trans people at border crossings.

#hallelujah

My only contact was some ongoing Facebook creeping—a few pictures of the chandeliers at the National Gallery of Art, the art deco above some random taco joint, and a video clip that briefly highlighted the Pentagon in the distance—reminiscent of the scene of the train coming into the Capitol in *The Hunger Games.*

iElla: MERM! I have no money!

Of course. Turns out she has hit her daily withdrawal limit before having even left the Metropolis airport . . . $11.97 at Starbucks, $41.99 at Apple . . . she was all Ella.

April 27, 2015

Caitlyn Jenner. It is possible this memoir wouldn't be complete without at least an acknowledgement of what was perhaps the most publicized transition of the decade.

I had no clue who this person was. I didn't know, nor follow, the Kardashians. I didn't read *People*, and rarely paid any attention to tabloids except while waiting in a checkout line.

She was an Olympian, a father to many, and ex-husband to a few, and then suddenly—the token trans woman in the U.S.A. I never did watch the "coming out" interview with Barbara Walters. I did not purchase a copy of the infamous *Vanity Fair*.

A few blogs reminded me that she was not the typical presentation of the trans population. She could afford surgeries and hormones, she was not a black woman at risk of sexual and overt violence—but neither was Ella. She did share many of the same struggles as Ella, though. A life of secrecy and dysphoria. Fear of the loss of affection from loved ones, loss of relationships, financial impacts, social stigma and being the target of harsh public discrimination and defamation.

My desire for Caitlyn is the same as I have for everyone—a life of love and light. She, by choice or design, is a new spokesperson for the gender-variant community, and I trust that she will use her position for the greatest good.

April 29, 2015

I relished in the calm of the PFLAG room. Other parents deal with LIFE, intertwined with gender.

A mom waging WAR against the Catholic School Board for not letting her daughter use the girls' washroom.

A mom struggling with the crippling anxiety of her high-school aged trans daughter.

A grandma grappling to understand her adult daughter's sexual identity as it changed along with each new partner.

A single father, with a child who recently revealed their gender dysphoria, who was mostly unsure how to deal with what was unfolding in front of him.

It was not rocket science—but there wasn't any easy answer book, either. No right or wrong. Just a place to share experience, strength, and hope . . .

May 5, 2015

I picked up Jet from daycare. He waved and smiled and ran away . . . throwing himself fully into the warm sandbox. I man-handled him out, holding him like a football under my arm—scratching and flailing and biting me—and deposited him in our own backyard.

The oversized space was a private paradise under construction. I painstakingly erected an 8-foot fence to the south a few years earlier, trying to shield myself from the unresolved emotional turmoil that spewed out of a fight with the neighbour over a retaining wall.

#fuckingpropertylines

When we first moved into the Gemstone, there was a large stump, bluntly massacred six feet above ground, that had grown into a tree-bush. The previous Gemstone owner had a dream one night of the ancient tree falling on the house and instructed her husband to cut it down. It was my reminder to resist the urge to make rash decisions that could irreparably stunt growth.

Slowly, the expanse of weedy grass had been reduced by multi-level decking and carefully planned flower beds. The dream was an oasis— with towering Red Maples and Double-Flowering Plums surrounding perennial beds that reminded me every year in the spring of the work I had done the previous year. As much as the dogs tried to foil my gardening dreams with acidic urine and puppy antics, my new watering-helper, Jet, helped me nurture it into life.

May 8, 2015

I went back on my diet of Diet Coke and beef jerky. My Step-Wife's awesome food coupled with my insatiable need to stuff myself had resulted in uncomfortably tight pants. I was bulging out everywhere.

What did I do about it? I told Arthur to get some exercise.

And I went to a meeting to wrap my head around my holistically addictive behaviours.

May 10, 2015

iGramma: Happy mama day!!
iMe: Thank you! And to you, too!
iGramma: Mama Burgers today? xox

iMe: Yep . . . wasn't sure it was going to happen, but we went after Acid's nap and then to a greenhouse where he terrorized the baby goats at the petting zoo . . .

May 15, 2015

I was so immersed in the gender-variant community by now that everything had become a somewhat new normal for me. Our reasonably well-adjusted transgender daughter was supported at home, school, and medical environments. I came across some recent Canadian data to bring it back into perspective.

#leftbrain

Being Safe, Being Me was the report, published in 2015, of the findings of The Canadian Trans Youth Health Survey. This was an electronic survey of 923 trans youth (aged 14-25), participants from all 10 provinces and one of the territories.[38]

Most youth (70%) reported sexual harassment; **more than 1 in 3 younger participants had been physically threatened or injured in the past year (36%)**; and nearly half of older youth reported various types of cyberbullying.

Family relationships are important, and while trans youth generally reported feeling their parents cared about them, **70% reported their family did not understand them**, and about 1 in 3 did not have an adult in their family they could talk to about problems.

Mental health issues were a key concern. Nearly **two-thirds reported self-harm in the past year**; a similar number reported serious thoughts of suicide; and **more than 1 in 3 had attempted suicide**.

Trans youth who had supportive adults both inside and outside their family were **four times more likely to report good or excellent mental health, and were far less likely to have considered suicide** [emphasis added].

#staggering #longwaytogo

38   Veale J, Saewyc E, Frohard-Dourlent H, Dobson S, Clark B & the Canadian Trans Youth Health Survey Research Group. (2015). Being Safe, Being Me: Results of the Canadian Trans Youth Health Survey. Vancouver, BC: Stigma and Resilience Among Vulnerable Youth Centre, School of Nursing, University of British Columbia.

May 16, 2015

Jet and I found my Uncle David sitting in a dark room, locked away on the second floor of his dementia wing. He was safe—but depressed and frustrated. We had come to jail-break him for an afternoon haircut and coffee. It had been way too long since we were here last, and I waffled between apologizing to him and wanting to tell him we were just there a week earlier because I knew he wouldn't remember that we weren't.

#terrible #youddoittoo

Hair Art was the outdated salon at the base of an outdated apartment building. It was barely marked and I doubted it was frequented by anyone but the most marginal of populations. Walking in reminded me a bit of the TV show *Cheers*—where everyone knows your name. Today there was Kent, the ever-faithful companion of the barber, Jim. There was a youngish man with dreadlocks who obviously didn't need a haircut, and his large, but gentle, German Shepherd who licked up Jet when we arrived. There was a very curvy lady sitting under an antiquated hair dryer with hair dye sloppily applied and dripping out of the plastic cap, and another woman killing a few hours sitting at one of two hair cutting stations that were no longer used for cutting hair.

They were all sipping alcohol out of plastic travel mugs while Jim struggled to stand long enough to cut David's hair. He was unable to breathe without his oxygen, but kept getting tangled in the tubing while trying to cut, so he took it off. Jim was awaiting a lung transplant—one which he was not likely to survive if he ever made it to the top of the list.[39]

Jet was a charmer, watching quietly as the sitcom unfolded in front of us. A man who emerged from downstairs demanded a ride from Kent to go find groceries for his old lady. She wanted that "chicken cordon bleu shit" and he had no idea where to start looking for it. The curvy lady protested the trip because her hair was going to be fried off by the time Kent got back to rinse it out. David enjoyed Jim's gentle manner and loving haircut—as rudimentary as it was for a man with shaky hands struggling physically.

---

39   Please sign your organ donor card and make your family aware of your wishes

Uncle David's haircuts were my favorite chore with him. The glimpse into another world, another surreal life.

May 18, 2015

Another fine example of poor parenting played out on the Monday of the long weekend. Arthur and I were puttering in the backyard growing paradise—me with my hands in the dirt and Arthur with his hands on the tools. Jet was spotted "mowing" the deck and enjoying the freedom of unstructured family time. Then . . . where *was* the baby?

Me: My 2-year-old just locked himself in my tool shed.

Locksmith: Oh my. Do you think you could talk him through fiddling with the lock on the inside?

Me: Nope—he is now hysterical.

Locksmith: I'll be there as soon as I can.

So, for $180 and an hour of stressful helpless waiting, Jet sobbed and called for his "mummy" with the sweetest little voice you've ever heard and made his little pick-me-up gesture, which I could see by peeking in the window. It was a blessing that he was upset enough by the situation to have not noticed the bone meal, malathion, and sharp hand tools that surrounded him.

#itonlytakesasecond #wewererightthere #parentingfail

May 20, 2015

iJackson: Can I go to the skate park?
iMe: Yes—take your phone
iJackson: thank you mom ♥ when do you want me jokes
*home
iMe: I'd rather have jokes than have you home
jk
iJackson: stop
iMe: What did the car say to the duck? #joke
iJackson: mom, just stop
and don't use #
i can't deal with a mom using #

May 22, 2015

Ella was smoking again. Not heavily and not perpetually, but enough that she was weighed down with the burden of her dirty secret. In a dramatic teenage-style apology, she charged into my room and threw her cigarettes out the window. For a moment, I contemplated going to retrieve them so I could have one—but of course I know there is never just one for me.

iMe: I have Ella's phone and iPad. She lost her tech privileges for unauthorized use. I haven't decided for how long yet.
iIain: Smoking or boobies?
iMe: I didn't demand she show me specifically, just caught a glimpse of one and her hysterical response was enough for me to know there was more she wasn't proud of . . .
I can't stop the behaviour, but I can revoke the privileges.

iIain: We can stop the behaviour.
iMe: We can try. She will find sneaky ways to do whatever she is going to do, regardless of rules.

This briefly reminded me of the unspoken benefits of having a daughter who identifies as transgender. She was advised against being on estrogens while smoking because of the increased risk of blood clots. Smoking or a flat chest. The choice was hers.

May 24, 2015

Jet turned 2.

There was no party—I hadn't mustered the energy to organize one. There was cake though, and a new sandbox for Jet to start bringing a beach into the house from—one shoeful of sand at a time. At the end of the day, I put him to bed with snuggles and smooches and ate the cake myself.

His birthday will always be a clear reminder for me that we were coming up on an anniversary of Ella's transition day. Jet's arrival coincided roughly with our last days of "Eliot"—Jet's eldest sibling will be known only as his sister. I have read about many families online that had chosen to celebrate the transition day (if one was identifiable), or the name change date, or the gender marker change date as a new birthday. We didn't follow suit, mostly because I'm sure Ella would have demanded we celebrate both, and I simply didn't have the money or the energy!

This day was also a reminder to start placing online orders for Jackson's gifts to ensure they arrived on time for his summer birthday.

May 25, 2015

This is my paralysing fear manifesting. The tragic story of this young man popped up on my newsfeed and bore a haunting resemblance to this of Ella taken 2 years earlier. My worries never go away. They just change.

San Diego Mourns Third Trans Teen to Die by Suicide

Kyler Prescott, a 14-year-old transgender boy, took his life on May 18, marking the third reported San Diego-area teen lost since March.

Kyler Prescott, an accomplished pianist and activist for marriage equality and animal rights in San Diego, Calif., died by suicide on May 18. The transgender boy was 14 years old . . .

Prescott's family was supportive of his identity, and attended local support groups for family members of trans youth. Prescott came to his family as trans "a few years ago," reports San Diego Gay and Lesbian News. His parents respected his wishes and referred to him using male pronouns, even asking the young man if he wanted the family to remove childhood photos of him wearing more feminine clothes . . .

"Some teens when they come out, they come out and that's it," explained [friend of the family]. "Other teens tend to flow between the genders. He chose male pronouns, but was completely comfortable with the family still having all the pictures up of his childhood. Because in Kyler's world a guy can wear a dress."[40]

June 1, 2015

I had taken on a few extra photography passion projects in addition to children on the autism spectrum and birth stories. Some of Ella's young friends were also transitioning, and I offered them a shoot every few months as they started on cross hormones to document their transition. I dreamed that at some point in their lives they would want to reflect and witness their emergence.

The bonus for me was not only in having the opportunity to spend time with these incredible youth, but also to become versed in the world of gaffs, binders, double-sided tapes, and cleavage creators. My young friend on that day described to me the "packer". A prosthetic penis. Apparently, it creates a bulge and a sense of having physical mass where none biologically exists. It is also, apparently, a great place to smuggle drugs into concerts.

---

40   Brydum, S. (2015). San Diego mourns third teen to die by suicide. Retrieved May 25, 2015 from http://www.advocate.com/politics/transgender/2015/05/25/san-diego-mourns-third-trans-teen-die-suicide

June 5, 2015

> iArthur: Jet was very snotty this a.m. At one point, I looked over at him and his whole face was wet with snot.
> iMe: Ahhhh. Poor Acid ☹
> iArthur: He kept sneezing on his iPad and wiping it off.

Gross and cute all at the same time.

June 7, 2015

It was my first PRIDE parade.

It wasn't lack of desire or lack of comfort that had kept me from attending such an event before. It was more like the sun beating down on me—with nowhere to hide my fair white freckled skin, and the childhood memory of jealousy that everyone got more candy or free giveaways to places I'd never even wanted to go.

The plan was for it to be a family event, but the reality for Jackson was that, although he had no problems supporting the LGBTQ community, his ball hockey game trumped his need to fly a rainbow flag. Arthur bailed last minute hoping to have some quiet deck-building time; the rest of us left in a hurry, late as usual.

We perched on the concrete, squeezed between people who I gathered were allies or voyeurs. Haters don't go to the PRIDE parade. Except for the soap-box preacher who stood on his resident corner with his sign reading "May God Forgive All Your Sins", distraught that the crowd of 50,000 had crashed his street-side pulpit. There may only be 30 people in a room for PFLAG, but the outpouring is obvious and the movement of acceptance and celebration *IS* happening, and continues to happen.

The mood was intoxicating—energy infused into people both by the fabulous weather and by the encompassing support. And, of course, there was some ethanol intoxication as well—evidenced by the smashed beer bottle behind us that made me long for the days of a smoke and a rye-and-coke for breakfast.

Army tanks, post-secondary institutions, dance squads.

Queens decked out in their finest, buff men decked out in their skimpiest . . .

Ella: "OMG, why can't they just cover *that* up."
"Put on a shirt."
"Why are they even allowed to do that?"

Police service, political parties, banks.

Home-schoolers, anti-circumcisers, banks and churches.

We rounded out the day with some vintage shopping and a donair. The exhausted sunscreen-smelling-sticky-dirty-baby (the best kind), the content almost 15-year-old girl pleased to have been adorned with some pride-rainbow My Little Pony socks and clear jelly shoes with heels, and I then encountered a priest back at the car.

Church parking squadron: We need these spots for *OUR people*. We have a big event.
Me: I needed this spot for *MY* people, just today.

June 8, 2015

I had reached the tipping point on Facebook where enough of my "friends" identify as trans or support a trans loved one, and belong to enough "transgender support groups" that a critical mass of my news feed now related to gender identity and expression. There was also a mix of photography, autism, and baby birth sites to round out my interests. I don't know if they have published a book called "What your Facebook Feed Says About Who You Are," but someone should.

The articles that I used to seek out seemed thrown in my face.

"What Every Trans Person Wishes You Knew"

"Misconceptions Every Trans Ally Needs to Know"

"10 Things You Must Do to Truly Support Your Trans Person"

"These 7 Assumptions About Non-Binary Folks May Be Hindering Your Trans Allyship"

Some were insightful and nourishing food for thought, some had a vigilante tone designed to strong-arm allies into acting and believing a certain way, some really used the concept of "white-skinned cis-gendered (and often male) privilege" as a sword to cut people who are not trans into shape. I admit to being an overly sensitive sort—taking comments and information very personally is often a curse.

They were correct, though, in saying that because I am not trans, I will never know what it is like. I am a steadfast ally. I have agonized many long nights about how to best love and support my child. I have dedicated time, energy, and money advocating. I have cried tears and dried Ella's sad, salty eyes. I have read articles, blurbs, blogs, books, and absorbed everything I could.

Don't hate me for being cisgender. It wasn't my choice, just as gender variance isn't a choice, either.

June 12, 2015

> iElla: If one more person tells me how bad I look, judges, or tells me to go change because I don't look normal I swear I will shoot them. FFS
>
> "Ella, take out those pigtails and take off that lipstick, it wrecks my reputation as a parent"
>
> Taking off black lipstick wasn't good enough, so I had to change, take off my hat, take off my sunglasses, redo my makeup, and so on . . .
>
> And yesterday, Dad went on and on about how terrible my makeup was. IT WAS EYEBROWS AND MASCARA. EYEBROWS AND MASCARA!!!
>
> iMe: He wants what's best for you. He learned, from his experiences, that people who fit into "normal" are more readily accepted by society

I love your style, Ella. I think it's awesome.

Sometimes it is over the top, though, and your world may not be ready for that yet.

June 15, 2015

After a few weeks of business, but relative normality, the wind changed and it felt a bit like the vortex of an energy storm had landed squarely on the Gemstone.

04:21 Jet awoke.

07:05 Jet and I investigated a baby blackbird that had fallen out of his nest and landed next to the driveway. We left him be.

07:36 I asked the driver to let me off the recently-departed city bus because I had an eerie suspicion I would need my car before the day was done.

09:34 Ella got "dress coded" at school.

She had pushed the boundary of acceptable for "girl" and for "14" and for "school" and had finally hit the line. I sided with the school. Cover up! For an attention seeking young lady who has seen the sexualization of women and nudity in every form of media, every day, every year—what other path could we have expected? Really?

She chose to "cover up" by putting a bra *over* her skimpy tank top. You know, the "over-under-garment" solution.

11:45 Arthur texts me. We now, apparently, had a pet bird. A blackbird.

13:03 Gramma canceled the weekend visit plans. She broke her foot—crutches and an air cast would be difficult to manage in a home with no bathroom on the main floor. Nor would it have been conducive to toddler chasing.

14:03 Kassandra's water breaks. 39

weeks and 6 days. The baby I had been on edge waiting for the "It's happening!" text to photograph the birth. I knew she had planned another natural delivery and she would stay home if possible to avoid unnecessary medical interventions—but being mindful of the fact that she lived 30 minutes from the hospital.

16:30 Poe, the baby blackbird, creeped me out. I was scared his beak would pinch and his claws would gouge. I dug up a few worms and fed them to him with tweezers and gloves. I did not regurgitate them.

02:59 Text summons—I leave for the hospital.

03:25 Kassandra emerges from her vehicle, on hands and knees facing backwards desperately trying to avoid a roadside delivery. ER staff wheel her in the same position with no resistance from security when they scream "She's *pushing*."

03:34 Baby emerges in a small assessment room filled with every available nurse and a doctor who barely had time to don gloves before catching baby. Perfection.

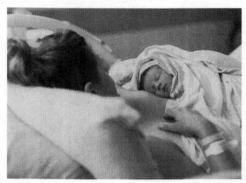

I spent the remainder of the dreamy night capturing many firsts and enjoying a few quiet baby snuggles of my own. That baby smell—intoxicating.

June 16, 2015

We continued to nourish Poe with a Suburbia-styled bird diet of smoked salmon and syringed water. I didn't know if that is the best for him, Google was not much help, and the bird sanctuary wasn't interested in our baby blackbird. I was hopeful that Angry Mama Blackbird would step back in and take over the baby bird feeding any day.

I admired her Angry Mama Blackbird's commitment to her child—I understood her. When we approached Poe, she squawked, dive-bombed us, and threw pinecones from the trees. It was a clear warning to not mess with her baby—though, she better than most mothers, was aware that one feisty mama has a hard time changing the course of nature. She didn't give up though, nor would I have. Until our babies can safely fly on their own, is that not our job?

It's not what Angry Mama Blackbird expected to be doing—I'm sure she would rather be breaking open garbage bags and shitting on clean cars than guarding her fallen baby, but nope—she is doing what mothers do. She accepted where Poe was at, and just did her thing, one moment at a time.

June 18, 2015

It had taken me a while to try to put my own vision of "beautiful" into a healthy place. I embraced stretch marks and scars and cherished personal style and expression in everyone, though I was finding this the most difficult with those closest to me. This seemed completely contrary to my nature or my values.

Was this just my own vanity? Was I worried I would be judged as a reflection of Ella? Or because I know that life is inherently easier for "pretty" girls in this masochistic, patriarchal society?

I begged Ella for a clean, glamorous look for her grade 9 graduation celebration. Her relentless begging for new clothes and more gowns had landed her a variety of lovely outfits to choose from. At the end of the debate, she chose the "grad dress" purchased for the afternoon assembly—with her hair, carefully straightened by me, with love, the night before, pulled into a big ratty mess that morning.

I arrived at the Suburbia Junior High gym with other uncomfortably hot parents, grandparents, and siblings sardined in, waiting for their child's 4.8 seconds of fame. The men were noticeably absent, off foraging for bison to feed and protect, I'd imagine.

Announcer: Fernando Pasquale Lamanini
Girly screams and cheers from the front of the gym.
Doug Ferguson
Voice-cracking baritone grunts from the football squadron.
Ella Grant
A variety of RRRROARING cheers and hollers from around the gym.

She marched across the stage, giving uncomfortably tight hugs to the administration in the receiving line.

Enthusiasm in the crowd is akin to Facebook likes. There were times during the processional that I longed for loud music—to equalize everyone's responses and eliminate the suffocating peer pressure. To hide the quiet grads in their silent moment.

It was all I could do to have Ella fix her hair and touch up her face so I could grab a few "nice" pictures of her special day. They went on Facebook and were circulated to my family—surely a testament to my hard work and vain efforts to have a "pretty" girl graduate grade 9.

What emerged just days later, however, was a bubble-gum goth chick with blue hair wearing a Vampira t-shirt, stripy cupcake skirt, glow-in-the-dark fishnets and a black beanie. Not my first choice—but the reality was that if it fell within the "no boobs, no bellies, no butts, and not provocative" rule. Who was I to complain?

The reality is that girls, transgender or not, fall on many different points on the "pretty" spectrum. Natural beauty, style, expression—simple loving acceptance was the answer for me.

June 20, 2015

I was excited to attend the first ever PRIDE event in Suburbia! I expected my PFLAG peeps, a token politician, and a handful of queer teens foraging for free hotdogs at the afternoon BBQ. I was pleasantly surprised by the hundreds of others—seniors who had walked over from the nearby centre with life-alert buttons in hand just in case things got too crazy: grandparents, parents, students, and . . . just people. The police toned down their "here to prevent trouble" demeanor with rainbow flags tucked in their pockets.

It was an outstanding success. "Genderbread"[41] men of every colour were carefully baked by the members of Outloud, their stories written and staked for people to read. A few Queens and some fabulous music rounded out the rainbow.

It was a majorly historical event on a minor scale.

June 24, 2015

iArthur: Poe is dead. Super sad feeling right now.
iMe: Let's bury him properly under the nice flowering tree in the back . . .
iArthur: Poe is laid to rest.
Please don't speak of him again.

June 25, 2015

Why don't we ask, "Why was I born heterosexual?" I suppose, statistically, it makes sense to differentiate the outliers, not the people in the middle of the bell-curve. By asking the question "How did this happen?" is there not an implication that it shouldn't have? Or that something went wrong? Or that something could be done to prevent or fix it?

Genetics and biology are SO very complicated we probably don't even have the test or technique to find what we think it is we may be looking for. Eons ago, the Romans did a stellar job of growing their populations and armies by policing the "sins" of masturbation, homosexuality, birth control, and divorce—all behaviours to encourage procreation. Perhaps those societal necessities aren't so true thousands of years later?

41   Appendix B

I trust in my Higher Power that everything is the way it should be—difficult or not. I hold this to be true because things *ARE* the way they are. If it was meant to be otherwise, it would already be.

June 27, 2015

> iArthur: I'm in serious need of sleep (I know you are, too) and my "asshole" mood is, directly and clinically, proven to be related to my lack of REM sleep.
> My ability to be social is, and has been, tied to my level of exhaustion.
> iMe: I do not think being an asshole is 100% caused by lack of sleep.
> iArthur: Agreed. I am working on the other 92.8%
> iMe: I hope so. I want nothing more than to be a healthy, strong family with you at the helm.
> iArthur: I want the same with you allowing me to be the co-pilot.
> iMe: Honestly, Arthur, I need to see some evidence of a willingness to move towards healthier behaviours. Stop analyzing the therapists. Deal with your shit. 💩 Our kids deserve that. So do I.
> iArthur: I love you.
> I think I've spent almost 2.5 decades in a war of attrition between me and altered states.
> iMe: I know how much dedication and hard work and surrender it takes to be well. I don't think you fully understand the depth of comprehension I have around the issue.
> iArthur: I will do anything and everything to be with you.
> iMe: I can only believe what you show me. Not what you tell me.
> iArthur: Agreed.
> And understood.

Things with Arthur were so far from perfect. But I remained 100% *in* and would continue to be until it was made crystal clear that I needed to be 100% *out*.

June 28, 2015

> iElla: #finallyihavesomegoodfriends
> iMe: Be nice to them! Not narcissistic! Ask questions. Be interested.
> iElla: Done, done, and done!

June 30, 2015

I wonder how many people have never had a need to engage their elected officials. We never had a Member of the Legislative Assembly at my parents' kitchen table. When Ella was first diagnosed with ASD, there was no funding for support services, and we spent thousands of dollars on private aides and therapies. A letter written in ALL CAPS in crayon on construction paper signed "Eliot" was enough to get someone's attention. Shortly after a few late-night political meetings at our kitchen table, a petition was tabled, and funding was allocated. Too bad we left the province before the money had time to trickle down to those that needed it, but someone along the way benefitted.

#squeakywheelgetsthegrease

There was a group of men, four or five, who sat in a comfortable cluster at the back of the bus every morning. I'd learned that they were neighbours who had been commuting together for going on 6 years. A tall, dark, and handsome young man sat in their territory on the bus in a new grey suit with a purple handkerchief thingy.

> Old guys on the bus: "New job?"
> New guy on the bus: "First day in the legislature!"
> *Straightened up an inch taller and brushed his brand-spanking new lapel in a pediatric kind-of way.*

The New Democratic Party had formed a majority provincial government in what was a historic election a few weeks previously—a landslide ousting of the ruling Progressive Conservative dynasty that had held power here for the previous 43 years. This was great news for me—left wing money for healthcare and education and a socially progressive party with openly gay MLAs being led by a mother with a special needs child. Financially, I imagined the province would be in trouble—and there would be big blunders, given the complete lack of know-how. The flip-side was that they were unlikely to be schooled in the ways of "abusing an expense budget" or "just leaving it because it has always been done that way" by the outgoing politicians.

I Googled the mystery bus man. He was "the" Starbucks Barista in his second year of political science turned well-paid elected official overnight. An article talked of how he thought "maybe his customer service experience would help him out", how "maybe he needed some new suits", and that "it might be time to move out of his parent's house". This man held the province's future in his hands.

He was asleep on the bus on his way home a few weeks later. Newly minted MLA pin on his new Armani jacket, and "Member of the Legislative Assembly" satchel clutched in his hands. I contemplated posting the photo on Twitter . . . but opted to hit him up for a business card instead. They hadn't even been printed yet.

This was my opportunity to dig into the top-surgery coverage and wait-list war. Ella was years away (if ever), but as of today, I'd be paying for it. Instead of financing boobs with my pocketbook, I would proactively finance it with time and energy spent hounding my new commuter friend, and befriending the new Minister of Health—also known to be a supporter of the LGBTQ community. New work had fallen into my lap.

August 12, 2015

Finally! A letter in the mail from the Metropolis Public School Board informing me of the new policies and procedures designed to streamline and alleviate roadblocks to being able to safeguard the private information of trans students; the desired outcome of the Freedom of Information and Privacy Complaint. This meant trans students would be able to guard their personal information at all Metropolis schools without parental (supportive or not), financial, or logistical roadblocks.

This was the product of years of persistence and red tape. It was not highly publicized. I did not receive credit or acknowledgement from anyone but a few. But it happened. I would still pursue the official inquiry to ensure a quasi-judiciary decision being made public so parents in other districts will have grounds to push for the same in their own communities.

I did get a GIANT hug from Ella. I also know it mattered, and youth will benefit in a tangible way.

September 16, 2015

Jackson was back on the ice. I was back in the stands with a camera and a bigger lens—thanks to the generosity of Arthur. The young men in bantam hockey now dwarf me. Where did my little guy go?

September 17, 2015

Ella had been waiting for this appointment for over 2 years—the first visit with the Endocrinologist following her 15th birthday. This was the arbitrary date we had set for the serious consideration of starting estrogens to try to quell the constant pestering about the subject. International guidelines, though not law, refer to an age of "informed consent" and others restrict the activity to 16 years and older for the commencement of cross-hormone therapy.

Why the hesitation and guidelines? Cross-hormone therapy causes permanent changes in the body. Estrogens will induce mammary tissue growth—breasts—that do not disappear if the hormones were stopped. There can also be a marked reduction in fertility. Other risks of therapy were similar in nature to those that come with taking birth control pills; increased risk of heart attack and stroke, as it did the risk of some breast cancers.

We had long, hard discussions with Ella about these issues. She *was* young to make such decisions about her future to have children, but she was open and interested in all possibilities. Estrogen therapy also meant a commitment from Ella to not smoke.

Not every trans woman chooses to go this route, nor should they. External physique and secondary sex characteristics do *not* equal gender. Some follow this path to align who they are inside with how they present to the world.

Ella literally leapt off the fragile paper sheet on the examination table to give the doctor the most uncomfortable hug—unlike anything he had received for a prescription for insulin, ever. For some immediate gratification, we feasted at an Indian buffet with extra naan for lunch and Ella started hounding me for a celebration of sorts. **A Pink Party**.

In some superhuman mustering of energy, after having not slept well and getting up with Jet shortly after 04:00, I purchased all the pink things I could see at the dollar store, including an assortment of pink helium balloons, pink party hats and a tiara with pink jewels. While waiting for the Rx to be filled at the pharmacy, I grabbed pink napkins, cream soda, pink hair ties, and then finally an ice cream cake with pink trim.

> Me: Can you write the word "Estrogen" on this?
> Dairy Queen man: Um. Can you write that out for me?
> Dairy Queen girl: You mind me asking what that is?
> Me: It's the "girly hormone".
> *Frightened that this young woman is probably of child-bearing age and doesn't know what estrogen is . . .*
> My transgender daughter is starting on hormones today.
> Dairy Queen girl: Cool. Like, we have an "all gender washroom" at my school!

I arrived home to find Ella and a friend dolled up in my best, and only, evening gowns, clicking around the kitchen in their tall heels. I threw the packages of decorations at them and gathered orders for pizza. A few more friends and allies gathered at the Gemstone—all teenagers show up for food. They partied like it was 2015 . . . pizza, pop, and pink. We cheered and watched Ella ceremoniously pop her fir

Let the mood swings begin!

September 18, 2015

On rainy days, we wear car jammies and play with tape.

I continue, one day at a time.

September 19, 2015

I am not one for big mushy farewells, and this won't be any exception.

I think I deserve a Giant Shiny Gold Star★ for having completed the task of putting the last few years into words; I will take great pleasure in crossing it off my "to do" list. I will give myself this pat on the back and not wait for someone else to validate my work, so I don't grow bitter about the long hours, late nights, and emotional turmoil that was this book—it was not a waste.

Through writing, I solidified my fluid concept of womanhood. It has changed a lot for me over the years. It is subjective. It's clear in my own journey, with that of Ella, Gramma, the women of rehab, the Serenity Sisters, the Quirky Moms, SuperJen, and the countless other women, that there is no one way to grow into a woman.

I have seen, and sown, seeds of compassion in many people around me; those willing to lend a helping hand to a mother struggling in public with a child in the middle of an autistic meltdown, to a trans person who simply needs to pee, or to an alcoholic who has lost their way. Just breathe, open your heart, and step into it.

Of course, much emphasis has been focused on Ella. Not a fictional character, or a star-struck celebrity, but a young adult with complex emotions, logistics, and struggles. I, alongside Ella, have gone from being admittedly ignorant about gender identity and expression to having a firm grasp on some of the basics. She is an unstoppable force, and I am nothing but honored to be her kick-ass mother and advocate. Jackson and Jet—the boys who light up my life—round out my "why".

I can already see the mountains still to climb on the horizon. I can't see the valleys and craters I will be forced to cross (or use grappling hooks to scale back out of when I stumble in) from today's vantage point, but I know they exist. Shit happens and some of it is going to come my way . . . maybe even an enormous pile of it. 💩 Regardless of this fact, I will trust in the knowledge that those in my life are tangible proof that obstacles can be overcome. People emerge stronger, and with any luck, wiser. They are also exhausted.

And the squirrels are back. I heard Pervis's little squirrel offspring clattering above my head behind the lath and plaster walls, still half painted, in the Gemstone. Their scratchy claws and foul mouths bark away.

Squirrels: Don't be too *busy* to have some damn fun, Carla.

Appendix A

	Remorse	Loneliness	Anger	Hurt	Confusion	Fear	Inadequateness	Depression	Caring	Happiness
Strong	Abashed, Debased, Degraded, Delinquent, Depraved, Disgraced, Evil, Exposed, Humiliated, Judged, Mortified, Shamed, Sinful, Wicked, Wrong	Abandoned, Cut off, Deserted, Destroyed, Empty, Forsaken, Isolated, Marooned, Neglected, Ostracized, Outcast, Rejected, Shunned	Affronted, Belligerent, Bitter, Enraged, Fuming, Furious, Heated, Infuriated, Intense, Outraged, Provoked, Seething, Storming, Vengeful, Vindictive	Abused, Aching, Anguished, Crushed, Degraded, Destroyed, Devastated, Discarded, Disgraced, Forsaken, Humiliated, Mocked, Punished, Rejected, Ridiculed, Tortured	Baffled, Befuddled, Chaotic, Confounded, Confused, Dizzy, Flustered, Rattled, Shocked, Speechless, Startled, Stumped, Stunned, Taken-aback, Thrown, Trapped	Alarmed, Appalled, Desperate, Distressed, Frightened, Horrified, Intimidated, Panicky, Paralyzed, Petrified, Shocked, Terrified, Wrecked	Blemished, Blotched, Broken, Crippled, Damaged, False, Feeble, Finished, Flawed, Helpless, Impotent, Inferior, Invalid, Powerless, Useless, Worthless	Alienated, Barren, Beaten, Dejected, Depressed, Desolate, Despondent, Dismal, Empty, Gloomy, Grieved, Grim, Hopeless, In despair, Woeful, Worried	Adoring, Cherishing, Compassionate, Devoted, Doting, Fervent, Idolizing, Infatuated, Passionate, Worship, Zealous	Delighted, Ecstatic, Elated, Energetic, Enthusiastic, Euphoric, Exhilarated, Overjoyed, Thrilled, Vibrant, Zippy
Medium	Apologetic, Ashamed, Contrite, Culpable, Demeaned, Downhearted, Flustered, Guilty, Regretful, Remorseful, Repentant, Sorrowful, Sorry	Alienated, Alone, Apart, Cheerless, Companionless, Dejected, Despondent, Estranged, Excluded, Left out, Lonely, Oppressed, Uncherished	Aggravated, Annoyed, Antagonistic, Cranky, Exasperated, Grouchy, Hostile, Ill-tempered, Irate, Irritated, Offended, Resentful, Sore, Spiteful, Testy, Ticked off	Annoyed, Belittled, Cheapened, Criticized, Damaged, Depreciated, Devalued, Discredited, Distressed, Impaired, Marred, Mistreated, Resentful, Troubled, Used, Wounded	Adrift, Ambivalent, Bewildered, Disordered, Disorganized, Disturbed, Foggy, Frustrated, Misled, Mistaken, Misunderstood, Perplexed, Puzzled, Troubled	Afraid, Apprehensive, Awkward, Defensive, Fearful, Fidgety, Fretful, Jumpy, Nervous, Scared, Shaky, Skittish, Spineless, Threatened, Troubled	Defeated, Deficient, Impaired, Imperfect, Incapable, Incompetent, Incomplete, Ineffective, Inept, Insignificant, Lacking, Lame, Overwhelmed, Small, Substandard, Unimportant	Awful, Crestfallen, Demoralized, Devalued, Discouraged, Dispirited, Distressed, Downcast, Fed up, Lost, Melancholy, Miserable, Regretful, Sorrowful, Tearful, Upset	Admiring, Affectionate, Attached, Empathetic, Fond, Kind, Kind-hearted, Loving, Partial, Sympathetic, Tender, Trusting, Warm-hearted	Aglow, Buoyant, Cheerful, Elevated, Gleeful, Happy, In high spirits, Jovial, Light-hearted, Lively, Merry, Sparkling, Up
Light	Bashful, Blushing, Chastened, Embarrassed, Hesitant, Humble, Meek, Reluctant, Sheepish	Blue, Detached, Distant, Insulated, Melancholy, Remote, Separate, Withdrawn	Bugged, Dismayed, Galled, Grim, Impatient, Irked, Petulant, Sullen, Uptight	Let down, Minimized, Neglected, Put away, Put down, Rueful, Tender, Touched, Unhappy	Distracted, Uncertain, Uncomfortable, Undecided, Unsettled, Unsure	Anxious, Careful, Cautious, Disquieted, Shy, Tense, Timid, Uneasy, Unsure, Watchful, Worried	Dry, Meager, Puny, Tenuous, Tiny, Uncertain, Unconvincing, Unsure, Weak, Wishful	Blah, Disappointed, Downcast, Funk, Glum, Low, Moody, Morose, Somber, Subdued, Uncomfortable, Unhappy	Appreciative, Attentive, Considerate, Friendly, Interested in, Like, Respecting, Thoughtful, Warm toward, Yielding	Contented, Cool, Fine, Glad, Good, Gratified, Keen, Okay, Pleasant, Pleased, Satisfied, Serene

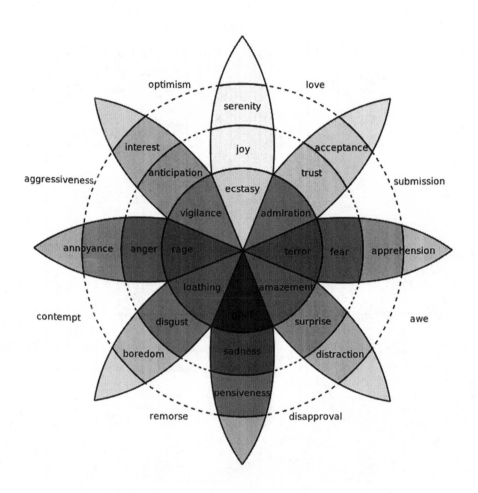

Appendix B

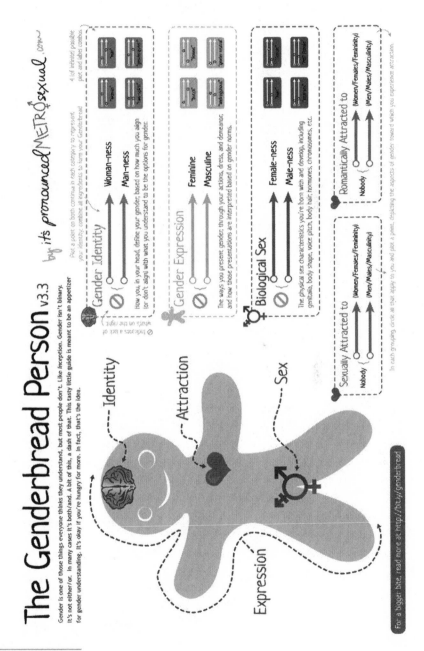

Carla Grant is a non-compliant pharmacist, award-winning post-secondary educator, author, photographer, and overachieving mother. She was born and raised in Canada, where she attended the University of Alberta. She is a study in contrasts—valedictorian at eighteen, recipient of the New York Festivals Grand Award for her radio documentary "The Cause of Thunder" at thirty, and rehab graduate at thirty-three. Carla has had lifelong struggles with mental health and addictions and is a testament of living recovery.

Carla manages the hectic schedule of a single parent of three kids and three dogs in a funky historic home constantly under renovation. She is a wholehearted LGBTQ2 advocate and ally, having launched and successfully challenged governments in precedent-setting cases to support her transgender autistic teen, and has spoken about gender diversity and autism at many educational events. She can be found in PFLAG support circles, behind her camera lens, backpacking the world—with or without the children—or simply in her yard, desperately trying to grow azaleas.